1. Gutachter: Prof. Dr. Ralf Möller, Technische Universität Hamburg-Harburg.
2. Gutachter: Prof. Dr. Friedrich H. Vogt, Technische Universität Hamburg-Harburg.
Tag der mündlichen Prüfung: 27. Februar 2009

Bibliografische Information der Deutschen Nationalbibliothek

Die Deutsche Nationalbibliothek verzeichnet diese Publikation in der Deutschen Nationalbibliografie; detaillierte bibliografische Daten sind im Internet über http://dnb.d-nb.de abrufbar.

ISBN 978-3-8325-2312-1

Logos Verlag Berlin GmbH
Comeniushof, Gubener Str. 47,
10243 Berlin
Tel.: +49 030 42 85 10 90
Fax: +49 030 42 85 10 92
INTERNET: http://www.logos-verlag.de

On the Formalization of
Model-Driven Software Engineering

Vom Promotionsausschuss der

Technischen Universität Hamburg-Harburg

zur Erlangung des akademischen Grades

Doktor-Ingenieur

von

Miguel Alfredo GARCIA GUTIERREZ

aus San Juan, Argentinien

2009

1. Gutachter: Prof. Dr. Ralf Möller, TU Hamburg-Harburg.

2. Gutachter: Prof. Dr. Friedrich H. Vogt, TU Hamburg-Harburg.

Tag der mündlichen Prüfung: 27. Februar 2009

Abstract

Model-Driven Software Engineering (MDSE) encompasses traditional areas of language design, tool engineering, and system validation and verification, following a unified conceptual and technical framework (metamodeling, declarative model transformations, model-based analysis). This work presents design cases of methodologies and tools for MDSE, where the state-of-the-art is advanced as a result of applying formal techniques. The contributions encompass (a) the application of metamodeling techniques to industrially relevant languages, capturing their static semantics in a machine-processable manner; (b) the formulation of a methodology for the design-time certification of transformation algorithms; (c) the design of algorithms for efficiently evaluating Object Constraint Language (OCL) invariants for both the secondary-storage and main-memory cases; and (d) several contributions focused on the generation of Integrated Development Environments (IDEs) derived from language definitions for Domain Specific Languages (DSLs). Venues for further progress and an appraisal of the impact of our research are also reported.

Kurzfassung

Modellgetriebene Softwareentwicklung (MGSE) umfasst die traditionellen Gebiete des Sprachentwurfs, der Werkzeugentwicklung, und der Systemvalidierung in einem einheitlichen konzeptuellen und technischen Rahmen (Meta-Modellierung, deklarative Modell-Transformation, und modellbasierte Analyse). Diese Arbeit untersucht Entwurfsfälle für Methodologien und Werkzeuge im Rahmen der MGSE, wobei der Stand der Kunst durch die Anwendung formaler Techniken erhöht wird. Die Forschungsbeiträge dieser Arbeit umfassen (a) die Anwendung von Techniken der Meta-Modellierung auf industriell relevante Programmiersprachen, (b) die Formulierung einer methodischen Vorgehensweise zur Zertifizierung von Transformations-Algorithmen zur Entwurfszeit, (c) der Entwurf von Algorithmen zur effizienten Evaluierung von in der Object Constraint Language (OCL) formulierten Invarianten im Sekundär- und im Hauptspeicher und (d) diverse Beiträge zur Generierung von Integrierten Entwicklungsumgebungen (Integrated Development Environments, IDEs) aus Sprachspezifikationen für Domänenspezifische Sprachen (Domain Specific Languages). Ebenso wird ein Ausblick für zukünftige Forschungsarbeiten gegeben, und der Einfluss unserer Forschungsarbeiten auf industrielle Praxis diskutiert.

Contents

List of Figures

List of Tables

List of Acronyms

ACID   Atomic, Consistent, Isolated, Durable

ASM   Abstract State Machine

AST   Abstract Syntax Tree

BDD   Binary Decision Diagram

BFS   Breadth First Search

BPEL   Business Process Execution Language

BPMN   Business Process Modeling Notation

CIM   Computation Independent Model

CMA   Concept Membership Assertion

CRUD   Create Retrieve Update Delete

CST   Concrete Syntax Tree

DbC   Design by Contract

DDG   Dynamic Dependency Graph

DDL   Data Definition Language

DL   Description Logic

DMVC   Declarative MVC

DQL	Data Query Language
DSL	Domain-Specific Language
EAI	Enterprise Application Integration
EBNF	Extended Backus-Naur Form
ECA	Event Condition Action
EJB	Enterprise JavaBeans
EJB3QL	EJB3 Query Language
EMF	Eclipse Modeling Framework
EMOF	Essential MOF
GC	Garbage Collection
GCI	Generalized Concept Inclusion
GMF	Graphical Modeling Framework
HCI	Human Computer Interaction
IDE	Integrated Development Environment
JDT	Java Development Tools
JIT	Just in Time
JML	Java Modeling Language
JPQL	Java Persistence Query Language
JSR	Java Specification Request
JVM	Java Virtual Machine
JVMTI	JVM Tool Interface

LINQ	Language Integrated Query
MDSE	Model-driven Software Engineering
MDT	Model Development Tools
MOF	Meta Object Facility
MVC	Model View Controller
OCL	Object Constraint Language
ODMG	Object Data Management Group
OQL	Object Query Language
PIM	Platform Independent Model
POJO	Plain Old Java Object
PSM	Platform Specific Model
QVT	Query, View and Transformation
RL	Relational Logic
RMA	Role Membership Assertion
RuleML	Rule Markup Language
SQL	Structured Query Language
STM	Software Transactional Memory
TGG	Triple Graph Grammar
TLC	The TLA^+ Model Checker
WFR	Well-formedness Rule
xEMOF	Executable EMOF
xUML	Executable UML

1 Introduction

Contents

1.1 Motivation for this Research

Experience has shown that the sharpening of requirements into specifications is a difficult task in software engineering, consuming resources that could otherwise be allocated to other phases in the software development process (e.g., verification and validation). Several lines of research aim at bridging the requirements-to-specifications gap:

- Ontologies, which allow jumpstarting system specifications with consistent formalizations, thus facilitating interoperability of the resulting systems.

- Advanced proof and model-checking techniques, with advances aiming at balancing the expressiveness of the formalisms vs. the time-space complexity of their decision procedures, so as to support abstractions conceptually closer to those in the problem domain.

- Platforms for custom model-driven tools, where previously separate tools are integrated to automate manual work in the practice of software engineering.

Increasingly, the design of programming languages reflects advances originating in all these fields: (a) innovative modularization constructs are being proposed to facilitate encapsulating the structure and dynamics of given problem domains (a goal shared with ontologies); (b) proposed type systems allow making finer predictions at compile-time about runtime program behavior (by relying on sophisticate decision procedures); and (c) the entry barriers to providing tool support for custom languages keep falling with the advent of building blocks for creating Integrated Development Environments (IDEs) for custom languages.

The current state of the art in software engineering has yet to embrace the possibilities opened by research progress. This PhD thesis contributes to realize some of these possibilities.

1.2 Thesis Statement

Our research hypothesis is: The application of formal techniques as part of the specification of programming languages, the design of translation techniques, and the design of supporting runtime systems, improves the productivity and quality of model-driven software development processes.

It is a goal of this thesis to offer existential proofs about our research hypothesis, i.e., we aim at presenting design cases of methodologies and tools for model-driven software engineering, where the advantages identified for this approach have been realized as a consequence of applying formal techniques.

As to the research methods and completion criteria, there is no algorithm on how best to apply formal techniques in the context of the current state of the art, as this design activity involves human cognition. However, there are established criteria to evaluate the fitness of new methodologies, languages, and tools in software engineering, criteria which are applied by specialists in this field. An external measure of such fitness is the degree to which proposals are adopted over time by the professional community.

1.3 Background

1.3.1 Design Patterns vs. Language Extensions vs. DSLs

The motivating force behind model-driven techniques is the realization that current languages are imperfectly equipped to express solutions in terms of a problem-domain formalization (i.e., in terms of an ontology defining the concepts, instances, relations, and dynamics of a subset of the world). Before adopting a custom domain-specific language embodying such means of expression, the usual evolutionary path consists in encoding recurring solutions as *design patterns*. In turn, those design patterns that stand the test of time become candidates for automation as *language extensions*. None of these partial solutions are without problems, as discussed next.

Design patterns. Manolescu et al. notice in their article *The Growing Divide in the Patterns World* [154] the limited adoption by software professionals of novel design patterns (with such design patterns focusing on particular usage situations, usually addressing specific software architectures or vertical domains such as healthcare). The reality of reuse reveals that most professionals are aware of a subset of the original 23 patterns described in the landmark *Design Patterns* book. Manolescu et al. go on to say: "*This gap is eroding the premise of patterns as an easily consumable form of expert knowledge and could ultimately cause an irreversible split between pattern experts — practitioners who advance the state of the art by identifying, refining, and documenting patterns — and those simply using patterns.*" [154, p. 61]. The MDSE advocate would quickly point out that sophistication is the very reason why novel patterns are not frequently used, although they should be. The solution cannot be other than encoding such sophisticate know-how in the model compilers that MDSE calls for. The design patterns advocate would argue instead that the community should push forward the way it has done so far (with better documentation, case studies where patterns are combined to solve a business problem).

Extending existing languages is a fertile ground for computer science researchers to put forward techniques. Frequently, such techniques focus on extending the syntax of a language in an upward-compatible manner. The necessary accompanying extension of the *semantics* are not so widely discussed, except for *translationist semantics* (desugaring new language constructs into the existing language). Mechanisms for achieving certain kinds of syntactic extension have been present in modern languages, e.g., operator overloading in C++ and function classes in Haskell. As an example of the latter, the embedding of a database query language was reported as early as (HaskellDB, [145, 29]). Crucially, the type system of the embedding language cannot be extended, a detrimental situation from the point of view of safety, as not all type-unsafe programs in the extended language may be amenable to sound and complete type checking. A successor to the approach initiated with HaskellDB is elaborated by Simon Peyton Jones and Philip Wadler in [123], endowing comprehensions with syntax for capturing the remaining expressive power of SQL (`ORDER BY`, `GROUP BY`, and `LIMIT`). Again, additional type checking rules are needed beyond those hardcoded in the existing type system.

More recently, language designers have recognized the need for planning ahead for extensibility [26], yet extending the type checking algorithm requires custom techniques as before. An example in this category is BPEL^{light} [167], where the existing constructs for message exchange are generalized into the concept of *conversations*, which allows for improved reuse by parameterizing the variable aspects of communication (e.g., whether an exchange is synchronous or consists instead of a two separate invocations between partners), to avoid overspecifying an algorithm. The extension in question relies on the BPEL 2.0 all-purpose `<extensionActivity>`. Falling just short of defining a completely new DSL, this technique cannot avoid the outcome where the same behavior can be expressed using different syntax, making programs more difficult to understand. As an aside, the periodic revisions of languages for enterprise computing should not be misinterpreted as a sign of reproachable design. After all, the domain they address is not nearly as well-behaved as the uniform closed world of discrete data structures, for which the palette of language constructs has remained stable for a long time. Rather, revisions reflect improved understanding of the economics of large-scale software development.

Summing up, the MDSE advocate would argue that, while building extensibility into the language is certainly a useful approach, it must be accompanied by other MDSE techniques, specially (a) specifying extended type checking rules in a declarative language such as OCL, and (b) compiling in stages by leveraging the customizable hooks in a model compiler framework.

1.3.2 Logical Consistency of Data Models

Not every syntactically correct software model is logically consistent: preventing a software specification from describing logically unsatisfiable situations requires extending the design-time analyses performed by model authoring tools with *logic engines*, as model-checking alone is not enough to detect unsatisfiability and state implicit consequences, in the general case.

As motivational example consider the data model depicted in Figure 1.1, proposed by Franconi in his lecture on Description Logics[1]. One of the (implicit) logical consequences resulting from the given constraints is that class `LatinLover` is inconsistent (no non-empty set of instances may simultaneously satisfy all invariants at runtime). In terms of DSL specifications, we want to make sure that language metamodels are satisfiable and make explicit its logical consequences to rule out unintended ones.

1.3.3 Logical Consistency of Behavioral Specifications

Some modeling languages allow expressing behavior. Behavioral specifications should also be checked for logical consistency, for example to detect whether all system states are reachable. Precisely specifying the dynamic semantics of modeling languages has proved to be a thorny issue, with different definition mechanisms having been tried for languages in industrial use. For example, Crane [47] points out the complications that current semantic definitions of three widespread versions of statechart languages exhibit (STATEMATE, Rhapsody, UML 2.0). The *UML 2 Semantics Project* has been tasked with the unenviable goal of sharpening post-fact the semantics of UML2[2].

---

[1]`http://www.inf.unibz.it/~franconi/dl/course`
[2]`http://www.cs.queensu.ca/~stl/internal/uml2/index.html`

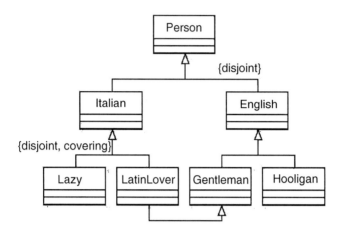

Figure 1.1: Enrico Franconi's Latin Lover example

A review of the many attempts at formalizing successive versions of UML 1.x can be found in [51]. Of the attempts reported, several fall under the category of "define the semantics of individual diagram notations". Given that diagrams are just views on one and the same underlying system description, such attempts resulted in incomplete, incompatible, and non-comparable accounts of UML semantics. Another dimension for classification regards the degree of formality given to concurrency [51]:

> *Another coverage level relates to the problems with possible concurrency as well as aspects of objects communication, which have been uncovered and not addressed in the original UML 1.x documents itself. Such open problems are typical for so called loose semantics, where the aspects of concurrency and object communication are not fixed to some design decision, but cover different implementations. Such loose semantics is not suitable for formal verification.*

Precise semantics have become more necessary with the advent of Domain Specific Modeling Languages (DSMLs). Some authors have gone as far as proposing a general-purpose *semantic anchoring methodology* to be routinely applied as new

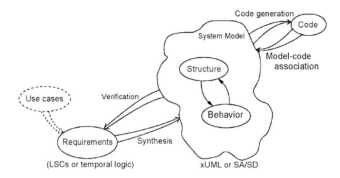

Figure 1.2: Interplay between specifications and implementations (Harel, [106])

DSLs become available [44], favoring the Abstract State Machine formalism [20] as target semantic domain. Besides the end-to-end tooling support thus made possible (involving, for example, simulation besides verification), another potential advantage of such technique is interoperability between separately specified DSMLs.

1.3.4 Verification of OO Programs

Figure 1.2 presents in a schematic manner the relationship between specification and implementation. The concepts mentioned in that diagram can be summarized as follows:

- **Model**: description of the statics and dynamics of a software system, expressed in a modeling language

- **Validation**: the process of determining the correctness of models, designs, and artifacts (*Are we building the right product?*).

- **Verification**: the process of determining whether an implementation corresponds to a model, and thus in a way exhibits the properties validated at the model level (*Are we building the product right?*).

In the definitions above a focus is already implicit in executable models, given that the properties of interest refer to the evolution of the system over time. Different modeling approaches and analysis techniques have been developed, aimed at answering different decision problems. Following a classification by Lamport [141], properties of interest comprise:

- **Safety properties**: something bad will never happen.

- **Liveness properties**: something good will eventually happen.

The textbook examples of them are (a) that an elevator door will not open between floors, and (b) that an elevator door will open after some time at the selected floor, respectively.

Reactive systems have resisted full verification as their complexity emerges not from the data they manage, nor from the algorithms they embody, but from the interactions with other systems. The techniques to verify reactive systems can be classified into:

- **Abstract Interpretation**: A partial execution of a program or system which gains information about its semantics (e.g., control structure, flow of information) without performing all the calculations. For example, we may take the abstract points "+", "0" and "-" to represent positive, zero and negative numbers and then define an abstract version of the multiplication operator, "*", which operates on abstract values. An interpretation is safe if the result of the abstract operation is a safe approximation to the abstraction of the concrete result. The meaning of "a safe approximation" depends on how we are using the results of the analysis.

- **Symbolic Model Checking**: An automated technique that, given a finite-state model of a system and a property (stated e.g., in a temporal logic) systematically checks the validity of this property. From the point of view of results, a model checker behaves as an exhaustive simulator (in that it returns counterexamples, i.e., traces of executions which violate a property of interest) but without necessarily performing an exhaustive state exploration.

- **Theorem Proving**: A theorem prover has a search component that sometimes finds the derivation tree (from premises to conclusion) that satisfies a proposed theorem, perhaps with the help of the modeler in the form of hints about proof tactics (e.g., "try induction"). Well known theorem provers are Isabelle/HOL, ACL2, PVS, Coq.

Although Abstract Interpretation is in principle more general than Model Checking, there is better agreement on algorithms for model checking, and the results achieved with them are more impressive than those using Abstract Interpretation. Theorem Proving is the most flexible technique of them all, and also the most difficult to use. Model checkers come with a pre-defined set of properties they can check (those supported by the space-reduction optimizations they rely on). For example, the models and properties of (a) SPIN are based on Linear Temporal Logic, while those of (b) SMV on Branching Temporal Logic and those of (c) UPPAAL on Real-Time Temporal Logic. The more expressive the behavioral model allowed by a logic, the more the model checker tooling relies on visual modeling. The toolset of UPPAAL has visualization facilities close to those found in UML tools.

1.4 Contributions

The contributions resulting from this PhD thesis span different development areas (language definition, tool engineering, verification techniques), comprising:

- A technique to improve the precision of metamodel-based language specifications [77, 79], applied to (a) a language used in the development of enterprise software systems (Java Persistence Query Language), and (b) the type checking rules of an industrially-relevant meta-modeling language (EMOF extended with Generics). Additionally, the technique in question is shown to simplify the construction of authoring tools for the language being specified [86].

- Also in the field of language design, a conceptual framework is proposed to integrate the specification of modeling views into DSL language specifications. A resulting advantage is the automatic synchronization between views and their underlying model, maintaining well-formedness at the same time [81].

- A methodology to automate the certification of translation algorithms common in the model-driven approach, by bridging the gap between the formalisms in which such transformations are expressed and the decision procedures required to certify properties of interest. Both imperative-style as well as declarative-style transformations are considered [84, 83].

- A scheme for software repositories to achieve efficient integrity checking of the artifacts they manage [82].

- A scheme to improve the efficiency of checking invariants at runtime over an object population residing in main memory by applying memoization, with an initial analysis of the application of transactional memory techniques [85].

- The integration of the Object Constraint Language (OCL) into a model-driven toolchain (the Eclipse Modeling Platform) (a) by providing a compilation component to translate OCL constraints into Java 5; and (b) by supporting the elaboration of OCL specifications with a custom IDE.

Although the description of each contribution necessarily focuses on its specifics, this PhD work makes the case for the integrated application of the proposed techniques. In addition to making results available to the research community, the prototypes accompanying some of the contributions provide a more direct venue for practitioners to adopt such techniques.

1.5 List of Publications

This thesis is a monograph, which contains some unpublished material, but is mainly based on the following publications, listed for each category in chronological order.

Journal Publication

- Miguel Garcia. Efficient Integrity Checking for Essential MOF + OCL in Software Repositories. *Journal of Object Technology*, vol. 7, no. 6, July-August 2008, pages 101-119.

Conferences

- Miguel Garcia and Ralf Möller. Certification of Transformation Algorithms in Model-Driven Software Development. In Wolf-Gideon Bleek, Jorg Räsch, and Heinz Züllighoven, editors, *Software Engineering 2007, volume 105 of GI-Edition Lecture Notes in Informatics*, pages 107- 118, 2007.

- Miguel Garcia and Ralf Möller. Incremental Evaluation of OCL Invariants in the Essential MOF Object Model. In Thomas Kühne, Wolfgang Reisig, and Friedrich Steimann, editors, *Modellierung 2008, volume 127 of GI-Edition Lecture Notes in Informatics*, pages 11–26, 2008.

Professional Magazines

- Miguel Garcia. How to process OCL Abstract Syntax Trees, Eclipse Technical Article, June 2007.

- Miguel Garcia. Automating the embedding of Domain Specific Languages in Eclipse JDT, Eclipse Technical Article, September 2008.

Workshops

- Miguel Garcia. Formalizing the Well-formedness Rules of EJB3QL in UML + OCL. In T. Kühne, editor, *Reports and Revised Selected Papers, Workshops and Symposia at MoDELS 2006, Genoa, Italy*, LNCS 4364, pages 66-75. Springer-Verlag, 2006.

- Miguel Garcia. Rules for Type-checking of Parametric Polymorphism in EMF Generics. In Wolf-Gideon Bleek, Henning Schwentner, and Heinz Züllighoven, editors, *Software Engineering 2007 Beiträge zu den Workshops, volume 106 of GI-Edition Lecture Notes in Informatics*, pages 261- 270, 2007.

- Miguel Garcia and A. Jibran Shidqie. OCL Compiler for EMF. Eclipse Modeling Symposium, co-located with Eclipse Summit Europe 2007.

- Miguel Garcia. Bidirectional Synchronization of Multiple Views of Software Artifacts. Workshop on Domain-specific Modeling (DSML'08), co-located with Modellierung 2008, Berlin, Germany.

- Miguel Garcia. Formalization of QVT-Relations: OCL-based Static Semantics and Alloy-based Validation. Second Workshop MDSD Today 2008, Elmshorn, Germany.

Technical Reports

- Miguel Garcia, Alissa Kaplunova, and Ralf Möller. Model Generation in Description Logics: What Can We Learn From Software Engineering?. Technical Report, Institute for Software Systems (STS), Hamburg University of Technology, Germany, August 2007.

- Miguel Garcia and Paul Sentosa. Generation of Eclipse-based IDEs for Custom DSLs. Technical Report, Institute for Software Systems (STS), Hamburg University of Technology, Germany, January 2008.

1.6 Dissemination in Industry and Standardization Bodies

Model compilers and modeling environments developed as part of this PhD thesis are being used by industry and by standardization bodies:

- An OCL compiler and accompanying text editor for OCL have been contributed as components to the Model Development Tools (MDT) subproject of Eclipse.

- Two software tools have been contributed as components in the Modeling Framework Tools (EMFT) subproject of Eclipse: (a) an extension of the Emfatic model editor to handle EMF Generics; and (b) a tool to automate the embedding of domain-specific languages in Java (DSL2JDT).

1.7 Outline of the Dissertation

The recognition that model-based techniques are advantageous when realizing language tooling has not been uniformly accompanied by industry-based efforts to formalize recent languages in terms of the Essential MOF + OCL datamodel [170]. In Chapter 2 we address one of the omissions by formalizing the static semantics of an industrially relevant language (JPQL, [66]), moreover comparing conformance aspects between model-based JPQL tools and their state-of-the-practice counterparts. In Chapter 3 we focus on formally specifying type checking rules, again supporting our claims in terms of an industrially relevant language (EMOF extended with parametric polymorphism). A strong measure of correctness for a DSL specification is *logical consistency*, formally ensuring that such specification is satisfiable, as discussed in Chapter 4.

All along, we aim at extending these techniques into the field of program verification, to certify the algorithms that realize model transformations in model-driven software engineering. To reach that goal, formalizations of both input and output (i.e., models expressed in EMOF + OCL) and of transformation algorithms are needed. The translation of OCL expressions is thus a pre-requisite and is covered in Chapter 5 in terms of an OCL to Java compiler which allows illustrating translation techniques. This chapter also conveys the operational semantics of OCL.

Without tools to support DSL usage, the language metamodeling technique would not be adopted in engineering practice. An efficient approach (*DSL embedding*, covered in Chapter 6) leverages the tooling of a host language yet enforces the static semantics of the embedded DSL. More complete tooling can be obtained as described in Chapter 7, by generating Integrated Development Environments out of (progressively more complete) language definitions. This activity is essential to establishing a toolchain for Model-Driven Software Engineering. Having made the case for IDEs for DSLs in general, a natural next step is the provision of one such IDE for OCL. After recognizing that current definitions of modeling languages neglect the specification of (bidirectional) view synchronization, a declarative approach is put forward in Chapter 8 to fill this gap.

With the previous elements in place, a procedure to certify model transformation algorithms is presented in Chapter 9. The approach is based on a model checker for a temporal logic, using $^+$CAL as high-level language which has the syntactic flavor of Algol. A glimpse of the difficulties faced when transferring such techniques to an industrial setting is offered in Chapter 10: not only new techniques but also detail-level engineering are required on QVT-Relations, a language for expressing model transformations, standardized by the OMG. After formalizing its static semantics, a validation technique is discussed, thus providing formal insight into the dynamic semantics of QVT-Relations.

The following two chapters focus on a runtime issue, namely the efficient evaluation of OCL invariants for finite object populations. The scenario addressed by Chapter 11 is that of software repositories, where the same problems faced by DBMSs are present (scalability, transactions) only that in the context of a very expressive datamodel and query language (EMOF and OCL, resp.) The problem is proved tractable by applying query optimization techniques based on monoid calculus. Addressing the same concern for the main-memory case presents a different set of design constraints, with the resulting balance being reached by adapting memoization techniques as described in Chapter 12.

Model-Driven Software Engineering is an active area of research, thus it comes as no surprise that further developments can be envisaged. Promising venues for further work, along with insights gained as a result of this research are brought together in Chapter 13.

1.8 Acknowledgements

I've learned quite a few things during my PhD time, and not just about academics. That has been possible thanks to the very talented and dedicated persons I've had the pleasure to work with and to get to know. I want to thank the professors at TUHH, my colleagues, and many students for all the interesting perspectives I've grown to appreciate over the years.

2 The Purpose of Language Metamodeling

Contents

Model-Driven Software Engineering (MDSE) encompasses traditional areas of both language design and software engineering (language definition and tooling, manipulation of programs and models, refinement of specifications into lower-level abstractions) following a unified conceptual and technical framework (metamodeling and declarative model transformations). By expressing a language definition as a metamodel, the information about abstract syntax and static semantics (including type-checking rules) becomes machine-processable, enabling language-aware manipulation along a toolchain in a reusable, declarative manner. In this work, metamodels are expressed in Essential MOF (EMOF) [170] (covering structural aspects), and are extended with constraints expressed in OCL [203], to be evaluated over finite populations of instances. An OCL class invariant is a boolean function over an object graph.

In the context of model-driven software engineering, the abstract syntax of a domain-specific language (DSL) is represented as an EMOF object-oriented model thus attaining a number of advantages compared to an Extended Backus Naur Form (EBNF) approach [137]. This object-oriented model additionally captures the static semantics of the DSL (e.g., declare-before-use) in the form of invariants expressed in the Object Constraint Language (OCL). As shown in [79], the type checking rules of a DSL are also amenable to an OCL formulation, unlike the situation in traditional DSL design where type-checking rules are treated separately. Additional benefits naturally emerge once the language definition is available as a metamodel:

- Abstract Syntax Trees (ASTs) can be exchanged with ease in a toolchain (e.g., between a compiler front-end and an static analyzer), fostering interoperability.

- The declarativeness of the OCL formulation allows applying formal techniques to language processing, in particular Hoare-style program verification of model-transformation algorithms, so as to know at transformation design-time whether well-formed output will always be generated for well-formed input [84].

- Prototypes exist [124, 49] where an AST definition is augmented with annotations to univocally determine a concrete syntax. From this augmented definition, a generator can derive: (a) grammars for different parser generators, making parsers interchangeable; (b) classes whose instances represent Concrete Syntax Tree (CST) nodes, thus allowing for OCL to be used to query and constrain a CST; (c) a visitor to transform a well-formed CST (as checked with OCL) into an AST; (d) an unparser from CST to textual notation (i.e., a pretty-printer); and (e) a text editor supporting usability features such as syntax-directed completion, markers for violations of well-formedness, navigation from usages to definitions, folding, and structural views.

- Following a similar approach, a concrete *visual* syntax can be defined, allowing for the generation of a diagram editor for the DSL in question [65, 90] as reviewed in Chapter 8.

This chapter reports the application of language metamodeling techniques to JPQL (Java Persistence Query Language), the query language for object-relational mapping standardized as part of the Enterprise JavaBeans 3.0 (EJB3) specification [66] (in that context, the language is also referred to as EJB3QL). Five years from now, today's EJB3 applications will be "legacy". We see our metamodel as an enabler for increasing the efficiency of reverse engineering activities. It has already proven useful in uncovering spots where the JPQL specification is vague. The case study reported in this chapter involved (a) expressing the abstract syntax and well-formedness rules of JPQL in EMOF and OCL respectively; (b) deriving from that metamodel software artifacts required for several language-processing tasks, targeting the Eclipse modeling platform; and (c) comparing the generated artifacts with their counterparts in the reference implementation of EJB3 (which was not developed following a language-metamodeling approach). The metamodel of JPQL constitutes the basis for applying model-checkers to assure conformance of tools claiming to follow the specification [84].

The structure of this chapter is as follows. Sec. 2.1 presents motivational examples of well-formedness rules and their formulation in the metamodel of JPQL. Sec. 2.2 discusses the impact of language metamodeling techniques on the consistency and completeness of a language specification. Sec. 2.3 summarizes places where the JSR-220 JPQL specification was found to be incomplete or imprecise. The schema language adopted in JSR-220 is formalized in Sec. 2.4. Sec. 2.5 discusses related work, with Sec. 2.6 offering conclusions and possibilities for further work. The software artifacts of this case study are available for download[1].

---

[1]http://www.sts.tu-harburg.de/people/mi.garcia/pubs/atem06/

2.1 Sample Shortcomings of the JPQL Spec

The JPQL specification includes an EBNF grammar which, as usual, cannot capture all well-formedness constraints relevant to the language being defined. Implementors of the specification cannot rely on a machine-processable specification of all relevant well-formedness rules (WFRs) thus leaving open the possibility for non-interoperable implementations.

The evaluation of WFRs that are not captured by an EBNF grammar becomes a responsibility of the semantic analysis phase of a language processing tool. As a simple example, JSR-220 [66, §4.3.1] requires *"Entity names are scoped within the persistence unit and must be unique within the persistence unit."* The OCL formulation is as follows:

```
context PersistenceUnit
  inv WFR_4_3_1 : self.entities->isUnique(name)
```

Beyond the productivity gain (once expressed in OCL, Java code to evaluate it can be generated automatically), the fact that this check is specified declaratively instead of implemented procedurally makes the resulting artifacts amenable to formal verification. For this particular WFR the "many-eyeballs principle" is enough for validating an implementation. This strategy does not scale to more subtle, intricate WFRs. Sec. 2.3 contains the OCL encoding of complex WFRs for which the correctness of a procedural evaluation is non-obvious.

As a further motivating example consider the case where the EBNF grammar underspecifies the WFR about expressions that compare values declared in enumerations. The production `comparison_expression` contains an alternative for just this case (`enum_expression` on Table 2.1), namely (in-)equality comparison of values coming from enumerations.

In fact, comparing values from different enumeration types makes no sense (doing so would defeat the whole purpose of enumeration types) but the grammar does not rule it out. This particular WFR is probably included in the semantic analysis phase of the reference implementation (but we haven't examined its source code to confirm it) while its OCL formulation is quite compact: the invariant `left.type()` = `right.type()` achieves just this in the context of `EnumCompExp`.

18

Table 2.1: EBNF for `comparison_expression`

```
comparison_expression ::=
  string_expression comparison_operator
    {string_expression | all_or_any_expression}
| boolean_expression { = | <> }
    {boolean_expression | all_or_any_expression}
|    enum_expression { = | <> }
    { enum_expression | all_or_any_expression}
| datetime_expression comparison_operator
    {datetime_expression | all_or_any_expression}
| entity_expression { = | <> }
    {entity_expression | all_or_any_expression}
| arithmetic_expression comparison_operator
    {arithmetic_expression | all_or_any_expression}
```

In another category, the grammar in the specification sometimes misses the opportunity to make distinctions that it *could* express, a fact that was brought to our attention by comparing it with its version for the ANTLR parser generator[2] in the reference implementation. From the specification:

> 4.6.9 Like Expressions
>
> The syntax for the use of the comparison operator *[NOT] LIKE* in a conditional expression is as follows:
>
> `string_expression [NOT] LIKE pattern_value [ESCAPE escape_character]`
>
> The `string_expression` must have a string value. The `pattern_value` is a string literal or a string-valued input parameter in which ...

According to this, `pattern_value` can be replaced by one of two specific constructs (`literalString` and `inputParameter`), for which grammar productions are defined. The normative document does not make this distinction (in that `pattern_value` is

---

[2]ANTLR parser generator, `http://www.antlr.org`

left undefined.) The reference implementation however reflects the intention of the spec, except that it calls `likeValue` what the specification calls `pattern_value` (Figure 2.1).

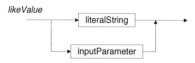

Figure 2.1: Reference implementation, what a pattern_value can be

We adopt the convention of displaying grammar productions from JSR-220 in EBNF notation. The names of OCL invariants have been chosen to allow for easy cross-referencing with the spec, each such name is prefixed with "WFR_" followed by the section number where the specification introduces the constraint.

2.2 Consistency and Completeness Enforced by Language Metamodeling

Expressing the structure and WFRs of a language as an EMOF+OCL metamodel forces the specification authors to consider corner cases that may be easily over-looked otherwise. While encoding in OCL the WFRs around type compatibility for comparison and for assignment expressions, we noticed that the specification is not clear about what combinations of (LHS type, RHS type) are valid in assignments (as part of the UPDATE statement), in case persistent entity types are involved. The specification is silent about whether assigning a B-typed value to a field with declared type A (where B is a subtype of A) is standard across implementations, implementation-dependent, or disallowed. Portability warnings for such cases are encoded in our metamodel as OCL invariants. For example, *"State-fields that are*

Table 2.2: EBNF fragment for the UPDATE statement

```
update_statement ::= update_clause [where_clause]
update_clause ::=
  UPDATE abstract_schema_name [[AS] identification_variable]
  SET update_item {, update_item}*
update_item ::=
  [identification_variable.]
  {state_field | single_valued_association_field } = new_value
new_value ::=
  simple_arithmetic_expression |   string_primary |
  datetime_primary |   boolean_primary |   enum_primary
  simple_entity_expression  |  NULL
```

mapped in serialized form or as LOBs may not be portably used in conditional expressions" [66, §4.6] can be found by searching for PORTABILITY_4_6. This section discusses in more detail our observations around the UPDATE statement.

Following the grammar in the spec, our metamodel allows an UPDATE statement to own one or more UpdateItem, each representing a LHS := RHS. All constructs that are allowed on the LHS support the EMOF interface LHSUpdateItem, similarly for those on the right hand side (Figure 2.2). For comparison, the EBNF counterpart is reproduced in Table 2.2. Notice that all shared properties of alternatives in a production rule can be factored out into the interface that covers them. In the UPDATE example, all constructs (and only those) on the RHS that may evaluate to a primitive type conform to the interface RHSUpdateItemSupportedJavaType, thus allowing an OCL expression to abstract away from the sub-cases.

The JSR-220 specification handles in §4.10 assignments involving primitive types only: *"The new_value specified for an update operation must be compatible in type with the state-field to which it is assigned."*

For completeness, the WFR for type compatibility for comparison (not assignment) between entities is also mentioned here, although it does not shed light on this issue: *"Two entities of the same abstract schema type are equal if and only if they have the same primary key value."* [66, §4.12].

Making explicit the underspecified assignment case is forced upon us by OCL type checking. It all starts when we consider the two sub-cases for a LHS: interface `LHSUpdateItem` is realized by the following two classes: `StateField` and `SingleValuedAssocField` (our metamodel faithfully enforces the partition semantics: the sub-cases cover the case completely and are disjoint with each other).

Listing 2.10 on p. 34 reproduces the OCL if-statement which specifies the compatibility condition for the primitive-types case (the then-branch) as well as the entity-types case (the else-branch). The else-branch in turn has to consider again the two partitioning sub-cases of the RHS: primitive or entity. For the first case, false should be returned as the types are not assignment-compatible. The second case embodies a conservative approach: only assignments of entities of exactly the same declared type are allowed, for lack of additional assurances from the specification, which is due for update in JSR-317.

Notice that the WFR discussion so far lies still within the realm of language structure, not operation. We don't claim that behavioral semantics should be specified in OCL. However, sooner or later, such additional information is needed for answering some decision problems. For example, without knowledge of the prescribed evaluation order of the LHSs in an UPDATE statement, what can be said about the following statement? Does it exchange the references in fields `workAddress` and `homeAddress`?

```
UPDATE Employee
SET workAddress = homeAddress,
    homeAddress = workAddress
```

The metamodeling approach allows expressing "details" which are taken for granted as unstated assumptions in most language specs. Continuing with the example of `UpdateItem`, it can be made explicit that the fields being assigned are actually visible (declared or inherited) at the type of the entity being updated:

```
context UpdateItem
  inv LHSVisibility:
    self.updateStmt.fromClause.type().isVisible(self.left)
```

Making explicit these assumptions is a precondition for applying formal approaches to reasoning about software artifacts.

2.3 Selected Examples of Additional Corner Cases

2.3.1 Visibility of Declarations

Just like in SQL, queries and subqueries may declare one or more identification variables in a FROM clause. The SELECT, WHERE, GROUP BY, and HAVING clauses may then refer to these variables. In case subqueries are present, the specification is not clear about how to interpret a nested variable declaration with the same name as a declaration in the outer scope. Is it disallowed or does it hide the outer declaration? For example:

```
SELECT c
FROM Customer c
WHERE c.balanceOwed < ( SELECT avg(c.balanceOwed) FROM Customer c )
```

Scopes for identification variables are not defined as such in Ch. 4 of the spec: *"An identification variable always designates a reference to a single value. It is declared in one of three ways: in a range variable declaration, in a join clause, or in a collection member declaration. The identification variable declarations are evaluated from left to right in the FROM clause, and an identification variable declaration can use the result of a preceding identification variable declaration of the query string."* [66, §4.4.2]. However, §4.6.2 implicitly introduces the notion of a visibility scope for identification variables: *"All identification variables used in the WHERE or HAVING clause of a SELECT or DELETE statement must be declared in the FROM clause, as described in Section 4.4.2. The identification variables used in the WHERE clause of an UPDATE statement must be declared in the UPDATE clause."*

Our interpretation of the scope rules can be summarized as: A FROM clause (and other constructs) introduces a new scope for identification variables. Scopes may be nested forming a tree hierarchy, with (new) variables declared in an inner scope hiding those with the same name in surrounding scopes. To confirm whether

Listing 2.1: Declarations-before-usages for a SelectStmt

```
context SelectStmt
  inv WFR_4_6_2_A:
    ( not self.whereClause->isEmpty()
      implies
      self.whereClause.areAllReferredVarsVisible (
        self.locallyDeclaredIdVars() )
    ) and (
      not self.havingClause->isEmpty()
      implies
      self.havingClause.areAllReferredVarsVisible (
        self.locallyDeclaredIdVars() )
    )
```

ORM (Object-Relational Mapping) engines conforming to the JSR-220 specification follow this interpretation, JPQL queries involving variable hiding were translated to SQL with two different engines. The resulting SQL exhibits variable hiding by explicitly renaming the declaration and usages of the inner variables.

In terms of our metamodel, we check in each query (including subqueries) whether all usages of variables refer to variables which are visible (Listing 2.1).

The argument received by function `areAllReferredVarsVisible()` is a set containing the declarations of visible variables. The recursive nature of the check performed by `areAllReferredVarsVisible()` can be seen at work for a subquery. The overriding OCL definition is shown in Listing 2.2 on p. 25. Before checking whether its WHERE and HAVING clauses (if any) fulfill the declares-before-usages constraint, the scope is augmented with the locally declared variables by using the OCL `union()` operator.

As in other situations, a visitor could have been written to procedurally validate scope visibility. Again, arguments related to the "productivity" and "correctness" categories can be made in favor of the declarative approach.

Listing 2.2: Declarations-before-usages for a subquery

```
context Subquery::areAllReferredVarsVisible ( varsInScope :
  Set(ejb3qlmm::idVarDecl::IdVarDecl) ) : Boolean
body :
( not self.whereClause->isEmpty()
  implies
    self.whereClause.areAllReferredVarsVisible (
      varsInScope->union(self.locallyDeclaredIdVars())))
) and (
  not self.havingClause->isEmpty()
  implies
    self.havingClause.areAllReferredVarsVisible (
      varsInScope->union(self.locallyDeclaredIdVars())))
)
```

2.3.2 Reduction of Datasets into Groups

GROUP BY (Figure 2.4) is a rich source of WFRs that amount to exceptions to otherwise valid queries. For example, groups can be formed based on the values of an entity-typed column, with an exception: *"Grouping by an entity is permitted. In this case, the entity must contain no serialized state fields or lob-valued state fields."* [66, §4.7], as encoded in Listing 2.3.

Some constraints stated in the specification are vague. For example, if a GROUP BY clause is used to reduce a dataset into groups, a boolean expression may be given in the HAVING clause to leave out some of the reduced groups. Such expression may refer only to the groups already reduced, not to their base data. The phrasing in the specification does not make it clear: *"The HAVING clause must specify search conditions over the grouping items or aggregate functions that apply to grouping items."* [66, §4.7]. Our reading is that a HAVING clause may contain usages of:

1. items which are grouped in the GROUP BY clause, as well as

2. aggregate functions on non-grouped items. Given that applying an aggregate function to a grouped item consisting of just one value always returns that single value, we rule out this possibility

Listing 2.3: Constraint on entities used as grouping criteria

```
context SelectStmt
inv WFR_4_7_B:
 let entitiesUsedAsGroupBy :
     Set(ejb3qlmm::schema::AbstractSchema)
 = groupbyClause->iterate(
     gbi : ejb3qlmm::selectStmt::GroupByItem ;
     r : Set(ejb3qlmm::schema::AbstractSchema) = Set{} |
     if gbi.oclIsKindOf(ejb3qlmm::idVarDecl::IdVarDecl)
        then r->including(gbi.oclAsType(
                   ejb3qlmm::idVarDecl::IdVarDecl).type())
        else r
     endif )
   in entitiesUsedAsGroupBy->forAll(
     as : ejb3qlmm::schema::AbstractSchema |
     as.lobFields->isEmpty() )
```

The set of item 1 consists of instances of any class implementing the interface `GroupByItem`. All usages in the HAVING clause not belonging to that set must be arguments to an aggregate function (i.e. must be an instance of a subclass of `AggregateExp`). An OCL function returning all data-access expressions being used in a `CondExp` returns the set for checking the condition in item 2. Such function is reused in the formulation of other WFRs.

2.3.3 Path Expressions

JPQL, like other OO query languages, allows dot-navigation syntax to express in a compact way what amounts to joins in a relational setting. Unlike its OCL counterpart, only the last association end in a path expression may have multiplicity > 1. In order to retrieve all objects reachable over some association from objects in a certain collection, a cartesian product can be specified. Together with other usual restrictions (only those associations ends that are visible can be navigated, fields for primitive values cannot be further navigated), the WFRs for path expressions amount to a number of constraints, which are formalized next, with reference to the

Listing 2.4: Navigability of path expression in JPQL

```
-- each association field should be visible
-- at the type of its predecessor
context AssocPathExp
inv : let pathLength : Integer = self.chainAssocs->size()
  in self.chainAssocs->forAll(f : ejb3qlmm::schema::AssocField |
    if self.chainAssocs->indexOf(f) > 1
    then let predec : Integer = (self.chainAssocs->indexOf(f))-1
        in self.chainAssocs->at(predec).type.
            associationFields->includes(f)
    else true
    endif )
```

Listing 2.5: Visibility for first navigation step

```
context AssocPathExp
inv : self.idVar.type().oclAsType(ejb3qlmm::schema::AbstractSchema)
      .associationFields->includes( self.chainAssocs->first() )
```

metamodel classes depicted in Figure 2.5.

In Listing 2.4, `forAll()` is used to iterate over the segments of a path expression to check whether each association end participating in the join is visible at the type (`AbstractSchema`) of its predecessor. Since a path expression always starts with an identification variable that stands for an entity, visibility should also be checked for it as shown in Listing 2.5.

JPQL allows non-single-valued association ends to appear only as the tail of a path expression. The invariant in Listing 2.6 checks whether every navigation step (except the last) is an instance of `SingleValuedAssocField`.

Not only path expressions should meet this chaining rule, but state fields too, given that a state field may contain a sequence of embedded class fields and only one simple field (Listing 2.7).

There are two kinds of state field path expressions in the JPQL metamodel: those starting with an identification variable and those starting with a single-valued as-

Listing 2.6: Navigations follow single-valued intermediate steps

```
context AssocPathExp
inv : let pathLength : Integer = self.chainAssocs->size()
  in self.chainAssocs->forAll( f : ejb3qlmm::schema::AssocField |
      if self.chainAssocs->indexOf(f) < pathLength
      then f.oclIsTypeOf(ejb3qlmm::schema::SingleValuedAssocField)
      else true
      endif )
```

sociation path expression. For a state field path expression starting with a single valued path expression, its state field should be visible at the type of its last association field. If the state field has a sequence of embedded class fields, the first one should be visible at the type of its last association field; if the state field has no embedded class field, the simple state field should be visible at the type of its last association field (Listing 2.8 on p. 29).

Join declarations in a FROM clause also form a chain, where the join fields should be visible at the type of its base, which in turn can be a range variable declaration or a join declaration (Listing 2.9 on p. 30).

2.4 Static Semantics and Database Schema

The well-formedness rules of JPQL can be made more precise by taking into account the particular database schema on which JPQL queries are to run. Also for other purposes, such as the translation from OCL into JPQL, the database schema has to be taken into account to obtain correct results. JPQL database schemas are instances of the metamodel depicted in Figure 2.3 on p. 33. The translation from OCL into JPQL surfaces in the context of the refinement of a Platform Independent Model (PIM) to a Platform Specific Model (PSM), as advocated by model-driven development. In this case, the PIM is expressed in EMOF+OCL and the PSM in terms of Java Enterprise Edition, including JPQL.

In a nutshell, PSM-level queries include details about tables and columns not present at the PIM level. For example, an EMOF+OCL model abstracts the re-

Listing 2.7: Chaining rule for embedded class fields

```
context StateField
inv : let pathLength : Integer = self.chainEmbedded->size()
    in if self.chainEmbedded->notEmpty()
      then self.chainEmbedded->forAll(
        f : ejb3qlmm::schema::EmbeddedClassField |
          if self.chainEmbedded->indexOf(f) > 1
          then let predec : Integer =
                  (self.chainEmbedded->indexOf(f))-1
              in self.chainEmbedded->at(predec).
                  type.embeddedClassFields->includes(f)
          else true
          endif )
      else true
      endif
```

alization mechanism for {ordered} association ends. A particular PIM to PSM refinement will choose one of several mapping patterns to realize the {ordered} feature (involving at least an additional column, possibly additional tables). As a result, the automatic translation to JPQL of OCL queries relying on ordered collections must take the chosen pattern into account, making explicit use of it in the platform-specific representation. Patterns for mapping OCL constructs to SQL'92 (with stored procedures) have been reported in [55].

Listing 2.8: Chaining rule for state field path expressions

```
context StateFieldPathExpwithSingleValuedAssocPathExp
inv : let sf : ejb3qlmm::pathExp::StateField = self.stateField in
    if sf.chainEmbedded->isEmpty()
    then self.path.type().oclAsType(ejb3qlmm::schema::Entity)
        .simpleStateFields->includes(sf.terminalField)
    else self.path.type().oclAsType(ejb3qlmm::schema::Entity)
        .embeddedClassFields->includes(sf.chainEmbedded->first())
    endif
```

Listing 2.9: Chaining rule in FROM clauses

```
context IdVarDecl
inv : self.branches->forAll( b |
      self.type().associationFields->includes(b.joinField) )
```

Another area where the information contained in the database schema influences the processing of JPQL ASTs is *schema evolution*. At the very least, whenever changes are propagated from a logical-level EMOF-based model to physical database schemas, an impact analysis to detect which queries become invalid is desirable. This scenario makes unavoidable the combined processing of JPQL ASTs and database schema information, as it implies cross-artifact consistency checks. This analysis is made simpler by having both kinds of information conform to EMOF + OCL models.

2.5 Related Work

2.5.1 Metamodeling-based Approaches

The automatic conversion of an EBNF-based language description into an EMOF-based one has been addressed before [3], and is covered in more detail in the larger context of Integrated Development Environments for DSLs (Chapter 7). The resulting class models are more compact than their EBNF counterparts, make use of generalization and namespaces, and may contain additional well-formedness rules.

Language metamodels based on EMOF+OCL ease the task of maintaining consistency across different software artifacts in a single software repository. For example, a repository may warn about JPQL queries requiring full table scans, resulting from Cartesian products where the fields involved in the selection condition are not indexed. Finding such queries involves access to both a representation of the database physical schema and to the AST of the JPQL queries.

2.5.2 Grammar-based Approaches

The hierarchies for word, tree, and hedge grammars are described in [24]. Language definition approaches based on *regular hedge grammars* enjoy an active community, as they are expressive enough to capture XML dialects. Initially, research focused on proving properties about the formalism itself: uniqueness of interpretation (of a given tree against a grammar), closure (of tree grammars) under union, algorithms for document validation, term rewriting properties (confluence and determinism). More recently, the focus has moved to establish such formalism in the state of the practice. This involves the engineering issue of inter-operating with existing (legacy) tools which use different internal representations (compilers, editors, source code navigators, documentation generators, style checkers and static analysis tools).

2.6 Summary

Improving the quality of enterprise-class software systems requires at some point advanced decision procedures, which in turn build upon precise language definitions. Our case study shows by construction how to achieve these goals.

It is difficult to process JPQL in the current state of the practice, where language aspects are not specified declaratively. For example, the type of the resultset of a SELECT statement can be determined statically (JSR-220 explains informally how). An OCL function encapsulating that algorithm can be used in deciding whether a dynamically built query will be rejected by the ORM engine. Ideally, such checks should be performe at compile time.

Language-processing algorithms can rely on tree walkers and visitor skeletons generated from language metamodels. For JPQL, visitors are needed for: translating to SQL'92, predicting execution time, or computing the depends-on relationships between materialized views. These and other use cases become possible once the metamodeling infrastructure reported in this chapter is in place.

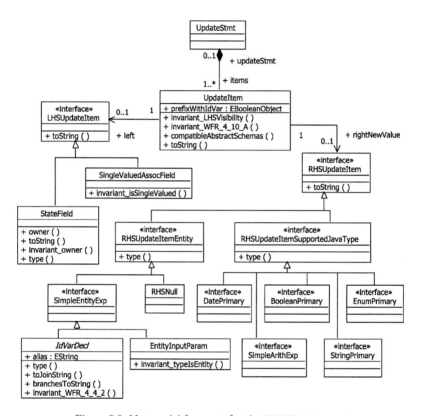

Figure 2.2: Metamodel fragment for the UPDATE statement

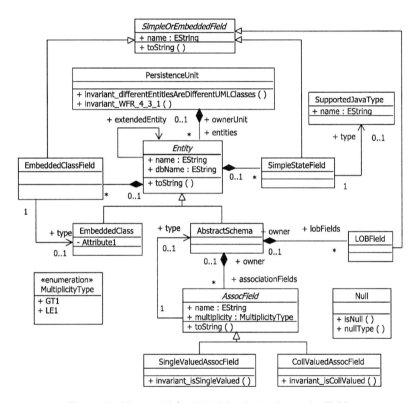

Figure 2.3: Metamodel for logical database schemas in JPQL

Listing 2.10: OCL encoding of type compatibility for assignments in an UpdateItem

```
-- "The new_value specified for an update operation must be
-- compatible in type with the state-field to which it is assigned"
context UpdateItem
inv WFR_4_10_A :
if left.oclIsKindOf(ejb3qlmm::pathExp::StateField)
  then
    -- LHS is typed with SupportedJavaType
    if not rightNewValue.oclIsKindOf(
      ejb3qlmm::stmts::RHSUpdateItemSupportedJavaType)
      then false
      else let
      t1 : ejb3qlmm::schema::SupportedJavaType
        = left.oclAsType(ejb3qlmm::pathExp::StateField).type(),
      -- RHS is either SimpleArithExp, StringPrimary,
      -- BooleanPrimary, DatePrimary, or EnumPrimary
      t2 : ejb3qlmm::schema::SupportedJavaType
        = rightNewValue.oclAsType(
          ejb3qlmm::stmts::RHSUpdateItemSupportedJavaType).type()
      in ejb3qlmm::schema::SupportedJavaType::
          areTypeCompatible(t1, t2)
    endif
  else
    -- LHS is typed with AbstractSchema
    if not rightNewValue.oclIsKindOf(
          ejb3qlmm::stmts::RHSUpdateItemEntity)
      then false
      else let
      t1 : AbstractSchema = left.oclAsType(
          ejb3qlmm::schema::SingleValuedAssocField).type,
    -- RHS is either RHSNull, IdVarDecl, or EntityInputParam
      t2 : AbstractSchema = rightNewValue.oclAsType(
        ejb3qlmm::stmts::RHSUpdateItemEntity).type()
      in t1 = t2 -- TODO spec incomplete: inheritance?
    endif
endif
```

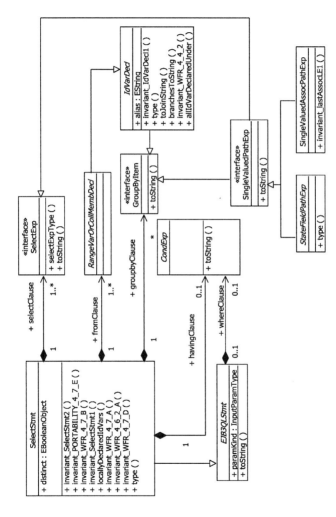

Figure 2.4: SELECT statement, including GROUP BY and HAVING clauses

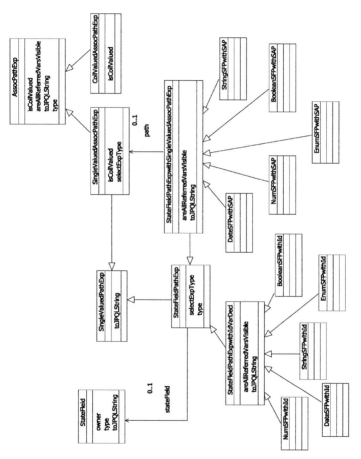

Figure 2.5: jpql.pathExp

3 Metamodel-based Specification of Type Safety

Contents

Type systems are an often neglected area in DSL language engineering. This state of affairs can be traced back to the perception that the specification and implementation of type-checking is too time consuming, given its interdependence with all the language constructs of the DSL in question. Additionally, most DSLs are translated into an statically type-safe language which provides a "safety net" to catch type unsafe programs. We present in this chapter a technique for the declarative specification of type-checking rules at the DSL metamodel level. Such rules rely on the same syntactic machinery as other well-formedness rules (i.e., are expressed in terms of EMOF + OCL) and are thus machine-processable. We show the resulting productivity and quality advantages in comparison to a manual implementation for

an industrially-relevant DSL, EMOF extended with Generics, which moreover has
a rich type system. The methodology described in this chapter can be applied to
specify the type-checking rules of other DSLs for which an EMOF metamodel is
available.

The EMF infrastructure allows the programmatic manipulation of models as first-
class citizens by making available (among others) reflection and persistence services
that significantly increase the productivity of the development of modeling tools.
A cornerstone of such infrastructure is the language in which models are expressed
(Ecore). The type system of Ecore adds generics to the type system of Essential
MOF [170]. Models expressed in Ecore can be seen in turn as a shorthand notation
for types in Java, thanks to the code generation capabilities delivered with EMF. It
is these generated classes that are used as a software component in tools for DSLs
(Domain Specific Languages), with the Ecore-based model specifying the abstract
syntax for the DSL in question [77]. Ecore can equally well be used to capture the
data model of a general-purpose application, although we focus on the DSL scenario
throughout this thesis.

The modeling abstractions supported by Ecore can be conceptualized as a subset of those available for UML2 class models. This subsetting does not reduce
expressiveness, as every datamodel expressed in UML2 can be reformulated as a
corresponding Ecore + OCL model. Several advantages result from focusing on a
well-defined set of constructs. For example, an implementation supporting Object-
Relational Mapping (ORM) of Ecore-based models must deal with considerably
fewer special cases than its UML2 counterpart.

The structure of this chapter is as follows. Sec. 3.1 reviews definitions around
type systems, serving as background for the characterization of EMF Generics in
Sec. 3.2, including the OCL formulation of well-formedness for type expressions.
Subtyping between parameterized types is formalized, after discussing conformance
of a parameterized type to its declaration. Related work, e.g. tooling support for
modeling with generics, is covered in Sec. 3.3. Conclusions and plans for future work
are discussed in Sec. 3.4.

3.1 Type Systems

The grammar of a programming or modeling language specifies the set of syntactically legal programs. Not all of them are useful: those (programs, models) on which the translator would fail are discarded by the well-formedness rules (WFRs) for sentences in the language. For example, requiring all usages of an identifier to refer to a declaration that is in scope is a common WFR. Typing rules add another hurdle that well-formed programs should overcome: they allow determining (preferably at compile-time) the most specific type of each expression, with the purpose of rejecting those programs that are type unsafe, i.e., those which may cause at runtime the assignment of a value of type T_1 to a location declared to hold values of type T_2, with T_1 not a subtype of T_2. Type safety alone does not rule out all unwanted runtime behaviors: correctly typed programs may crash, never terminate, or produce incorrect results. The decision procedures for analyzing properties of interest beyond type-safety are the realm of Hoare-style program verification [94] or model-checking tools [142]. In contrast to these specialized techniques, type systems have a successful track record in terms of cost/benefit (specification effort vs. variety of unsafe situations detected), thus explaining all the effort that goes into their engineering. The designers of a type system must balance natural tensions among expressiveness, performance of type inference, and usability of the resulting type system.

More in detail, specifying a type system involves:

1. Making explicit the rules by which new types can be defined. Together with the set of built-in types, types so constructed constitute the *universe of types* for a given program or model.

2. Building upon this vocabulary of valid types, the link to the grammar of the language is established in the form of *typing rules*, i.e., a procedure to assign (sometimes infer) a unique type for each well-formed expression in the language. This inference is not performed in isolation but taking into account an *environment* of visible ⟨*identifier, type*⟩ pairs.

3. Finally, the subtyping relationship between types allows determining, in con-

junction with the type annotations from the previous item, whether the program is type safe. This algorithm is embodied in the *type checker*

The mechanism of choice to define type construction expressions is usually an EBNF grammar with additional WFRs, generating a set of valid types instead of valid sentences. The need for WFRs for type expressions can be seen for example in the context of *generic type declarations*, i.e., those owning one or more type parameters which may impose constraints for type arguments to fulfill. Not every syntactically-correct *parameterized type* (listing *type substitutions*) conforms to its type declaration. Types are generally compile-time entities, but EMF always reifies them at runtime for reflection. Java 5 supports reflection of typing information in the form of `java.lang.reflect` classes, with much improved support available in Java 6 (`javax.lang.model.util.Types`).

Similar to Java before generics, a classifier declaration in Ecore before 2.3 did not own any type parameters and thus was a constructor for just one type. Instead, a classifier with type parameters defines a *set of types*, one for each conformant substitution by a type argument. For example, a list that keeps its items automatically sorted may be declared as

```
class OrderedList<T extends Comparable<? super T>> { . . . }
```

The declaration above makes clear that `T` admits any type argument as long as it conforms to `Comparable<? super T>`. Interface `Comparable` allows comparing two values of type `T` or supertypes thereof. For example, if an ordered list is to contain `String` items a comparator for `Object` will also do, as strings are objects. Bounded generics allow writing generic algorithms which minimally depend on the type of the input, while preserving static type-safety. The idea of factorizing object capabilities into fine-granular types was first introduced by ML [89].

Angle brackets are used for two different purposes in Java 5. In the example above, the outermost pair of angle brackets encloses a *type parameters section*, while the innermost pair encloses a *type arguments section*. A type parameters section occurs in the context of type construction, while no new type is introduced by type arguments (they act like queries returning types already defined). In the example, the fragment `? super T` denotes a set of types, each of them lower bounded by `T` (*lower bounded by* being generics-speak for *supertype of*). Subtyping is formalized in Sec. 3.2.3. The ? is not actually a type argument but a wildcard standing for any of several possible type arguments. A wildcard can only be used in places where a type argument is expected, however it should not be considered to be the name of a specific type. For instance, each occurrence of ? in Pair<?,?> in general stands for different types, and ? is *not* a subtype of ?. By convention, the unqualified wildcard ? is a shorthand for ? `extends Object`.

3.2 Well-formed Types in EMF Generics

Two main constructs are subject to well-formedness checking: (a.1) the declaration of a generic type, and (a.2) a parameterized type, i.e., an invocation of (a.1) with type arguments. The OCL WFR for (a.1) is given in Sec. 3.2.1, as a prerequisite for answering:

(b.1). whether a given parameterized type is a valid invocation of its declaration (Sec. 3.2.2)

(b.2). subtyping relationship between two parameterized types (Sec. 3.2.3)

The precise formulation of these queries over ASTs is not straightforward given the rich structure of references that (a.1) and (a.2) may exhibit. For example, determining (b.1) must take into account two different scopes for type parameters (that of the declaration and that of the invocation) where moreover wildcards may occur (except in bounds of type parameters in a.1). For the same reason, the case-analysis of transformation algorithms operating on ASTs of type expressions is intricate.

Figure 3.3 shows the new classes (`ETypeParameter` and `EGenericType`) added to the metamodel of Ecore to support genericity. Only legal instantiations of this metamodel will result in legal Java types. The reader is invited to compare the readability of the OCL formulation vs. the current realization in EMF, which takes the form of commented procedural code in `org.eclipse.emf.ecore.util.EcoreValidator` ("specification by reference implementation"). Moreover, OCL invariants can be compiled into Java, allowing the automatic detection of violations of WFRs during

AST tree-building or transformation, before further processing takes place. The WFRs for the non-generics fragment of Ecore are covered elsewhere [193, 170].

3.2.1 Declaration of a Generic Type

Informally, well-formed ASTs of (a.1) consist of an `EClassifier` with a non-empty list of `ETypeParameter`, which from then on are in scope for the whole type declaration (e.g. `class C <T extends C<T>>` is legal, §8.1.2 in [95]). A type parameter owns a possibly empty list of upper bounds, later used to answer (b.2). Each such bound is represented in the AST as an `EGenericType` which may represent:

- a reference to a type variable (in scope for a.1), acting as a terminal node, as no type arguments can be specified

- a reference to a non-generic type

- a reference to a generic type, either with or without type arguments (in the latter case a so called *raw* type reference).

Listing 3.3 on p. 48 contains the OCL formulation of the sketched WFRs.

3.2.2 Type Invocation

Again informally, a parameterized type (a.2) consists syntactically of a name reference to a generic type (a.1), followed by one or more type arguments. At the AST level, all these constructs are instances of `EGenericType`, with conventions on their connectivity used to determine the role played by the instance (conventions fixed when the abstract syntax was chosen). Details are given below as individual WFRs are reviewed. Syntactically valid type arguments can be any of:

- references to type variables in scope for the type invocation. This scope is introduced by a generic type or operation declaration in which the type invocation occurs, and is not to be confused with the scope of type variables for the referred generic type declaration,

- references to types (raw type reference, parameterized type reference, or reference to non-generic type),

- wildcards (?, ? extends *oneUpperBound*, ? super *oneLowerBound*). Each of these bounds, just like bounds in a generic type declaration, cannot be a wildcard itself. Instead, it can assume any of the forms described in the two previous items.

The start situation when answering (b.1) are ASTs for a parameterized type $P_1 = G < T_1,..T_n >$ and its declaration $D_1 = G < A_1,..A_n >$. P_1 and D_1 are not directly comparable as usages of type variables belong to disjoint scopes and as P_1 may contain wildcards. A process termed *capture conversion* ([95], §5.1.10) rewrites those wildcards into appropriately bounded fresh type variables (whose lifetime is limited to answering b.1). The resulting type invocation has the form $P_2 = G < X_1,..X_n >$. The next rewriting takes place on the declaration D_1 by substituting all occurrences of type variables declared in D with the type arguments from P_2. Each $A_i, i = 1..n$ is rewritten to $A_i[V(A_j) \leftarrow X_j, j = 1..n]$, where $V(A_j)$ stands for the type variable introduced by A_j. The resulting working expression D_2 is not a declaration anymore but a parameterized type (a.2) sharing the same scope of type variables as P_2. The final step involves iterating over each actual type argument tp_i in P_2, checking if it is a subtype of each upper bound of the type argument at the *ith* position in D_2. In case any of these comparands refers to a type variable, *type argument containment* (explained in the next subsection) is used.

3.2.3 Subtyping Between Two Parameterized Types

Subtype and *Supertype* are binary relations on types. They are partial orders (i.e., reflexive, antisymmetric, and transitive) and transpose of each other. It is sufficient to define *directSubtype* (or *directSupertype*) to have *Subtype* and *Supertype* univocally determined. Direct subtype, symbolized $<_1$, consists of:

- an enumeration of pairs of predefined types (i.e., for the $BuiltInType \times BuiltInType$ subset of $Type \times Type$)

- a partition of the remaining cases into categories with a membership condition for each. For example, in the type system of Java 5, the partition with pairs of the form $\langle NullType, C \rangle$ (where C is a class or interface type) has the constant

membership condition *True*. As a consequence, `null`, the only value conforming to the type *NullType*, can always be assigned to a location declared to
hold instances of C, for any declared type C.

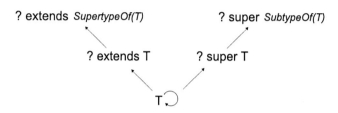

Figure 3.1: Graphical display of the rules for Type Argument Containment. Arrows
point at the container argument

Besides answering whether subtyping holds between two types, it is sometimes
possible to conclude whether two type expressions T_1, T_2 (involving type variables
and wildcards) exhibit subtyping, i.e., whether the set of types denoted by T_1 is
necessarily a subset of that denoted by T_2. This procedure, *type argument containment* (§4.5.1.1 in [95]) is depicted visually in Figure 3.1 and formalized for the Ecore
metamodel in terms of OCL as shown in Listing 3.1.

A type argument is either a wildcard, a raw type invocation, a parameterized type
invocation, or a reference to a type variable. Therefore, type argument containment
alone does not provide an answer in all cases where two arbitrary type arguments are
compared for subtyping. An important special case is the comparison of two parameterized types without wildcards or type variables: it succeeds only when they refer to
the same generic type and their arguments match exactly: none of `List<String>`,
`List<Object>` is subtype of the other, for otherwise type-unsafe updates would be
allowed. The rules in Figure 3.1 imply that upper-bounded wildcards exhibit covari-
ant subtyping with respect to their bounds. In contrast, lower-bounded wildcards
give rise to contravariant subtyping.

Listing 3.1: Type Argument Containment

```
context EGenericType::contains(TA : EGenericType) : Boolean
def: (self = TA) or
    if self.isUpperBoundedWildcard()
    then -- left branch in Figure 3.1
        if TA.isUpperBoundedWildcard()
        then self.eUpperBound.isSuperTypeOf(TA.eUpperBound)
        else self.eUpperBound = TA
        endif
    else if self.isLowerBoundedWildcard()
        then -- right branch in Figure 3.1
            if TA.isUpperBoundedWildcard()
            then self.eUpperBound.isSuperTypeOf(TA.eUpperBound)
            else self.eUpperBound = TA
            endif
        else false
    endif
```

3.3 Related Work

3.3.1 Typing of Object-Oriented Programs

Emfatic [50] is an Eclipse-based text editor that simplifies the creation of Ecore-based models thanks to an intuitive textual notation. As part of the activities reported in this PhD thesis, Emfatic was extended to handle generics, allowing bidirectional translation .emf ↔ .ecore. Generics-aware type checking of Ecore models is relevant for the Eclipse MDT implementation of OCL. A discussion of typing for Generics OCL can be found in [138].

Bruce explains in [30] the formal machinery required for analyzing the type system of OO languages, including a discussion of the design decisions made for several languages currently in use. Determining whether the rules of a proposed type system (defined as in Sec. 3.1) actually reject all type-unsafe programs is a topic on its own, with researchers increasingly relying on mechanized proofs, for example for Java [175].

Before generics, EMF developers would routinely add potentially unsafe downcasts. A refactoring to automatically parameterize Java classes [129] can be used to remove them. Another discussion of type inference in Java 5 can be found in [179].

3.3.2 Improvements to the Java Type System

A proposal has recently been made to extend the type checking rules of Java to support *immutability* [211], without extending the syntax of the language (initially, by relying on custom type arguments for Generic types, and in a second stage, by using the type-level annotations made possible by the ongoing JSR-308, Annotations on Java types[1]).

Under the proposed scheme, an object may be *mutable* or *immutable*, and a reference may be *mutable, readonly,* or *immutable*. Their differences are as follows [211]:

- *Class immutability*: No instance of an immutable class may be changed; examples in Java include `String` and subclasses of `Number` including `Integer` and `BigDecimal`. Java's type system has no way of expressing or checking this property.

- *Object immutability* guarantees that an object cannot be modified, even if other instances of the same class can be. For example, some instances of `List` in a given program may be immutable, whereas others can be modified. Object immutability gives strong guarantees that can be used for pointer analysis and optimizations, such as sharing between threads without synchronization, and to help prevent hard-to-detect bugs. For example, the documentation of the `Map` interface in Java states that *"Great care must be exercised if mutable objects are used as map keys. The behavior of a map is not specified if the value of an object is changed in a manner that affects equals comparisons while the object is a key in the map."*

- A *readonly reference* (or a `const` pointer in C++) cannot be used to modify its referent. However, the referent might be modified using an aliasing mutable

---

[1]http://groups.csail.mit.edu/pag/jsr308/dist/jsr308-checkers.html

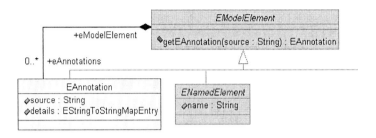

Figure 3.2: Annotations in the EMF implementation of EMOF

Listing 3.2: Different cases for JSR-308 annotations on Java types

```
@Interned String intern() { ... }            // return value
int compareTo(@NonNull String other) { ... } // argument
String toString() @ReadOnly { ... }          // receiver
@NonNull List<@Interned String> messages; // generic argument
myDate = (@ReadOnly Date) readonlyObject; // cast
```

reference. Reference immutability is required to specify interfaces, such as that a procedure may not modify its arguments (even if the caller retains the right to do so) or a client may not modify values returned from a module.

The type checking rules for immutability could also be applied to executable languages that adopt EMOF as native object model. JSR-308 and the immutability check are initially planned to become generally available in the Java 7 timeframe.

In the EMF implementation of EMOF, annotations are less structured than in JSR-308: each model element may contain a number of annotations, each consisting of a `String` (its *source*) and dictionary of *(key, value)* pairs, both `Strings`, as depicted in Figure 3.2. Executable DSLs aimed at EMOF would also benefit from structured annotations as those made possible by JSR-308. For illustration, examples from usages of JSR-308 annotations are shown in Listing 3.2.

3.4 Evaluation

Type-checking rules formulated as OCL invariants at the DSL metamodel level are
necessary to achieve certified model transformations (Chapter 9). This certification comprises the design-time (symbolic) analysis of behavior of a transformation
algorithm, for all possible executions that satisfy stated preconditions, to ensure
termination and the establishment of stated postconditions.

Listing 3.3: WFRs for generic type declarations

```
context EClassifier
inv consistentTypeParameters :
  allDifferent( eTypeParameters.name ) and
  eTypeParameters->forAll( tp | tp.isConsistent(eTypeParameters) )

context ETypeParameter::isConsistent( tpsInScope :
  Collection(ETypeParameter)) : Boolean
def: self.name <> '' and ( self.eBounds->isEmpty() or
  self.eBounds->forAll(tr|tr.isConsistentTypeReference(tpsInScope)))

context EGenericType::isConsistentTypeReference(
  tpsInScope : Collection(ETypeParameter)) : Boolean
def: not isWildcard() and ( ( self.isReferenceToTypeParameter()
  and tpsInScope->includes(self.eTypeParameter) )
xor (self.isReferenceToClassifier() and
    -- self.eClassifier declares a generic type
    self.eClassifier.isValidTypeInvocation(self.eTypeArguments)))

context EGenericType::isReferenceToTypeParameter() : Boolean
def: eClassifier->isEmpty() and
    not eTypeParameter->isEmpty() and eTypeArguments->isEmpty()

context EGenericType::isReferenceToClassifier() : Boolean
def: not eClassifier->isEmpty() and eTypeParameter->isEmpty()
```

Listing 3.4: WFRs for type invocations

```
context EClassifier::isValidTypeInvocation( -- see 4.5 in JLS3
  -- typeArgs contains the type arguments of the type invocation
  typeArgs : Sequence(EGenericType) ) : Boolean
def: if not self.isGenericTypeDeclaration()
    then typeArgs->isEmpty()
    else typeArgs->isEmpty() -- raw type
        or isValidTypeInvocationAfterCaptureConversion(
             captureConversion(typeArgs) )
    endif


context EClassifier::isValidTypeInvocationAfterCaptureConversion(
  typeArgs : Sequence(EGenericType) ) : Boolean
pre: typeArgs->isEmpty()
    or typeArgs->forAll( ta | not ta.isWildcard() )


context EClassifier::isValidTypeInvocationAfterCaptureConversion(
  typeArgs : Sequence(EGenericType) ) : Boolean
def: -- this operation has an OCL-specified precondition, see above
  typeArgs->isEmpty()
  or Sequence( 1..typeArgs->size() )->forAll(index |
      eTypeParameters->at(index).isValidTypeSubstitution(
        typeArgs->at(index), typeArgs ) )


context ETypeParameter::isValidTypeSubstitution( -- 4.10.2 in JLS3
  -- ccta is a capture-converted type argument, i.e. not a wildcard
  ccta : EGenericType,
  typeArgsForAllTypeParams : Sequence(EGenericType) ) : Boolean
def: self.eBounds->forAll(si |
      si.isSuperTypeOf(ccta,typeArgsForAllTypeParams) )
```

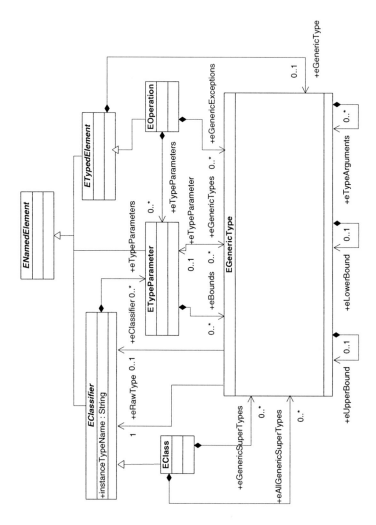

Figure 3.3: Fragment of the Ecore metamodel dealing with Generics

4 Logical Consistency of Metamodels

Contents

The transformation components in a model-driven toolchain manipulate program and model representations. Such components are expected to enforce contracts of the form: *whenever a transformation receives well-formed input and terminates, its output will be well-formed.* Implicit is the possibility for such well-formedness rules (WFRs) to be satisfiable for finite program and model representations. We call the WFRs in that case to be *logically consistent* and set out to find an automated procedure to determine whether an arbitrary EMOF + OCL metamodel is logically consistent. As pointed out by Calvanese and De Giacomo:

> *The properties of various classes and associations may interact to yield stricter multiplicities or typing than those explicitly specified in the class*

diagram. Detecting such cases allows the designer for refining the class diagram by making such properties explicit, thus enhancing the readability of the diagram. [40, p. 74]

For example, the following consequences from the class model in Figure 4.1 render it logically inconsistent [40]:

- the cardinality of the extent of class `CellPhone` is zero

- same goes for `MobileOrigin`

- the concepts `Phone` and `FixedPhone` are synonyms (i.e., they always overlap exactly)

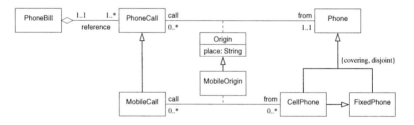

Figure 4.1: An unsatisfiable class model for a phone system [40, p. 80]

This chapter focuses on answering the question whether the static semantics of a DSL are logically consistent, by finitizing this decision problem for a Relational Logic formulation. The presented decision procedure is applicable outside the EMOF + OCL context. For this reason, the reported case study is formalized in terms of Description Logics ($\mathcal{ALC}$ and $\mathcal{SHIQ}$).

The structure of this chapter is as follows. A more detailed motivation and terminology is introduced in Sec. 4.1. The translation from $\mathcal{ALC}$ and $\mathcal{SHIQ}$ into Relational Logic is covered in Sec. 4.2. Two sample case studies are analyzed in

Sec. 4.3. The chosen logic engine also allows for visually inspecting, in an interactive manner, the obtained *counterexamples*. We argue that the capability to perform *model exploration* (in addition to *model finding* and *model checking*) is essential when working with complex formalizations. The performance measurements of Sec. 4.4 reveal the strengths and weaknesses of the approach. Sec. 4.5 concludes by providing an outlook on future applications of SAT-based model finders.

4.1 Application of Alloy Model Generation to Description Logics

Model checking and model generation (aka model finding) are well-established methodologies for formally verifying properties of possibly time-evolving systems. A recent survey can be found in [118]. Usually, some aspects of real-world systems have to be abstracted away in order to make them accessible to formal logical modeling: continuous vs. discrete behavior, granularity, stochasticity, etc. Nevertheless, model-checking tools are successfully applied in practice. Indeed, improvements in the underlying decision procedures (most notably SAT and BDDs [22]) together with higher-level specification languages have broadened the applicability of these techniques. New application fields have been identified recently. One such field comprises solving selected problems arising in ontology management and evolution as a complement to dedicated DL engines.

The *model generation problem* for Description Logic is postulated as follows. Given an ontology O, which is a pair $(\mathcal{T}, \mathcal{A})$ of a TBox $\mathcal{T}$ and an ABox $\mathcal{A}$, find an interpretation $\mathcal{I}$ which satisfies all axioms of $\mathcal{T}$ and $\mathcal{A}$. In case of a *model checking problem* the goal is to prove whether a given interpretation is a model.

In order to support the ontology development process in an incremental way, our thesis is that well-known model-generation tools can be adopted accordingly and provide major benefits for human ontology designers. In this work we evaluate pros and cons of applying an existing model checking and generation tool in this context.

In fact, the ontology designer is often not interested in just testing the satisfiability of an ontology by checking whether one single model exists, but possibly wants to inspect a number of generated models instead. This way, unintended models might be identified. This kind of modeling methodology has been proven to be very effective in software engineering (e.g., [120]). The ontology designer should be offered a possibility to adjust the ontology by examining automatically generated relational model structures. Model generators support this process quite well whereas for checking the satisfiability of ontologies and computing the taxonomy tableau algorithms have been proven to be very effective. Thus, it seems attractive to augment tableau provers to also support model generation. Current tableau algorithms are not well applicable as model generation procedures since they only return (a description of) a so-called single canonical model. Instead, model finders are able to enumerate all models systematically. This can indeed be useful for ontology design tasks.

To illustrate this, we discuss the following simple example. Let A, B be concepts and R be a role. Suppose the satisfiability of the following concept is checked by both a DL system and a model finder: $(\exists R.A) \sqcap (\exists R.B)$. The model generated by a tableau algorithm is shown on the left-hand side of the vertical bar in Figure 4.2. However, the ontology designer may be more interested in inspecting models computed by a model finder (see Figure 4.2, to the right of the vertical bar). The latter four models are not considered by the rules of tableau prover because if the left structure is model, then the structures to the right of the bar are also models. Thus, it suffices to consider only one model (the one to the left of the bar) in order to show satisfiability. In order to evaluate an ontology (i.e., the concepts, roles, and axioms in it), considering all models is nevertheless interesting as we argued above. Thus, it makes sense to investigate contemporary model finders, study the state of the art in this field from a practical point of view, and identify possible limitations.

In our case study, we adopt a particular finite model finder, namely Alloy Analyzer 3.0 [120], whose language is based on relational calculus and thus allows for straightforward representation of $\mathcal{ALC}$ knowledge bases. The technique reported here is not the first attempt at rephrasing ontology languages in Alloy, yet it has been developed independently. In [201], case studies have been published where an ontology has been formulated (and further analyzed) in Alloy, Z, and (recently) HOL. Unlike our approach to capture the semantics of $\mathcal{ALC}$ constructs directly, the authors define a translation schema that considers the meta-level of the ontology

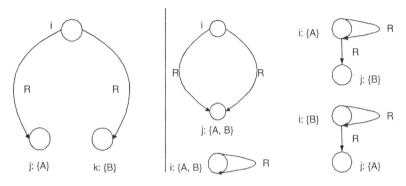

Figure 4.2: Models of $(\exists R.A) \sqcap (\exists R.B)$

language in terms of individuals for concepts and properties as well as relationships among these individuals. We show results achieved so far for several case studies:

- Model inspection (Sec. 4.3.1);

- Visual display of counterexamples for a subsumption assumption (Sec. 4.3.2) and for a concept equivalence assumption (Sec. 4.3.3);

- Finding models for $\mathcal{ALC}$ terms whose satisfiability analysis is expensive for contemporary tableaux-based reasoners (Sec. 4.4).

In the next section we address the translation rules for DL into Alloy, starting with the base logic $\mathcal{ALC}$.

4.2 Translation from Description Logics

The logic underlying the Alloy Analyzer is Relational Logic (RL) whose syntax, type rules and semantics are described in [119]. This logic is more than a syntactical variation of first-order logic, because it includes transitive closure. An automatic model finder requires the specification of a *scope*, a bound on the number of atoms in the universe (cardinalities of concepts). This limitation is not as dramatic as it might seem, given the so-called *small-scope hypothesis*:

First-order logic is undecidable, so our analysis cannot be a decision procedure: if no model is found, the formula may still have a model in a larger scope. Nevertheless, the analysis is useful, since many formulas that have models have small ones. [...]   Given a relational formula, we can construct a boolean formula that has a model exactly when the original formula has a model in some given scope. [119]

Given that $\mathcal{ALC}$ exhibits the finite model property, it is thus amenable to circumvent the finite-scope limitation. In fact, we can compute worst case concept cardinalities according to the maximum concept branching factor and the maximum depth of nested existential quantifiers.

4.2.1 Translation Rules for $\mathcal{ALC}$

Definition 1 (Alloy Translation Rules for $\mathcal{ALC}$ Concepts) If A is a concept name, C, D are concepts, R is a role name, the following translation rules can be applied to $\mathcal{ALC}$ concepts in order to obtain semantically equivalent Alloy formulas:

A	A
$C \sqcap D$	C & D
$C \sqcup D$	C + D
$\neg C$	univ - C
$\forall R.C$	univ - (R.(univ - C))
$\exists R.C$	R.C

Here, A, C, D, R denote Alloy relations, &, +, - are set operators (intersection, union and difference, respectively), "." stands for the relational join operator. The unary relation univ represents the set containing every instance of the universe (interpretation domain).

Definition 2 (Alloy Translation Rules for $\mathcal{ALC}$ TBox and ABox axioms) We summarize translation rules for $\mathcal{ALC}$ terminological and assertional axioms into Alloy.

- In $\mathcal{ALC}$, expressions $\top$ (universal concept) and $\bot$ (unsatisfiable concept) are used as abbreviations for $A \sqcup \neg A$ resp. $A \sqcap \neg A$, where A is a concept name.

In Alloy, we define the `TOP` relation as a covering subset of `univ`, and `BOTTOM` as the subset of `TOP` containing no instances:

`sig BOTTOM in TOP {} fact { #BOTTOM = 0 }.`

A signature (denoted as `sig`) introduces a set of atoms. The declaration `sig A { }` introduces a set named `A`. An `abstract` signature has no elements except those belonging to the extension of its subsignatures.

- Elementary descriptions are atomic concepts and atomic roles.

  Atomic concepts are declared in Alloy as non-empty subsets of `TOP`. For example, A is declared as atomic concept: `sig A in TOP {} fact { }`.

  Atomic roles are specified in Alloy with a set `TOP` as both domain and range. For example, the role `hasChild` is an atomic role:

  `abstract sig TOP { hasChild : set TOP }.`

- If C is an atomic concept and D is a concept, then $C \sqsubseteq D$ is called generalized concept inclusion, or GCI. GCIs are translated into Alloy using the set operator `in` (subset): `fact { C in D }`.

- Concept definitions of the form $A \equiv C$, where A is an atomic concept, are called equality axioms. Equalities are translated using Alloy's set equality operator: `fact { A = C }`.

- Instances of a given concept description are called individuals. If i is an individual, then it can be defined in Alloy as follows: `sig i in TOP {} fact { #i = 1 }`.

  In Alloy, a multiplicity keyword placed before a signature declaration constrains the number of elements in the signature's set. For example, the keyword `one` allows for defining a signature whose set contains exactly one element. Thus, `one sig i in TOP {}` declares instance i, having the same effect as the specification above. To implement the unique name assumption, additional constraints are generated to ensure that these singleton sets are pairwise different, for example: `fact { no ( polyneikes & iokaste ) }`.

- If a, b are individual names, C is a concept and R is a role name, than the following assertions about named individuals can be built by using constructs above: $C(a)$ (concept membership assertion), $R(a, b)$ (role membership assertions). In terms of Alloy we define concept membership assertions as `fact { a in C }` and role membership assertions as `fact { a -> b in R }` (`->` denotes the relational product operator).

4.2.2 Translation of $\mathcal{SHIQ}$ and $\mathcal{SROIQ}$

Alloy's underlying logic is expressive enough to encode $\mathcal{SHIQ}$ or even $\mathcal{SROIQ}$ formulas. As an outlook, tables below depict the Alloy formulation of $\mathcal{SHIQ}$ and $\mathcal{SROIQ}$ concepts and role constructors as well as of additional role constructs possible in Alloy. Here, `:>` denotes the range restriction and `~` is the relational transpose operator defined over binary relations. The operator `#` applied to a relation gives the cardinality of the relation as an integer value. The binary relation `iden` relates all the instances of the universe to themselves.

$\mathcal{SHIQ}$ concepts	Alloy translation
$\leq nR.C$	`{ a : univ	#(a.(R :> C)) =< n }`
$\geq nR.C$	`{ a : univ	#(a.(R :> C)) => n }`
inverse	`~R`
$\mathcal{SROIQ}$ concepts	**Alloy translation**
$\{o\}$	`sig i in TOP { } fact { #o = 1 }}`
$\exists R.Self$	`(R & iden).univ`
Further role terms	**Alloy translation**
$R \sqcap S$	`R & S`
reflexive transitive closure	`*R`

$\mathcal{SHIQ}$ allows for defining role hierarchies, which is a finite set of role inclusion axioms $R \sqsubseteq S$ where R and S are roles, and transitive roles ($R \circ R \sqsubseteq R$). In Alloy, we achieve the same expressibility using the set operator `in` and the relational composition (join) operator `.` as in the expressions `R in S` and `(R . R) in R`.

In $\mathcal{SROIQ}$, a role inclusion axiom is of the form $w \sqsubseteq R$, where w is a finite string of roles (e.g., $S1$, $S2$) and R is a role name. The appropriate translation into Alloy is: `(S1 . S2) in R`.

4.3 Case Studies

In what follows, we illustrate advantages of our proposal in the context of ontology design by discussing several case studies.

4.3.1 Model Inspection by Counterexample Extraction

As an introductory example of model inspection, we use the Oedipus example (see [13, p. 73]). In this example, the following ABox with some facts about the Oedipus story is supposed:

$$hasChild(iokaste, oedipus) \qquad hasChild(iokaste, polyneikes)$$
$$hasChild(oedipus, polyneikes) \qquad hasChild(polyneikes, thersandros)$$
$$Patricide(oedipus) \qquad \neg Patricide(thersandros)$$

Now, we want to find out whether some individual exists that have a child that is a patricide and that itself has a child that is not a patricide. This can be seen as a problem of checking the satisfiability of the concept

$$hasPatricideChildWithNonPatricideChild$$

$$\equiv$$

$$(\exists hasChild.(Patricide \sqcap \exists hasChild.\neg Patricide))$$

Applying $\mathcal{ALC}$ translation rules to the Oedipus knowledge base, we obtain the Alloy specification shown in Listing 4.1 on p. 66.

Alloy presents the following model (Figure 4.3 on p. 60). We will discuss next how it relates to the ontology given above. In summary, Iokaste is shown to have a patricide child (Oedipus in this model) who in turn has a non patricide child (a choice of individuals in this model).

Alloy offers a choice of customization capabilities for visualizing models but we will stick with the default settings. Particular models can be shown graphically as "snapshots" where individuals are represented as rectangles. Each such rectangle is identified by the internal name used by Alloy (e.g., "TOP1") which appears on the up-

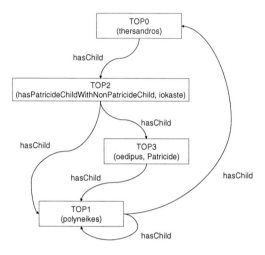

Figure 4.3: Oedipus example

per part of the rectangle. Arcs between rectangles stand for binary relations (roles), a label on the arc makes clear which role is being referred to. For each individual, the sets (concepts) it belongs to are shown as a comma separated list of labels on the lower part of the rectangle in question. Absence of one such label means that the individual does not satisfy that concept. For example, the labels of the node "TOP2" "iokaste, hasPatricideChildWithNonPatricideChild" reveal that individual iokaste is described by concept hasPatricideChildWithNonPatricideChild. Browsing further models will show other constellations under which this concept is satisfied. Note however that in this particular model, polyneikes is considered to have himself as child (nothing in the TBox prevents this). Inspecting models may lead to adjust the ontology with further axioms.

4.3.2 Counterexamples for a Subsumption Assumption

We use the following example from [13, p. 82] to demonstrate how a subsumption relation can be explained using Alloy. Assume that we want to check whether $(\exists r.a) \sqcap (\exists r.b)$ is subsumed by $\exists r.(a \sqcap b)$. This is equivalent to the satisfiability test of the concept $ifUnsatisfiableThenSubsumes \equiv (\exists r.a) \sqcap (\exists r.b) \sqcap \neg(\exists r.(a \sqcap b))$

Letting Alloy analyze the predicate $ifUnsatisfiableThenSubsumes$ results in several models. If left to its own devices, Alloy presents a model that minimizes the number of individuals. Alloy can be instructed however to look for models of a certain shape. We will do just that in order to display the solution presented in [13, p. 82], which is computed by a tableau algorithm. In order to achieve this, we will constraint those model we are interested in to those having exactly three individuals, with no individual in a nor b having a role filler over r. The model we are looking for is depicted in Figure 4.4. The technique described above is, of course, generally applicable and results in shorter response times as only a subset of all possible models is explored.

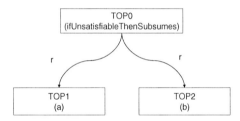

Figure 4.4: Model of the concept $ifUnsatisfiableThenSubsumes$

Figure 4.5: Model of the concept $counterExample$

To gain a better understanding for this result, one must recall that labels of particular individuals (nodes) contain concept names the individual belongs to. Absence
of some concept name C in the label of an individual means that the individual
belongs to the concept $\neg C$. Therefore, the node TOP1 explicitly has b in its label
and implicitly $\neg$a. A similar explanation holds for the node TOP2.

4.3.3 Counterexamples for a Concept Equivalence Assumption

As a next test case we assume the following simple TBox:

$$
\begin{aligned}
dogholder &\equiv (person \sqcap (\geq 1\ hasdog.dog)) \\
houndholder &\equiv (person \sqcap (\geq 1\ hashound.hound)) \\
dog &\equiv hound,\ hashound \sqsubseteq hasdog
\end{aligned}
$$

Suppose we expect that concepts *dogholder* and *houndholder* must be equivalent.
In order to check this automatically, we can let the Alloy Analyzer generate models
of the concept:

$$counterExample \equiv (dogholder \sqcap \neg houndholder) \sqcup (\neg dogholder \sqcap houndholder)$$

One model found by Alloy as a counterexample is shown in Figure 4.5 on p. 61.
In this model, the individual named TOP is found that belongs to the concept
dogholder but not to the concept *houndholder*. The reason is that the roles *hasdog*
and *hashound* are not equivalent.

4.4 Evaluation of Practical Usefulness

In order to empirically study the performance of model generation with Alloy we
have chosen a benchmark originally proposed for comparing DL systems (DL-98
systems comparison). We consider k-branch, which evaluates satisfiability-testing
performance for large concept expressions without reference to a TBox. Progressively larger expressions (for increasing sizes) are presented in two variants: all
k-branch-p expressions are unsatisfiable while all k-branch-n expressions are satisfiable. These (and other) benchmarks are available online[1]. We also used the

---

[1] http://dl.kr.org/dl98/comparison/data.html

solver RacerPro 1.9.1 beta to measure the times for (un)satisfiability checking with a tableau prover.

Summing up, Alloy exhibits a competitive performance for satisfiable input concepts if models can be found with up to 10 individuals. If models have more than 10 objects, performance quickly degrades (in particular, if unsatisfiable concepts are used as input). Apparently, BDD optimizations used in these systems cannot cope with combinatorial explosion, as more models are explored by Alloy than by tableau-based algorithms. Thus, there is good news when models are small enough (as full information can be presented to the ontology designer). If large model structures have to be explored, we found that model generators such as Alloy are not applicable.

As explained in the Alloy literature, the guiding principle for their construction was the "small scope hypothesis", which k-branch does not exhibit. Had we chosen a benchmark where this is the case, the results would have been more favorable to Alloy. For comparison, the time spent by RacerPro in this problem for different problem sizes is also shown in Table 4.1 and Table 4.2. The results of Alloy's runs are shown for different scope sizes (we did not yet implement an algorithm to compute the scope size according to the maximum concept branching factor and maximum depth of nested existential quantifiers as mentioned in Sec. 4.2).

As can be concluded from the measurement results, modern highly-optimized tableau-based provers far outperform model finders such as Alloy. However, in order to improve the usefulness of tableau-based reasoners also for ontology design tasks, it may be a good idea to equip them with model generation capacities like those provided by model finders for identifying unintended models. In the other direction, namely for increasing performance of model finders, DL prover techniques might also be helpful (given the expressivity of the input formulas is in the DL fragment). A tableau prover could be used for satisfiability checking. If there exists a model, the tableau describes a canonical model, which could be further modified in order to derive all models in the sense of model finders. If the expressivity is too high, models might be infinite, however, so the details of this idea have to be investigated carefully.

#	Alloy, 10 inds	Alloy, 15 inds	RacerPro
1	265	110	3
2	110	328	5
3	1,797, NMF	5,281	24
4	1,422, NMF	21,921, NMF	31
5	2,562, NMF	43,687, NMF	164
6	1,469, NMF	31,125, NMF	288
7	6,828, NMF	61,625, NMF	681
8	6,906, NMF	42,625, NMF	1,809
9	6,250, NMF	53,000, NMF	4,392
10	7,375, NMF	4,970,229, NMF	9,714
11	7437, NMF	3,024,688, NMF	23,623
12	17,50, NMF	575,407, NMF	51,266
13	27,640, NMF	4,215,123, NMF	119,628
14	4,281, NMF	3,654,211, NMF	294,519
15	38,577, NMF	1,282,483, NMF	765,325

Table 4.1: Concept satisfiability benchmarks (k-branch-n, all times in milliseconds, NMF = no model found, # = problem size)

#	Alloy, 10 inds	Alloy, 15 inds	RacerPro
1	47	94	1
2	1,532	531	2
3	875	44,624	4
4	1,281	34,421	5
5	2,610	30,953	11
6	9,828	56,422	24
7	5,781	63,935	29
8	1,984	41,578	218
9	6,578	70,466	113
10	58,718	716,200	225
11	12,500	520,077	638
12	30,484	345,288	711
13	6,500	409,849	1,099
14	10,624	811,636	3,517
15	11,719	3,129,982	4,143
16	5,066	845,979	11,742
17	7,219	1,204,383	24,594

Table 4.2: Concept unsatisfiability benchmarks (k-branch-p)

4.5 Outlook

While originally addressing interactive systems, in particular communication protocols, model-checking techniques are now applied to general imperative algorithms, as exemplified by the $^+$CAL algorithm language [142]. Given that $^+$CAL allows specifying pre- and postconditions alongside imperative statements, it constitutes a viable mechanism for automatically testing the optimized implementation of a decision procedure. Indeed, model checkers might also be successfully applied to develop robust and scalable optimized description logics systems. Unlike testing, model checking may dramatically reduce development effort.

The crucial requirement for integrating model finders in practical applications like model-driven and ontology development tools is the efficiency of constraint-solving engines they are based on. One of the recent investigations in producing high-performance tools is a Kodkod, a SAT-based model finder designed for a relational logic [196]. Besides of promising performance results, the system provides for further relevant features like optimized handling of assertional knowledge (in Alloy, specifying partial solutions is possible only in the form of additional constraints that increases the complexity of the solving process). Also looking into the future, SAT-solving algorithms designed to take advantage of multicore processors show promise [147].

Listing 4.1: Oedipus knowledge base expressed in Alloy's Relational Logic

```
module oedipus
   abstract sig TOP { /* atomic roles */ hasChild : set TOP }
   sig BOTTOM in TOP {} fact { #BOTTOM = 0 }
/* atomic concepts */
   sig hasPatricideChildWithNonPatricideChild in TOP {}
   sig Patricide in TOP {}
/* individuals */
   one sig polyneikes in TOP {}      one sig iokaste in TOP {}
   one sig thersandros in TOP {}     one sig oedipus in TOP {}
/* pairwise disjointness of individuals */
   fact{no(polyneikes & iokaste)} fact{no(polyneikes & thersandros)}
   fact{no(polyneikes & oedipus)} fact{no(iokaste & thersandros)}
   fact{no(iokaste & oedipus)} fact{no(thersandros & oedipus)}
/* equality axioms */
   fact { (hasPatricideChildWithNonPatricideChild) =
        (hasChild.(Patricide&(hasChild.((univ - Patricide)))))}
/* concept assertions */
   fact { oedipus in Patricide }
   fact { thersandros in ( univ - Patricide ) }
/* role assertions */
   fact { oedipus -> polyneikes in hasChild }
   fact { iokaste -> polyneikes in hasChild }
   fact { polyneikes -> thersandros in hasChild }
   fact { iokaste -> oedipus in hasChild }
pred show() { #univ = 4 } run show for 4
```

5 Translation of OCL Specifications

Static semantics play a crucial role in DSL metamodeling as they shape the contracts that model transformations should abide by. Additionally, well-formedness rules are also leveraged in authoring environments to catch malformed DSL expressions at their origin, before further inconsistencies are introduced in the software development process.

In this work, static semantics are formulated in OCL. An important language service, compilation from OCL to Java, was not supported by the Eclipse Modeling infrastructure which focused instead on parsing, AST building, and interpretation of OCL. In the context of that infrastructure, OCL compilation is more than a nice-to-have:

- DSL programs constitute the Model in an MVC (Model-View-Controller) architecture. For example, a graphical editor generated with Eclipse GMF follows the MVC paradigm. Response time determines the user acceptance of interactive authoring environments. OCL compilation is thus an important factor for DSL tooling.

- Outside the context of static semantics, OCL is a viable means to encode a number of functional requirements in general software development (pre- and postconditions, queries).

- Attempting to manually formulate usages of OCL collection operators in terms of Java Collections is error prone, given that there is no one-to-one correspondence between the semantics of similarly named operators.

This chapter discusses the design decisions made when developing our OCL to Java compiler integrated in the Eclipse Modeling infrastructure. The structure of this chapter is as follows. The interplay between that infrastructure and our compiler is covered in Sec. 5.1. The techniques for OCL translation described in Sec. 5.2 can be applied to other target languages (e.g., database query languages).

Sec. 5.3 provides details about the compilation algorithm, which comprises a conversion from OCL types to Java counterparts (Sec. 5.3.2) and the translation of OCL constructs proper (Sec. 5.3.3). The architecture of our compiler is extensible, Sec. 5.4 presents candidate extensions after reviewing representative LHS → RHS translation patterns. A particular case of OCL AST processing is refactoring, the topic of Sec. 5.5. Sec. 5.6 delves into performance evaluation. The integration of compiled code with other artifacts produced in an MDSE toolchain is the focus of Sec. 5.7. Finally, Sec. 5.8 discusses related work and concludes the chapter by evaluating the benefits of the approach.

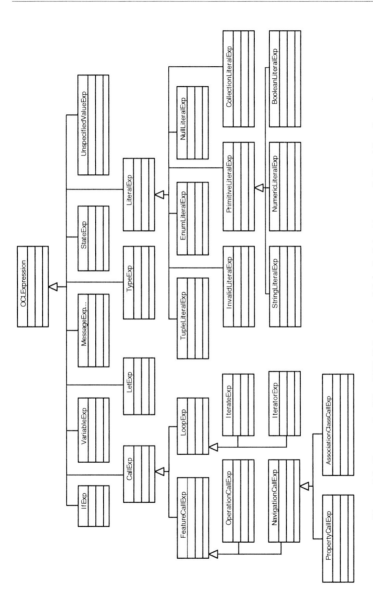

Figure 5.1: Fragment of the OCL 2.0 metamodel (only inheritance relationships shown)

5.1 Target Software Architecture

The operation of a compiler [12] can be broken down into phases: (1) lexical analysis; (2) parsing a stream of tokens into a language-independent Concrete Syntax Tree (CST); (3) transforming such CST into a language-specific Abstract Syntax Tree (AST). During this phase, usages are resolved to their declarations, and symbol tables are built for later use in succeeding phases, as for example during (4) semantic analysis, where the static semantics are checked. For example, a program may be syntactically valid yet not pass type checking, with type checking being a case in point of well-formedness. For input that has progressed this far, the remaining phases can generate executable code: (5) translation to intermediate code, (6) detection of unreachable blocks, (7) optimization (e.g. constant propagation) based on control and dataflow analyses, (8) instruction selection and register allocation.

In our setting, the output language is a high-level language (Java 5), moreover constrained to a number of code idioms. The particular patterns to generate partly depend on user preferences. For example, either (a) POJO-style (Plain Old Java Objects) or (b) EMF-enabled style can be chosen. The latter is suitable whenever EMF services will be accessed at runtime (reflection, dynamic object model, interaction with Eclipse editors). As an example of (b), method signatures generated for OCL invariants follow the contract expected by the EMF Validator Framework.

Similarly, there are code idioms resulting from OCL itself (most notably, the implicit *source* argument resulting from OCL's compact syntax).

Regarding the input languages, the basic activities of parsing, AST building, and well-formedness checking for Ecore + OCL are carried out by reusing building blocks provided by the Eclipse Modeling infrastructure [78] (compare with the effort required to access, for example, the ASTs and symbol tables prepared by the front-end of a C++ compiler). Although well-formed ASTs are available, the translation algorithm still has to account for the mismatch between OCL and Java:

- OCL is (mostly) a function-based language, where functions are not first-class citizens. No OCL constructs allow returning arbitrary functions as values or receive them as arguments. A limited form of lambda abstraction is available in loop expressions, where the body defines a function for mapping each element in the source collection, with an accumulator to reduce the final result.

- Some OCL types have no direct counterpart in the Java libraries. For example, `OclInvalid` represents the result of applying a function outside its domain, while `Bag` represents an unordered collection allowing duplicates.

- OCL defines a number of built-in functions (the OCL Standard Library) whose Java counterparts are defined in `org.eclipse.ocl.util`.

- Some capabilities expected by OCL are not provided by either the EMF or Java object systems, and have to be provided by generated code, e.g. keeping track of `allInstances()` of a given type.

On the plus side, EMF support for parametric polymorphism (Chapter 3) is in line with the strongly-typed nature of OCL and makes for a seamless transition from OCL collection types to those from the `java.util` package.

5.2 Processing of OCL Abstract Syntax Trees

The techniques applied to process OCL Abstract Syntax Trees (ASTs) are summarized in this section, including (a) patterns for OCL visitors, (b) taking advantage of Java 5 Generics when customizing visitors, (c) achieving conciseness by encapsulating the walking order, and (d) keeping track of input-output relationships across a chain of visitors. These techniques allow for the formulation of translation algorithms as sets of $LHS \rightarrow RHS$ substitutions (thus facilitating their analysis), at the same time having a straightforward realization in terms of visitors.

The MDT OCL framework supports all the way from parsing a textual OCL expression to interpreting it on some object population, for both Ecore and UML2 class models. This requires some infrastructure, which MDT OCL provides as visitors for:

- validating the concrete-syntax tree (CST) prepared by the parser

- resolving identifiers to declarations, i.e., transforming a CST into an abstract syntax tree (AST)

- interpreting an OCL AST against an object population

Listing 5.1: Handler to unparse an `IteratorExp`

```
protected String handleIteratorExp(IteratorExp<C,PM> callExp,
  String sourceResult, List<String> variableResults,
  String bodyResult) {
  StringBuffer result = new StringBuffer();
  String name = callExp.getName();
  result.append(sourceResult).append("->").append(name).append('(');

  for (Iterator<String> iter = variableResults.iterator();
    iter.hasNext();) {
    result.append(iter.next());
    if (iter.hasNext()) { result.append(", "); }
  }

  result.append(" | ").append(bodyResult).append(')');
  return result.toString();
}
```

The functionality listed above is accessed over an interface following the façade design pattern, `org.eclipse.ocl.OCL`. Although this section does not focus on issues related to concrete-syntax trees, two remarks are in order. First, CST classes are internal, i.e. not part of the public API of the MDT OCL component. And second, the validation of a CST is actually performed by the same visitor in charge of the CST to AST conversion.

OCL expressions cannot be understood in isolation, they always appear in the context of some model element, which determines the other model elements that are in scope. For example, the formal arguments to an operation can be referred in a precondition but not in a class invariant. Any of the following model elements may office as context:

- a class (each OCL invariant has a class as context)
- a class property (for example, an OCL query to compute a derived attribute has that attribute as context)
- an operation (pre- and postconditions, body expressions)

Unparenthesized form	`currentLevel.name = 'Silver' implies`
	`card.color = Color::silver and`
	`currentLevel.name = 'Gold' implies`
	`card.color = Color::gold`

Correct interpretation	`( (currentLevel.name = 'Silver')`
	`implies (card.color = Color::silver)`
	`) and (`
	`(currentLevel.name = 'Gold'`
	`implies card.color = Color::gold))`

Table 5.1: Revealing precedence rules of operators in an expression

For the sake of clarity, OCL ASTs can be depicted as in Figure 5.4 on p. 82. The algorithm to build such views has been implemented as part of the tool OCLASTView [78]. These views make clear the structure of OCL ASTs. For example, given an unparenthesized fragment, realizing the correct interpretation (based on operator precedence rules) is immediate with the visual depiction, as shown in Table 5.1.

5.2.1 Basic API for Visitors

The occurrences of OCL language constructs are internally represented as instances of the OCL metamodel classes (depicted in Figure 5.1 on p. 69). In the AST shown in Figure 5.4 on p. 82, the root is an `IteratorExp`. This particular iterator (a `forAll` with two iterator variables) evaluates whether the boolean condition expressed in its body is true for all pairs of items in the source collection (the source collection being `self.participants`, whose type is `OrderedSet(Customer)`). As a whole, this `forAll` reports whether items with duplicate names exist. The tree representation depicts iterators with the source collection as first child, the iterator variable(s) as next children, and the body as last child (in keeping with the lexical order in the textual syntax). More diagrams of the OCL 2.0 metamodel can be found in the latest specification by the OMG (May 2006, [171]).

The nodes in an OCL AST stand for a function application (internal node) or for a read access (leaf node). The default post-order visit order for internal nodes (implemented in class `AbstractVisitor`) is usually satisfactory, as it accommodates for nodes standing for arguments to be visited before the function application itself.

Listing 5.2: The default visit order for an `IteratorExp`

```java
public T visitIteratorExp(IteratorExp<C, PM> callExp) {
   T sourceResult = callExp.getSource().accept(this);
   List<T> variableResults;
   List<Variable<C, PM>> variables = callExp.getIterator();
   if (variables.isEmpty()) {
      variableResults = Collections.emptyList();
   } else {
     variableResults = new java.util.ArrayList(variables.size());
     for (Variable<C, PM> iterVar : variables) {
        variableResults.add(iterVar.accept(this));
     }
   }
   T bodyResult = callExp.getBody().accept(this);
   return handleIteratorExp(callExp, sourceResult,
           variableResults, bodyResult);
}
```

For example, the default visit order for an `IteratorExp` is determined by the Java method `visitIteratorExp` and its accompanying `handleIteratorExp` shown in Listing 5.2. Informally speaking, an OCL iterator expression evaluates its body for each item in the source collection. Such body expression usually involves an accumulator variable, with the value computed for the body being assigned to the accumulator variable, thus making it available for the next iteration (an OCL iterator combines map and reduce of functional programming [110]). The metamodel of `IteratorExp` is depicted in Figure 5.2. Incidentally, `forAll` is special in that it is the only OCL iterator construct allowing more than one variable, as a shorthand to nesting `forAll`s. The example in Figure 5.4 on p. 82 employs this shorthand to evaluate the body expression over the Cartesian product of the source collection.

The implementation in Listing 5.2 performs no processing at all, it just visits all nodes. Instead, an unparsing visitor (to obtain the textual representation back from an AST, shown in Listing 5.1) returns a string of the form:

sourceCollection→iteratorName(iteratorVariables | iteratorBody)

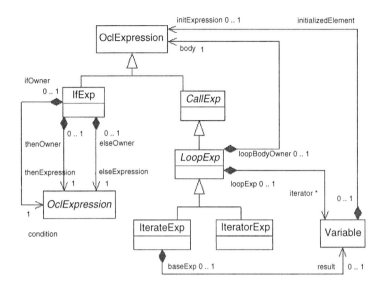

Figure 5.2: Containment associations for IfExp and LoopExp

An unparser needs only override handleIteratorExp(), as visitIteratorExp() takes up the recurrent duty of visiting the children nodes, moreover passing results (Strings in this case) as actual arguments to handleIteratorExp(). In case the default visit order is not deemed appropriate for some particular scenario, its visit... methods can be overridden to achieve another order. This is necessary, for example, when evaluating an OCL if-then-else-endif: the else part is to be evaluated only in case the condition part evaluates to false. This is what EvaluationVisitorImpl.visitIfExp() does.

5.2.2 Usage of Generics when Processing OCL ASTs

Given that MDT OCL aims at supporting both Ecore and UML2 class models, the decision was made by its authors to use Generics [79] (also known as parametric

Type parameter	org.eclipse.emf.ecore (unless otherwise specified)
PK	EPackage
C	EClassifier
O	EOperation
P	EStructuralFeature
EL	EEnumLiteral
PM	EParameter
S	EObject
COA	org.eclipse.ocl.ecore.CallOperationAction
SSA	org.eclipse.ocl.ecore.SendSignalAction
CT	org.eclipse.ocl.ecore.Constraint
CLS	EClass
E	EObject

Table 5.2: Expected type arguments in the Ecore-specialization of MDT OCL

types) to avoid duplicating the code base. This was a tradeoff, as Java 5 supports *intersection types* (e.g., a type argument T may be required to implement two interfaces A & B) but not *union types*, which would be fitting to the need to specify that the class context of an OCL invariant can be either an Ecore class, i.e., an `org.eclipse.emf.ecore.EClassifier`; or an UML2 class, i.e., an `org.eclipse.uml2.uml.Classifier`. Still, static type-safety is achieved by following programming conventions about type substitutions, summarized in Tables 5.2 and 5.3.

5.2.3 Common Steps in Writing OCL Visitors

Usually it makes sense to consider first what output is wanted for leaf nodes in OCL ASTs. These nodes are recognized because `AbstractVisitor` defines their handler to simply return `null`; no children nodes are visited, and thus no `handler...` methods are defined for such constructs. In summary, leaf nodes are handled by the methods shown in Listing 5.3 on p. 78 (where the return type T is a type parameter of the visitor class).

Some notes on the usage of these methods follow: `visitVariableExp()` han-

Type parameter	org.eclipse.uml2.uml (unless otherwise specified)
PK	Package
C	Classifier
O	Operation
P	Property
EL	EnumerationLiteral
PM	Parameter
S	State
COA	CallOperationAction
SSA	SendSignalAction
CT	Constraint
CLS	Class
E	org.eclipse.emf.ecore.EObject

Table 5.3: Expected type arguments in the UML2-specialization of MDT OCL

dles *usages* of variables in OCL expressions. From a `VariableExp` it is possible to access the declaration of the referred variable, i.e., to access an instance of `org.eclipse.ocl.expressions.Variable<C, PM>`. Two novelties of OCL 2.0 are the built-in literal values `null` and `OclInvalid` which may appear in the textual syntax. Generally the result of an operation invocation on `OclInvalid` or with an undefined argument is undefined except in the following cases, as prescribed by the OCL specification [171, pp. 2-10 in Sec. 2.4.11], all of them irrespective of the lexical order of the arguments:

- `true` or *Anything* is `true`

- `false` and *Anything* is `false`

- `false` implies *Anything* is `true`

- `if` *Condition* `then` *thenPart* `else` *elsePart* `endif` has the value dictated by the condition regardless of the value of the not-chosen branch (in particular, such branch may evaluate to `OclInvalid`).

In terms of the OCL metamodel, non-leaf nodes are those whose metaclasses define one or more composition associations, as for example `IfExp`, `IterateExp`,

Listing 5.3: Methods in a visitor to handle leaf nodes

```
public T visitVariableExp(VariableExp<C, PM> v);
public T visitTypeExp(TypeExp<C> t);
public T visitUnspecifiedValueExp(UnspecifiedValueExp<C> unspecExp);
public T visitStateExp(StateExp<C, S> stateExp);

public T visitIntegerLiteralExp(IntegerLiteralExp<C> literalExp);
public T visitRealLiteralExp(RealLiteralExp<C> literalExp);
public T visitStringLiteralExp(StringLiteralExp<C> literalExp);
public T visitBooleanLiteralExp(BooleanLiteralExp<C> literalExp);
public T visitNullLiteralExp(NullLiteralExp<C> literalExp);

public T visitInvalidLiteralExp(InvalidLiteralExp<C> literalExp);
public T visitEnumLiteralExp(EnumLiteralExp<C, EL> literalExp);
public T visitUnlimitedNaturalLiteralExp(
        UnlimitedNaturalLiteralExp literalExp)
```

and `IteratorExp` (Figure 5.2). Their handlers in a visitor usually piece together the results of visiting the owned parts.

The metamodel classes which are subtypes of `CallExp` contain a reference to an additional implicit argument (not shown in the textual syntax between the parentheses of the argument list). This *source expression* can be obtained by invoking `getSource()` on the `CallExp`.

For example, the metamodel fragment in Figure 5.1 on p. 69 shows that a `CallExp` is a supertype of `PropertyCallExp`. Accordingly, the grammar allows: `self.age >= 18`, where `age` stands for a property (an attribute), with `self` being the source expression (an instance of `VariableExp`). This implicit source should be visited just like other arguments. Additional OCL constructs that own sub-expressions occur in connection with the initializers of variables and with the arguments of operation calls.

Besides the handlers discussed so far, the remaining methods follow similar patterns, however some comments are in order:

- some types in the method signatures are not shown in the fragment of the

OCL metamodel depicted in Figure 5.1 (that is the case for the constructs `TupleLiteralPart`, `CollectionItem`, `CollectionRange`, `Variable`, and also for `CollectionLiteralPart`). As Figure 5.3 shows (p. 80), not all OCL constructs have counterparts subtyping `OCLExpression` in the metamodel (Figure 5.1 depicts only the classes branching off from `OCLExpression`).

- MDT OCL follows Chapter 12 of the OCL specification [171] and includes the `ExpressionInOcl` metaclass. This metaclass does not subtype `TypedElement` but `Visitable` and constitutes the container for context variables (`self`, `result`) and for those variables standing for operation parameters (if any). `AbstractVisitor.visitExpressionInOCL()` will visit those owned parts, invoking method `AbstractVisitor.handleExpressionInOCL()` for each of those results.

- `@pre` may be used in a postcondition as the postfix of a property, to indicate the value the property had before execution of the operation. More in detail, the `FeatureCallExp` metaclass defines the `isMarkedPre` property. Unfortunately, Section 8.3.2 "FeatureCall Expressions" of the OCL spec [171] omits the description of the `FeatureCallExp` metaclass. However, it is at least clear that a `VariableExp` cannot be marked `@pre`.

5.2.4 Further Techniques to Process OCL ASTs

A visitor is not limited to letting other components know of its processing only through return values, it may also update instance state at the visitor level. This is frequently the case with chains of visitors: a visitor receives as argument in its constructor the previous one, in order to access the updated instance state (after the received visitor has completed its processing).

Also in the context of visitor chains, it is possible to keep track of the input-output relationships at the node level in the form of bidirectional maps (one-to-one, one-to-many, or many-to-many). This practice enables use cases such as round-trip engineering (updating the output expression modifies the input, or at least signals what nodes in the input AST are out-of-synch with their counterpart). For example,

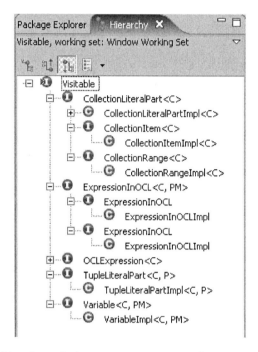

Figure 5.3: Metaclasses for language constructs not subtyping `OCLExpression`

when using the OCL → Java compiler, offering the capability to debug at the OCL source-code level requires keeping track of the correspondence between OCL AST nodes and generated Java statements, as the Java debugger reports its progress in terms of Java line statements (this is related to JSR–45: *Debugging Support for Other Languages*, [126]).

Whether an OCL expression is interpreted or compiled, one way to make OCL evaluation faster consists in computing at compile-time as much as possible of the expression, as a result of analyses such as *constant folding* or *strength reduction* or *common sub-expression elimination* (compiler-implementation terminology) or *partial evaluation* (functional programming terminology).

Listing 5.4: Code sketch of AST rewriting relying on an AST cloning utility class

```
@Override
protected Visitable handleOperationCallExp(
    OperationCallExp<C, O> callExp,
    Visitable sourceResult,
    List<Visitable> argumentResults) {

  int opcode = callExp.getOperationCode();
  if (!isArithmeticOp(callExp)) {
    return super.handleOperationCallExp(
      callExp, sourceResult, argumentResults);
  }
  OCLExpression<C> newSource = (OCLExpression<C>) sourceResult;
  OCLExpression<C> newArg =
    (OCLExpression<C>) argumentResults.get(0);
  if (!(newSource instanceof NumericLiteralExp)
      || !(newArg instanceof NumericLiteralExp)) {
    return super.handleOperationCallExp(
      callExp, sourceResult, argumentResults);
  }
  /*
  * actual reduction comes here
  */
```

In general, AST rewritings usually involve leaving most of the input AST as-is, which requires most handlers in a visitor to just return a cloned version of the input. It would be cumbersome to duplicate over and over that strategy whenever a reducer visitor is written. Instead, utility classes such as OCLCloner [78] encapsulate such behavior by default. A new visitor need only override those methods where it may detect an opportunity for applying a reduction, invoking the non-overridden version in case the preconditions for the reduction are not fulfilled. For example, in the context of compile-time arithmetic simplification, the method visitOperationCallExp() is shown in Listing 5.4.

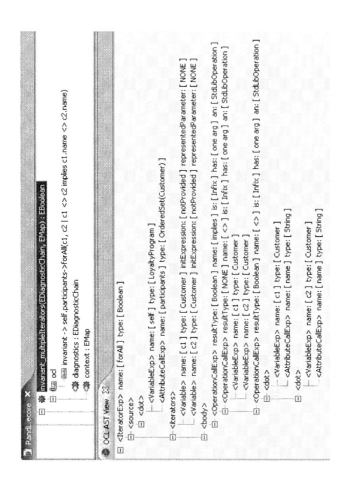

Figure 5.4: Visual depiction using OCLASTView [78] of the AST for the invariant self.participants→forAll(c1,c2 | c1<>c2 implies c1.name<>c2.name)

5.3 Compilation Phases

5.3.1 Information Initially Available to the Compiler

The ASTs prepared by MDT OCL encode not only structural aspects of OCL (operators, operands, precedence) but also reveal the statically computed types for each sub-expression, down to the leaf nodes (literals, read access to variables). Not all of this type information has been explicitly stated by the developer, but is inferred from the types of arguments and the involved operation. Less frequently, a type declaration itself may be implicit and the resulting type has no user-visible name (this is the case for tuple literals and for implicit iterator variables in loop expressions).

The translation algorithm comprises (a) types conversion and (b) expressions translation. The latter involves a structural mapping that considers one node at a time of the input OCL AST, and produces a Java counterpart. This translation has to abide by the type conversion, i.e. the Java type of an output expression has to conform to that specified by the rules elaborated in Sec. 5.3.2. Translation (b) requires information available locally at each input node. Such nodes stand for a function application (internal node) or for a read access (leaf node). As explained in detail in Sec. 5.3.3, the translation of a function application is constructive: provided that the arguments have already been translated, the output for the function application as a whole will be well-formed.

Regarding the possible OCL constructs, Figure 5.1 depicts the relevant fragment of the OCL metamodel [171], i.e. the classes whose instances are nodes in an AST (for more details, see [78]). For illustration, one such AST is shown in Figure 5.4, depicting the *static dataflow* of an OCL expression. For simple expressions, such AST depiction has the same shape as the *dynamic dataflow* (i.e., the tree of call stack activations). For OCL expressions involving recursion or loops, the dynamic dataflow is data-dependent and a visual representation would involve unwinding the call hierarchy for a particular execution trace.

The OCL Standard does not specify the order in which AST building should take place, but it cannot be arbitrary: `def` statements can be used to add: (a) attributes, (b) references and (c) operations to a class model specified in Ecore. In order for other OCL expressions to parse correctly (as they may contain usages of these newly added model elements), the declaration part of all `def` statements is processed first, affecting an in-memory copy of the original input model. Thereafter, ASTs are built for the initialization part of the `def` statements and for the remaining OCL statements. An example of mutual forward references occurring in the initializers of `def` statements is depicted in Figure 5.5.

```
                                      context A
 refToA  0..1                         def dA: sa : String = refToB.sb
             refToB
  ClassA              ClassB          context B
           0..1                       def dB: sb : String = refToA.sa
```

Figure 5.5: Mutual forward references in the initializers of `def` statements

5.3.2 Types Conversion

The declared types appearing in a particular Ecore + OCL specification are a subset of the *universe of types* resulting from applying OCL type construction operators to the union of the OCL built-in types and those in the user-specified class model. The subtype relationship over the types universe is a partial order. The types conversion implemented by our compiler must map this graph G into an isomorphic graph H (whose nodes represent Java 5 types). This isomorphic mapping is a bijection f between the vertices of G and H such that any two vertices u and v from G are adjacent if and only if $f(u)$ and $f(v)$ are adjacent in H. This ensures that, if two nodes in the target graph are connected, such statement about subtyping is valid under the subtyping relationship of Java 5 (§4.10 in [95]).

Type formation in OCL is summarized in Figure 5.6 and covered in Sec. 8.2 of the OCL 2.0 Standard [171]. In fact, the OCL → Java types conversion can be made more concise by translating into Ecore types [79] (which are shorthands for the Java 5 types that will appear in the code generated by the EMF CodeGen component). The algorithm to achieve this conversion appears on Tables 5.4 and 5.5, as pairs of $LHS \rightarrow RHS$ transformations from OCL types into Ecore types.

This algorithm is applied to instances of Ecore's `ETypedElement` (attributes and references in classes, formal parameters and return type in operations) after ASTs have been built as discussed at the end of Sec. 5.3.1.

OCL type	Ecore counterpart
	(wrapped inside an `EDataType<T>` with `instanceClassName` as below)
Collection(T)	`java.util.Collection<? extends T>`
Sequence(T)	`java.util.ArrayList<? extends T>`
Set(T)	`java.util.HashSet<? extends T>`
OrderedSet(T)	`java.util.LinkedHashSet<? extends T>`
Bag(T)	`org.eclipse.ocl.util.Bag<? extends T>`
Boolean, Integer	`EBoolean`, `EInt`
String, Real	`EString`, `EDouble`
TupleType	A dedicated `EClass` is added to the in-memory copy of the input model, with structural features standing for the tuple's fields
VoidType	All OCL-defined expressions return some value, including `body` statements defining `EOperations`. The Java counterpart of VoidType is a `void` method return type, but such methods cannot be defined with OCL.
MessageType	Not handled by our compiler, MessageTypes denote method invocations, which are not reified in Java.
ElementType	This metaclass appears in the OCL standard just to introduce vocabulary for later use in English sentences. There is no "ElementType" as such, the item type of a collection must be one of the types defined above.

Table 5.4: Types present in OCL since version 1.0

OCL type	Ecore counterpart
AnyType	`EObject`
InvalidType	As in Java, there is no name in Ecore for the type whose only allowed value is `null`. Whenever an OCL expression would evaluate to InvalidType, the Java counterpart will compute `null`.
TypeType	"TypeType" appears in the OCL specification only in diagrams (in particular, no definition for it is given). Its apparent intent, type reification, is already handled by the Ecore metamodel and the above definitions, which suffice for ASTs involving `oclIsTypeOf()`, `oclIsKindOf()`, and `oclAsType()`.

Table 5.5: Types added to OCL 2.0

5.3.3 Expressions Translation

The internal nodes in an OCL AST stand for the application of a function to its arguments. The OCL constructs subclassing `CallExp` receive, besides the argument list, an additional *source expression* as implicit argument. In the example shown in Figure 5.4 on p. 82, `self.participants→forAll(c1,c2 | ... )`, the source expression of the `forAll` is `self.participants`.

In general, the Java code generated to compute the function application could assume that the values of arguments are available in local variables. This recursive pattern fits perfectly the visit order that can be followed by subclassing `org.eclipse.ocl.utilities.AbstractVisitor`. To enforce this recursive pattern, each method in the compilation visitor (one for each OCL construct) should abide by the following contract:

(a) visit nodes standing for arguments so that Java statements to compute them are added to a visitor-local running list; and

(b) return the name of the local variable where the result of the expression rooted at the visited node will be available (the upstream node will need this name to complete its own code generation)

While performing (a) for each argument to an OCL function invocation, the name

Listing 5.5: Template of the code generated for an `IfExp`

```
/* 'NCS' below stands for the nearest common supertype
for the types of the Then and the Else branches */
NCS if123 = null;
// statements generated by getCondition().accept(this)
// returning the local variable name 'cond456'
if (cond456) {
    // statements generated by getThenExpression().accept(this)
    // returning the local variable name 'then789'
    if123 = then789;
} else {
    // statements generated by getElseExpression().accept(this)
    // returning the local variable name 'else789'
    if123 = else789;
}
```

of the local variable holding the argument's value can be obtained: this name was returned as per (b).

For example, the code generated for an `if` C `then` E_1 `else` E_2 `endif` appears in Listing 5.5, making clear that generated local variables will be in scope (and assigned) by the time they are used: the local variable containing the result of C is in-scope and assigned by the time it is referred in the generated `if` statement. The above scheme also "scales down" to AST leaf nodes, as shown in Listing 5.6. As a further example, the visitor method in charge of compiling an OCL `let` statement is shown in Listing 5.7. A more comprehensive input-output pair (involving iterators and implicit variables) can found in Listing 5.15 on p. 99.

The compilation algorithm is encapsulated in class `CompilationVisitor`. The implementation of OCL visitors in general is discussed in [78], including techniques such as the encapsulation of walker code, instantiation of type-parametric visitors with type substitutions, and tracking the input-output relationship between AST nodes along a chain of visitors.

The complete list of translation rules cannot be reproduced here because of space reasons (such rules are, in essence, syntax-triggered substitutions). The analysis

Listing 5.6: The translation of an OCL primitive literal is a Java literal

```
@Override
public String visitBooleanLiteralExp(
    BooleanLiteralExp<EClassifier> literalExp) {
    return literalExp.getBooleanSymbol().toString();
}
```

Listing 5.7: Visit order for a `let` expression: initializer, in-part

```
@Override
public String visitLetExp(LetExp<EClassifier, EParameter> letExp) {
    OCLExpression<EClassifier> initExpr =
        letExp.getVariable().getInitExpression();
    // add the Java stmts for the initializer part of the letExp
    String srcInitVal = initExpr.accept(this);
    String srcJavaType = getSrcType(letExp.getVariable().getType());
    String srcVarName = letExp.getVariable().getName();
    addAssignment(srcJavaType, srcVarName, srcInitVal);
    // add the Java stmts for the in part of the letExp
    String res = letExp.getIn().accept(this);
    return res;
}
```

around termination and determinism of the compilation algorithm relies on its formulation as a number of pattern-based substitutions of the form $LHS \rightarrow RHS$,
where each OCL construct is matched by only one LHS. The transformation algorithm can be shown to correctly preserve meaning if each rewrite transformation is
proved meaning-preserving. The rewrite rules are terminating because they decrease
the number of occurrences of OCL constructs available for matching, and are confluent given that the LHSs partition the set of shapes that OCL constructs may take
(each OCL construct being matched by one rewrite rule). In this pattern-matching
strategy, translation operates bottom-up from the leaves of the AST.

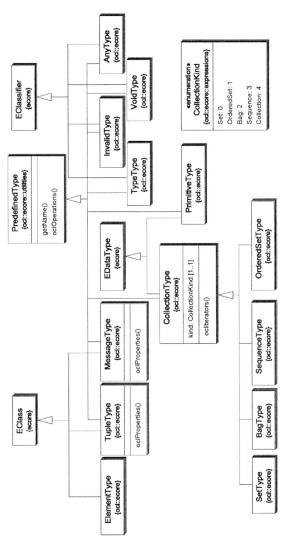

Figure 5.6: Type information in MDT OCL

5.4 Translation Patterns

After the semantic analysis phase is complete, a 3GL compiler translates abstract
syntax into abstract machine code, pending detailed instruction selection. To avoid
the combinatorial explosion between compiler frontends and target processor architectures, an *intermediate representation* is used (Figure 5.7). In case of our
OCL compiler, the target architecture consists of generally accepted mechanisms in
stack-based, garbage-collected OO programming languages (C#, Java, Smalltalk).
Therefore, some translation patterns are presented at a conceptual level in terms of
Java syntax for the RHS part, with the assurance that no Java-only mechanisms are
being resorted to.

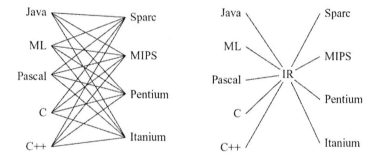

Figure 5.7: Compilers for five languages and four target machines: (a) without an
IR, (b) with an IR (reproduced from [12])

OCL loop operations, of both the iterator and `iterate()` varieties, constitute
frequently used collection operations that deserve custom code to be generated for
each. The distinction follows the abstract syntax (Listing 5.14 on p. 98).

Usually, an invocation of `iterate()` contains only a single iterator variable, and
thus the resulting RHS looks as reproduced in Listing 5.8. As for more than one
iterator variables, nested loops are added.

Listing 5.8: Pattern for the translation of OCL loop operations

```
... compile sourceResult here
... compile initialValue here
<accumulatorType> <accumulatorVarName> = <initialValue>;
for (<iterVarType> <iterVarName> : <sourceResult>) {
   <accVarName> = ... compile iterate body here
}
```

5.4.1 Extending the Compiler

Early on the decision was made to base our compiler on Ecore instead of UML2. The modeling abstractions in Ecore are a subset of those in UML2. In detail, Ecore does not allow: class-scoped features or operations, association classes, association-end qualifiers (which office as primary keys to identify an item in a collection), and the marking of operations as `isQuery()`. With the expressive power of OCL however, every datamodel that can be expressed in UML2 can be reformulated as a corresponding Ecore + OCL model (for example, a Singleton pattern can be stated with an invariant of the form $Type \rightarrow$`allInstances()`$\rightarrow$`size()` = 1). MDT OCL provides uniform support for both UML2 and Ecore, by relying on bounded type parameters. We thus see no principle obstacle to refactor the codebase of the compiler to take as input an UML2-based model instead of an Ecore-based one.

The detection of the minimal subset of invariants that need rechecking (due to updates to the object population, intercepted at runtime) has been addressed a number of times. One technique to achieve detection relies on AspectJ and is described by Dzidek [27]. Altenhofen et al. also address this problem [7]. Existing approaches re-evaluate from scratch each invariant in the potentially affected set, upon detecting an update to any location referred from the AST of the invariant. However, it would be enough to evaluate those nodes upstream of the updated one, propagating values as long as the new value differs from the cached previous value (using memoization, Chapter 12). Recursion and looping result in the dynamic dataflow not matching the shape of the compile-time AST (Sec. 5.3.1), an issue to consider to avoid false-positives (invariants that actually need no rechecking) as well as, more importantly, mispredictions (overlooking re-evaluating an invariant whose value has actually changed).

Another area for future work consists in re-architecting our (batch) compiler to support incremental compilation. This would require reacting to the deltas that the Eclipse workspace notification mechanism provides.

5.5 Refactoring of OCL Expressions

The presence of OCL constraints in an integrated Ecore + OCL model implies that refactorings at the class model level can no longer ignore their effect on the syntax, well-formedness, and semantics of the associated OCL constraints. A desirable property for refactorings is for them to be *semantics preserving*. What exactly is meant by that requires more precision. For example, every refactoring loses *some* semantics: a refactoring for speed results in programs having a different observable behavior from the original ones (which are slower).

Kniesel [132] frames the problem of refactoring in the context of *conditional program transformations*, where preconditions guard against unwarranted applications of a source-level transformation. In the case of OCL, the authors of [155] cleverly define an OCL refactoring to be semantics preserving provided the following conditions are met: (a) there is a one-to-one correspondence between old and new OCL constraints; and (b) every possible evaluation of each new constraint results in the same value as its old version on the image of the system snapshot (how to compute the image function for each refactoring is not spelt out in detail).

Taking as starting point the list of refactorings proposed by Fowler [75], an adaptation to the OCL language is made. Exemplarily, one refactoring is proved to be semantics preserving (by structural induction on the shapes of the fragments of OCL ASTs participating in the refactoring), although in the chosen case (moving an attribute to another class over an association with one-to-one multiplicity) the result is intuitive. The Eclipse-based tool RoclET[1] aims at implementing the refactorings described in [155].

Sometimes, a simpler version of a verbose expression can be obtained without

---

[1]RoclET, http://www.roclet.org/

Listing 5.9: Example of Verbose Expression

```
context LoyaltyProgram
def verboseTransactions : Set(Transaction) =
  self.partners->collect ( i_ProgramPartner : ProgramPartner |
    i_ProgramPartner.deliveredServices )->collect (
      i_Service : Service | i_Service.transactions )->asSet()
```

Listing 5.10: Concise formulation of the fragment in Listing 5.9

```
context LoyaltyProgram
def conciseTransactions : Set(Transaction) =
  self.partners.deliveredServices.transactions->asSet()
```

change in meaning, thus promoting readability. Listing 5.9 shows a sample verbose version, while Listing 5.10 displays its simplified counterpart. Rules for simplifying expressions (for both improved performance and readability) can be found in [88].

Correa and Werner [46] offer a catalog of *code smells* for OCL, i.e., patterns that go against established programming practice, for example by impairing readability or by complicating the evolution of the expressions. Typical smells include *magic numbers, and-chain* (several Boolean expressions anded together instead of broken apart into separate definitions), Law of Demeter [148], and duplicate code. To overcome their shortcomings, a number of refactorings are put forward. For example, *Implies Chain* denotes a chain of `implies` operators, that can be simplified by replacing the occurrences of `implies` with `and` except for the last one. Line 1 of Listing 5.11 shows the example of Implies Chain and the next line shows the result after refactoring.

To our knowledge, no detailed algorithms have been presented in the literature

Listing 5.11: Example of Implies Chain

```
a1 implies a2 implies .. implies aN implies b
(a1 and a2 and .. and aN) implies b
```

Listing 5.12: Nested loop in an invariant, resulting in a cartesian product

```
context LoyaltyProgram
inv: self.participants->forAll( c1 |
      self.participants->forAll( c2 |
        c1 <> c2 implies c1.name <> c2.name ))
```

for the following language processing tasks: (a) detecting unused derived operations or attributes (not an error, but a symptom that a typo may have occurred); (b) replacing an arbitrary (complex) subexpression with the invocation to a `defined` operation. Notice this may involve passing as explicit arguments some bindings in the scope of the caller but not in the scope of the callee; (c) finding unused explicit arguments; (d) computing the average complexity of an expression in *big-O* notation; (e) inlining a `def` usage (also called macro expansion). This is the counterpart to factoring a subexpression into a separate definition.

5.6 Performance

Measuring wall-clock time, compiled code runs up to six times faster than its interpreted counterpart (twice as fast on average). In all cases, elapsed times for the interpreter do not include runtime parsing and AST building, as these operations can be amortized among several evaluations. The largest speedups correspond to nested loops, as is the case for the invariant shown in Listing 5.12 evaluated over 10000 instances (84 sec vs. 580 sec). Better speedups could be achieved if our compiler were an *optimizing* compiler [206]. Some compile-time optimizations (e.g. constant propagation) are performed by the JIT (Just-in-Time) compiler of Java anyway. Additional algorithms for OCL rewriting appear in [78] and [88].

The remaining examples in this section are also based on the Royal & Loyal case study [78]. The chart displayed in Table 5.6 compares the elapsed times for the constraints shown in Listing 5.13 (the first two bars corresponding to the first OCL expression, and so on).

Listing 5.13: A representative set of OCL expressions

```
context Customer
  def a: wellUsedCards : Set( CustomerCard )
       = cards->select( transactions.points->sum() > 10000 )
context Customer
  inv b: self.programs->collect(partners)
         ->collectNested( deliveredServices )->isEmpty()
context ProgramPartner
  inv totalPointsEarning: deliveredServices.transactions
    ->select( oclIsTypeOf( Earning ) ).points->sum() < 10000
context TransactionReport
  inv cycle: card.transactions->includesAll( lines.transaction )
```

OCL query	Interpreted (sec)	Compiled (sec)
Customer.a	0.31	0.16
Customer.b	1.41	1.28
ProgramPartner.totalPointsEarning	2.50	1.69
TransactionReport.cycle	0.16	0.03

Table 5.6: Execution time of representative OCL expressions

5.7 Integration in an MDSE Toolchain

Ecore + OCL specifications, while declarative, still lack any form of behavioral specification, as is possible with statecharts, or Event-Condition-Action rules. If such behavioral specifications were available, fully working components could be generated by a model compiler (as done by Executable UML [182] tools, which usually target the C programming language). Even without behavioral specifications the productivity and quality gains are significant: Figure 5.8 on p. 97 depicts a screenshot of an EMF-generated tree editor that allows authoring sentences of a custom DSL. Ad-hoc queries and method invocations can be performed through a (generated) OCL Interpreter. A problems view contains entries for OCL invariants currently broken for the object population being edited. No single Java statement was manually written to realize this editor. Alternative concrete syntaxes (embedded, textual) are the topic of Chapters 6 and 7 resp.

5.8 Related Work and Evaluation

Another OCL $\to$ Java compiler has been available for Eclipse since 2005, the Octopus IDE[2] (developed by Warmer and Kleppe, the original authors of OCL). Octopus provides syntax-aware text editors for integrated UML + OCL specifications. The main differences with our work are: (a) Octopus adopts a code generation strategy where separate helper methods compute subexpressions, we inline instead such computations; (b) the notification, serialization, and reflection mechanisms that most EMF-based editors rely on are not present in the POJO-style code generated by Octopus. In particular, (c) ad-hoc OCL queries (i.e., known only at runtime) cannot be evaluated, a task that MDT OCL supports with OCL Interpreter (and associated GUI).

The availability of compilers constitutes an acid-test for the specifications of their input languages. The metamodel approach to language specification [77] has proved to be a step forward, provided that the same level of precision attained by previous language definition techniques is followed (i.e., formulation of static semantics as OCL invariants, including typing rules). Several synergy effects can be realized from the unified mechanism for constraining object models that OCL offers (synergies in the fields of program verification, software repositories, and automatic generation of tools, to name a few). Their impact is amplified by the availability of such capabilities on the Eclipse platform.

---

[2]http://octopus.sourceforge.net/

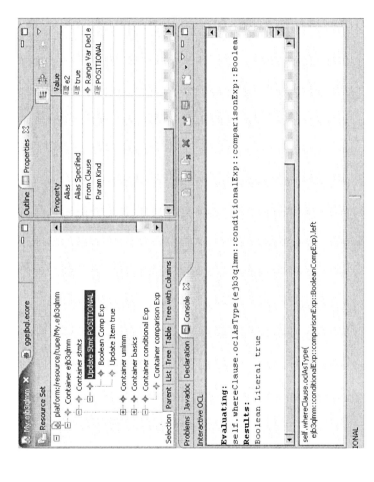

Figure 5.8: Querying an object population (sentences of a custom DSL) during editing

Listing 5.14: Case selection for `iterate()`

```
@Override
public String visitIteratorExp(
    IteratorExp<EClassifier, EParameter> iteratorExp) {
    String sourceResult = iteratorExp.getSource().accept(this);

    switch (OCLStandardLibraryUtil.getOperationCode(
            iteratorExp.getName())) {
    case PredefinedType.EXISTS:
        return createExistsIterator(iteratorExp, sourceResult);
    case PredefinedType.FOR_ALL:
        return createForAllIterator(iteratorExp, sourceResult);
    case PredefinedType.SELECT:
        return createSelectIterator(iteratorExp, sourceResult);
    case PredefinedType.REJECT:
        return createRejectIterator(iteratorExp, sourceResult);
    case PredefinedType.COLLECT:
        return createCollectIterator(iteratorExp, sourceResult);
    case PredefinedType.COLLECT_NESTED:
      return createCollectNestedIterator(iteratorExp, sourceResult);
    case PredefinedType.ONE:
        return createOneIterator(iteratorExp, sourceResult);
    case PredefinedType.ANY:
        return createAnyIterator(iteratorExp, sourceResult);
    case PredefinedType.SORTED_BY:
        return createSortedByIterator(iteratorExp, sourceResult);
    case PredefinedType.IS_UNIQUE:
        return createIsUniqueIterator(iteratorExp, sourceResult);
    case PredefinedType.CLOSURE:
        return createClosureIterator(iteratorExp, sourceResult);
    }
    assert false;
    return null;
}
```

Listing 5.15: The noAccounts invariant translated into Java

```
public boolean invariant_noAccounts(DiagnosticChain diagnostics,
   Map<Object, Object> context) {
/* context LoyaltyProgram
  inv invariant_noAccounts :
  -- when the LoyaltyProgram does not offer the possibility to earn
  -- or burn points, the program members do not have LoyaltyAccounts
  partners.deliveredServices
  ->forAll(pointsEarned = 0 and pointsBurned = 0)
  implies memberships.account->isEmpty() */
  org.eclipse.ocl.util.Bag<RandL.Service> collect1 =
    org.eclipse.ocl.util.CollectionUtil.createNewBag();
  for (RandL.ProgramPartner i_ProgramPartner :
    org.eclipse.ocl.util.CollectionUtil.asSet(this.getPartners())) {
    collect1.addAll(org.eclipse.ocl.util.CollectionUtil.asSet(
      i_ProgramPartner.getDeliveredServices()));
  }
  Boolean forAll2 = true;
  for (RandL.Service i_Service : collect1) {
    if (forAll2) { Boolean equal3 =
        Boolean.valueOf(i_Service.getPointsEarned() == 0);
      Boolean and4 = equal3;
      if (and4) { Boolean equal5 =
          Boolean.valueOf(i_Service.getPointsBurned() == 0);
        and4 = equal5;
      }
      forAll2 = and4;
    }
  }
  Boolean implies6 = forAll2;
  if (!(implies6)) {
    implies6 = Boolean.TRUE;
  } else {
    java.util.List<RandL.LoyaltyAccount> collect7 =
      org.eclipse.ocl.util.CollectionUtil.createNewSequence();
    for (RandL.Membership i_Membership :
      org.eclipse.ocl.util.CollectionUtil.asOrderedSet(
        this.getMemberships())) {
      collect7.add(i_Membership.getAccount());
    }
    implies6 = (new Boolean(collect7.isEmpty()));
  }
  if (!(implies6)) {
    if (diagnostics != null) { diagnostics.add( . . . ); }
    return false;
  }
  return true;
}
```

6 Automating the Embedding of Domain Specific Languages

Contents

The Eclipse Java Development Tools (JDT) excels at supporting the editing and navigation of Java code, setting the bar for newer IDEs including those for Domain Specific Languages (DSLs). In spite of the progress made by IDE generation (covered in Chapter 7), it may not initially be clear for a new DSL whether its later use will justify the development of dedicated tooling. In order to avoid falling back to encapsulating new language abstractions as "frameworks and XML dialects", we explore in this chapter an alternative path, *embedded DSLs*, by automating the generation of the required APIs from EMOF models describing the abstract syntax of the DSLs in question [80]. To evaluate the approach, we present a case study (statecharts) and discuss the pros and cons with respect to other approaches.

Most embedded DSLs, while offering a user-friendly syntax, are fragile in the sense that their expressions may not comply with the full static semantics of the DSL in question. Productivity studies recommend that errors should be reported while the frame of mind is still focused in the error location. To address this issue, we leverage the extension capability of Eclipse to detect at compile-time malformed DSLs expressions. The technique relies on mainstream components only: Eclipse Modeling Framework, OCL, and JDT. Additionally, support for embedded DSLs can be improved beyond well-formedness checking by performing language processing as a background task. The prototype described in this section (DSL2JDT) has been contributed to the Eclipse Modeling Framework Tools project[1].

The structure of this chapter is as follows. Sec. 6.1 examines current support for embedded DSLs specially focusing on the (lack of) static semantics checking. Once the value proposition of this technique is clear, Sec. 6.2 covers the patterns in the generated API that support guided interactive editing, a feature not present in traditional DSL embedding. Sec. 6.3 discusses how compile-time checking is actually realized, this turns out to be pleasantly simple (but not simplistic) given our decision to leverage existing infrastructure. The situation is different for DSL-aware language processing proper (i.e., beyond well-formedness checking) as reviewed in Sec. 6.4. Related work and an appraisal of the proposed technique conclude this chapter.

6.1 Embedded DSLs and Static Semantics

Nowadays, software development involves a number of DSLs, yet no first-class citizenship is given to them, i.e. IDEs are not aware of the full static semantics for (combinations of) DSLs. Popular examples of DSLs used in combination with Java include SQL, BPEL, and JSP, but the list can also be extended to include notations focused on certain aspects of system functionality (business rules, access control,

---

[1]Eclipse Modeling Framework Tools project, http://www.eclipse.org/emft

databinding between GUI forms and underlying model objects, etc.). Providing integrated IDEs for such DSLs has proven hard. A Java IDE aware of SQL would for example flag those embedded SQL statements that become invalid after refactoring the database schema. Supporting such scenarios is easier if both host and embedded languages are designed with cooperation in mind, as is the case with Microsoft's LINQ (Language INtegrated Query) [160]. Experience has also shown that any complex-enough DSL is doomed to reinvent constructs that are taken for granted in general-purpose languages (cf. control-flow constructs in RDBMS stored procedures, in the XSL language by the W3C for XML transformation, and in QVT-Operational [173]), thus strengthening the case for integrated tool support.

The conventional wisdom around DSL tooling is that one may either:

1. provide minimal compile-time checking of DSLs. This is the path followed by XML practice with errors being discovered at runtime when document instances are interpreted, or

2. invest effort in developing dedicated plugins for editing DSLs with custom syntax (be it textual or diagram-based), checking at compile time the Abstract-Syntax-Trees (ASTs) for all involved software artifacts.

The economics of the two alternatives are clear: the "dedicated IDE" approach is technically better but also justifiable only for DSLs with a large user base. Actually, most of the tooling cost for a DSL comes from supporting its concrete syntax. Most of the benefits of a DSL however result from the analyses and transformations performed on its abstract syntax. Given that this "back-end infrastructure" is common to all DSL implementation alternatives we take it as starting point for our generator of APIs for DSL embedding. Besides allowing for early feedback on the DSL being engineered, the resulting risk minimization is useful in another way: if the DSL proves successful enough to warrant development of a dedicated IDE, no development effort is thrown away. With DSL2JDT the embedded DSL code can still be used in such IDE, as it depends only on the abstract syntax of the DSL, which is independent from its concrete syntax.

As far as we know, the APIs of all existing embedded DSLs have been developed

Listing 6.1: Relational calculus expressions for the KodKod relational engine

```
public class KodKod {
  /**
   * Returns a formula stating that all vertices
   * have at least one color, and that no two adjacent
   * vertices have intersecting colors.
   * @return a formula stating that all vertices
   * have at least one color, and that no two adjacent
   * vertices have intersecting colors.
   */
  public Formula coloring() {
      final Variable n = Variable.unary("n");
      final Formula f0 = n.join(color).intersection(Color).some();
      final Formula f1 =
      n.join(color).intersection(n.join(graph).join(color)).no();
      return (f0.and(f1)).forAll(n.oneOf(Node)); }
  }
```

manually. The code snippet in Listing 6.1 (for a relational calculus DSL[2]) illustrates some frequent idioms. Basically, repetition of enclosing lexical contexts is avoided, thus reducing syntactic noise.

In effect, the Content Assist feature of the JDT and the type system of Java 5 are leveraged to enforce some of the well-formedness rules of the embedded DSL (KodKod) when expressing ASTs for it in the host language (Java 5). Additionally, method chaining facilitates editing when used in conjunction with so called *progressive interfaces*: whenever the DSL grammar calls for a mandatory construct, the preceding method in the chain returns an interface with a single method declared in it (standing for the successor in lexical order in the underlying DSL grammar) so that the IDE offers a single choice.

Java APIs like those used above, by themselves, do not capture all relevant well-formedness rules (WFRs) of any but the simplest DSLs. Our approach toward DSL embedding allows evaluating at compile-time such constraints, provided they can be discovered by the EMF Validation Framework using reflection (as is the case when

---

[2]KodKod relational engine, http://web.mit.edu/emina/www/kodkod.html

using our OCL Compiler). The combination of generated APIs and compile-time well-formedness checking surpasses the "DSL in XML" approach in terms of usability and safety, moreover relying on mainstream technologies. Additional techniques (in-place translation, statement-level annotations, and DSL-specific views) may be optionally adopted to further increase the usability of embedded DSLs, as discussed in Sec. 6.4.

6.2 Code Idioms in APIs for Embedded DSLs

Statecharts often serve as examples in discussions on model-driven tooling and this section follows that tradition. Being a graphical formalism, any usability points that their embedding can attain should be welcomed with appreciation: a basic statechart metamodel (Figure 6.1) devoid of any annotation for concrete syntax is given as sole input to our translation procedure. The screen capture in Figure 6.2 shows the resulting API being used to instantiate a statechart describing the behavior of a telephone.

What does the generated API for the statechart DSL look like? Consider for example class `Region` containing zero or more `Vertex` and zero o more `Transition`. At edit time, Content Assist should offer first `subVertex(...)` as completion proposal (only). After accepting that suggestion, the next method in the chain should be `transition(...)` (only). And that's just two structural features. Well, the fragment of the *expression builder* defining such API is reproduced in Listing 6.3 on p. 116. As can be seen, three parts are generated for each concrete class:

- a factory method that encapsulates a more verbose factory invocation.

- The AST node freshly instantiated as per the previous item is not directly returned but wrapped first in a decorator (class `RegionBeingBuilt` in this case) which selectively discloses update methods on the wrapped AST node. Such update methods are grouped into batches (three in this case, starting with `RegionBeingBuilt0` and up to `RegionBeingBuilt2`).

- the last invocation in a method chain will be `toAST()`, which unwraps the AST node from its *expression builder* and returns it.

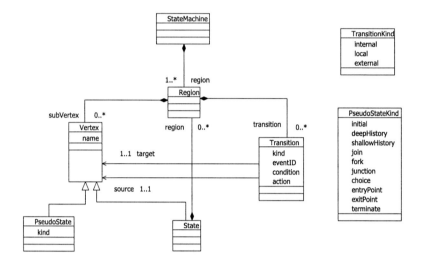

Figure 6.1: Metamodel for the Mini Statechart DSL

The choices offered by a progressive interface are not as linear as the example above might suggest. One of the heuristics applied by DSL2JDT to improve usability involves optional fields. A contiguous run of optional fields is offered in a single batch of options, allowing to spring any of them. In order to access the next batch of options, the mandatory constituent (the one coming up right after the run of contiguous options) is to be chosen from Content Assist. Other rules include:

- Alternative items, i.e. those resulting from an enumeration, result in content suggestions being packed in a single batch of options. For example, the items for the `kind` enumeration result by default in methods `kindLocal()`, `kindInternal()`, and `kindExternal()` being generated. If the number of options becomes unwieldy, one may choose instead to have a single update method (an update method taking an enumeration literal as argument).

- For boolean fields so called yes/no methods can be specified. For example, `off()` is more readable than invoking `setIsOn(false)`.

```
Region regionActive = S.region().subVertex().transition().toAST();
State stateActive = S.state().name("active").region(regionActive).to
PseudoState topTerminate = S.pseudoState().name("terminate").kindTerr
Transition liftReceiver = S.transition().source(stateIdle).target(sta
        .toAST();                                    Vertex arg
Transition callerHangsUp = S.transition().source(s)
Region topRegion = S.region().subVertex(stateIdle     ⊚ stateActive        t
StateMachine telephone = S.stateMachine().region(     ⊚ stateTopInitial    ;
                                                      ⊚ stateIdle
return telephone;
```

Figure 6.2: Embedded DSL statements for a Statechart DSL

- Classes owned over strong composition and declaring only primitive fields are instantiated with a single method invocation, where the field values are received as arguments. For example, a field xyPos with type Point2D will be set with the method invocation xyPos(-1,1) rather than the more verbose setXYPos(new Point2D(-1,1)).

6.3 Checking Static Semantics During Editing

As already stated, we want to engage the IDE in checking the static semantics of DSL expressions. Given the reflection capabilities of EMF and the existing GUI for JUnit in the Eclipse Java editor, this task is greatly simplified:

1. each group of embedded DSL statements (making up a DSL expression) is encapsulated in a dedicated Java method that returns a self-contained AST, obtained by finishing a method chain with toAST()

2. a JUnit test is created for each method above, invoking the default EMF validation on the AST root node. That way, the particular WFRs of all the nodes in the tree will be evaluated, without having to enumerate them explicitly (EMF determines all the applicable validators using reflection).

3. Although not shown here, debugging the unit tests with an exception breakpoint of AssertionError allows inspecting detailed diagnostic messages for

each malformed AST node. In a generated IDE such functionality has to be implemented from scratch (Sec. 7.4.1).

For example, the static semantics for the AST of Figure 6.2 on p. 107 can be checked with the code in Listing 6.2 on p. 109. Semantics checks need not be limited to those expressible in OCL. If embedding XQuery[3], full static type analysis can be performed by reusing existing Java libraries[4]:

Given an XQuery expression, the tool uses the normalization rules speci-
fied in the W3C XQuery Formal Semantics document to convert the given
expression to an expression in a core grammar (a subset of the XQuery
grammar). . . . Given a normalized expression, the tool again uses the
static typing rules specified in the W3C XQuery Formal Semantics doc-
ument to determine the output type of the expression. . . . The Static
Analyzer also checks for semantic errors (such as passing an empty ex-
pression to a function call where an integer argument is expected).

As long as tests are manually coded following the pattern above, all embedded DSL statements will be checked for well-formedness. If the developer overlooks testing some embedded expression, its well-formedness will be known only at runtime (potentially remaining as a bug waiting for happen). This problem is due to the opaque nature (as far as the JDT is concerned) of the embedded DSLs: there is no infrastructure so far to explore the Java code being edited, looking for occurrences of DSL embeddings to check, thus ensuring coverage of WFRs. Achieving such coverage automatically is possible with JDT extensions for DSL-awareness, the topic of next section.

---

[3]XQuery, http://www.w3.org/XML/Query/
[4]XQuery Normalizer and Static Analyzer, http://alphaworks.ibm.com/tech/xqnsta

Listing 6.2: JUnit test for compile-time checking of static semantics

```
public class TestTelephone extends junit.framework.TestCase {
  public void testTelephoneExample() {
    StateMachine dslExpr = C.telephoneExample();
    assertTrue(MyEcoreUtil.isWellFormed(dslExpr));
  }
}
```

6.4 Processing DSL Statements Beyond Checking of Static Semantics

6.4.1 Existing IDE Infrastructure for DSL Processing

The Eclipse Java editor incrementally checks static semantics during editing. A similar capability for embedded DSLs can be achieved by implementing a *compilation participant*[5], which allows extension plugins to (a) be notified when a full or incremental build is starting or when a working copy (in a Java editor) has been updated. *"During these notifications, types can be added, changed or removed, build markers can be created, or errors can be reported to the Java editor"* (reproduced from the Eclipse Developer documentation[3]). For the record, there are at least two other approaches for performing Java language processing: (a) annotation processors and (b) an Eclipse workbench builder. Annotation processors are ruled out as they cannot explore the AST of Java method bodies, and thus cannot access the embedded DSL statements. A workbench builder can inspect the AST of the Java compilation units being built, and would otherwise be a viable solution were it not for one of the use cases of interest, in-place translation, where such Java AST is modified, as will be seen shortly.

Although a compilation participant can be directly written to support the use cases in this section, existing tools and frameworks that simplify the inspection and manipulation of Java 5 ASTs are another implementation venue. For exam-

---

[5]http://help.eclipse.org/help33/index.jsp?topic=/org.eclipse.jdt.doc.isv/
  reference/api/org/eclipse/jdt/core/compiler/CompilationParticipant.html

ple, SpoonJDT[6] allows defining *spoonlets*, Java classes that can be plugged in a pipes and filters architecture to process Java ASTs. SpoonJDT also contributes preference pages to configure spoonlets to be active on a per project basis. Interestingly, spoonlets can be developed (and debugged) in the same workspace where the target projects reside (with a compilation participant a second Eclipse instance is required). Finally, a converter from JDT Core ASTs to EMF-based counterparts is available. SpoonJDT has been used to perform in-place code additions (not in-place translations, however) such as adding Javadoc and preconditions to existing methods.

We review next by means of example the requirements for an IDE to qualify as DSL-aware, beyond checking of static semantics. The areas to cover include (a) in-place translation, (b) statement-level annotations, and (c) DSL-specific views.

We believe that the additional implementation effort can be justified if such functionality is encapsulated for reuse across DSLs. Given our intention to explore the IDE generation approach (the topic of Chapter 7), full DSL-awareness for the JDT was not realized as part of this PhD thesis. However, most if not all of the issues that embedded DSLs aim to solve will also show up in dedicated IDEs, and thus an analysis of design decisions proves useful.

6.4.2 In-place Translation

GUI programming using APIs like Swing or JFace can get quite verbose, a situation that has sparked a number of GUI description languages (mostly in the form of XML dialects, usually for interpretation at runtime). Representative examples include XUL[7], AIUML[8], and XForms[9], but there are many others[10].

Such languages are a prime candidate not only for embedding, but also for in-place translation: we want a JDT extension to expand snippets in a GUI description language into their verbose Swing (or JFace or ...) formulation. That way, Java code appearing afterwards may refer to the GUI widgets implicit in the GUI description

---

[6]http://spoon.gforge.inria.fr/TutorialJDT/TutorialJDT
[7]XUL, https://www.mozilla.org/projects/xul/
[8]AIUML, http://www.alphaworks.ibm.com/tech/auiml
[9]XForms, http://www.w3.org/MarkUp/Forms/
[10]http://en.wikipedia.org/wiki/List_of_user_interface_markup_languages

snippet (for example, to wire event handlers to the widgets, as many GUI description languages only specify the structural and layout aspects of a user interface, not its behavior).

```
   .  .  .
 menu item {
    text = "Both text and icon"
    icon = "images/middle.gi
    mnemonic = b
 }
 menu item {
    icon = "images/middle.gi
    mnemonic = d
 }
 menu separator
 menu radiobutton {
    text =
    "A radio button menu ite
    group = a
    selected = true
    mnemonic = r
 }
   .  .  .
```

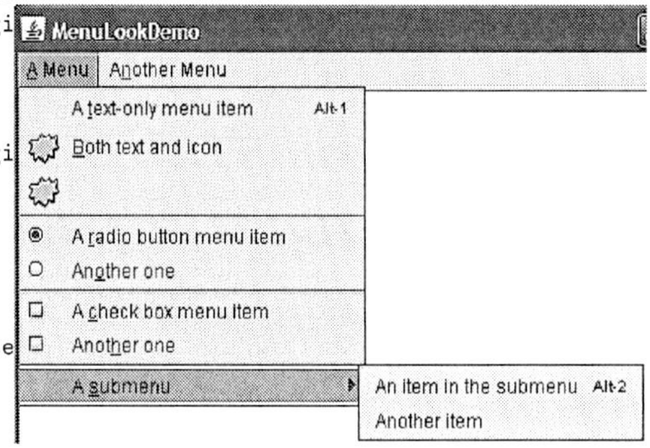

Figure 6.3: DSL snippet declaratively describing a GUI (left) and runtime rendering (right)

The idea is so compelling that others have already implemented it, however not in the interactive Eclipse JDT but as a batch compiler. This compiler can process the *JavaSwul* DSL. For example, a GUI may have a menu hierarchy, that a compact JavaSwul snippet can describe in just a few lines (Figure 6.3). Its Java counterpart stretches over 63 lines and refers to classes JMenuBar, JMenu, JMenuItem, JRadioButtonMenuItem, JCheckBoxMenuItem. Several methods appear: setMnemonic(), getAccessibleContext(), setAccessibleDescription() (among others) as well as enumeration literals of non-obvious interpretation such as KeyEvent.VK_1 and ActionEvent.ALT_MASK. It can thus be concluded that Swing programming is low-level.

JavaSwul is a language extension rather than a language embedding. Similar to any extension, providing tool support for it requires (a) extending the Java grammar with new productions and (b) writing so called *assimilators* to desugar JavaSwul snippets into Java ASTs. The resulting syntax looks better (once the user has managed to get it right without Content Assist) and has more degrees of freedom than the Java idioms used so far (method chaining, static imports, variable length argument lists). In contrast, the approach to embedding favored by DSL2JDT does not require up-front knowledge of the productions of the Java grammar. Moreover, one could in principle use a compilation assistant to behave as an assimilator (i.e., weave information gathered from the surrounding Java AST nodes and the embedded snippets into the output). In contrast, self-contained embeddings include all the input required for expanding a DSL snippet into plain Java, because of a simple reason: whenever missing input is detected, the DSL metamodel can be updated to make room for it.

6.4.3 Statement-level Annotations

Several language processing applications call for decorating Java programs with additional structured information. A lightweight approach to providing such metadata (short of extending Java syntax) involves defining custom annotations. These and other usages of annotations will only increase. Two examples can be mentioned:

- As part of the ongoing JSR-308 (Annotations on Java types), extensions to the Java 7 syntax are proposed[11]. The current prototype patches OpenJDK for parsing and for generating bytecode in an extended class format.

- Similarly, Harmon and Klefstad [107] propose a standard for worst-case execution time (WCET) annotations at the statement level, metadata that is important for Real-Time Java.

The JSR-308 project and the proposal about annotations for WCET require modifications to the Java grammar, parser, and compiler, thus explaining why those efforts take so long in the making. This integration burden is unfortunate as it stifles innovation, making more difficult the early adoption of language extensions. As we

---

[11]JSR-308 (Annotations on Java types), http://groups.csail.mit.edu/pag/jsr308

have seen, embedded DSLs are a non-intrusive way to enrich Java programs with non-Java information. From the point of view of language processing, they lower the cost of proofs of concept. If implemented together with the other use cases described in this section, the resulting IDE extensions are also comparable in usability with dedicated IDEs, given that the additional language constructs they manipulate are just that: syntactic extensions to Java, not completely new grammars.

6.4.4 DSL-specific Views

Some graphical notations are considered standard, with textual counterparts playing a minor role although they convey the same information (for example, musical notation vs. MIDI sequences, bond diagrams vs. chemical formulas, etc.) In these cases, the usability of an embedded DSL would be increased by displaying alongside the textual formulation a read-only view of its 2D or 3D representation. This may be derided as a poor man's WYSIWYG, but as with DSL embedding we see instead a lot of leverage being gained from a no-frills architecture. And not to be forgotten, textual notations improve the accessibility of IDE tooling for the visually impaired.

In fact, some Eclipse-based plugins already adopt this "editable text mapped to readonly diagram" metaphor, only that one-way view update is triggered by the build process or a user action. This to make sure that the data source has reached a stable state, unlike the case during interactive editing.

6.5 Related Work

Language tooling is a vast field. We summarize two areas directly related to DSL embedding: (a) proposed embeddings in a functional/object language (Scala[12]), and (b) well-formedness checking over XML artifacts.

6.5.1 DSL Embedding in Scala

The syntax of Java 5 contributes to the readability of internal DSLs (variable length argument lists, static imports). Still, DSLs embedded in Java cannot circumvent the

---

[12]Scala programming language, http://www.scala-lang.org

`subject.verb(object)` bias of the language: no additional infix operators can be defined nor existing ones overloaded. In Scala, binary operators can be overloaded. The resulting advantages for DSL embedding are reported by Dubochet [62]. In turn, DSL embedding in functional languages has a long tradition, Leijen and Meijer were already reporting in 1999 how to embed SQL in Haskell [145]. Although superficially similar to other embedding efforts like SQL/J, the DSL embeddings we're talking about do not require modifying the front-end of a compiler, as is the case with SQL/J.

Scala allows for a more compact notation, and the same techniques reported in this chapter can be applied in its IDE to take care of well-formedness checking at compile time. That might suggest Scala is a better choice for DSL embedding. We see it differently. To us, what all these examples have in common is the tension between *language-level* as opposed to *IDE-level* extensibility, a matter that exceeds the particular host-embedded language pair being considered. Our reasoning can be summarized as follows: as long as the JDT (including extensions) allows for reasonable solutions, it pays off to stick with it for DSL embedding. In any case, the debate will likely go on among the language camps.

Improvements to Content Assist in JDT can be leveraged by all DSL embeddings in Java. For example, ideas around *framework-completion as a planning problem* have been explored in Prospector [153]. Unlike with custom generated IDEs, they benefit users of DSL embedding without additional effort from their part.

6.5.2 Static Analysis of XML Artifacts

The proliferation of XML dialects has prompted checking good old static semantics for them too. Hessellund [112] has identified typical kinds of integrity constraints to check across XML artifacts developed for consumption by some framework (for example, referential integrity constraints across configuration files in projects extending the Apache Open for Business (OFBiz) framework). Once such constraints have been made explicit in Prolog, a tool takes charge of checking them. Additionally, those editing operations that are feasible for the current editing state are found, much like Content Assist works in the JDT:

> *Given a portfolio of metamodels specified in SmartEMF, i.e., DSLs con-*
> *forming to Ecore, we can represent languages, domain constraints, and*
> *models in a uniform way. All artifacts are mapped into a single con-*
> *straint system implemented in Prolog that facilitates constraint checking*
> *and maintenance, and allows us to infer possible editing operations on a*
> *set of models.*

Taking into account the large number of XML dialects in use today, it makes sense to think about ways to embed them in Java, while keeping the XML format as a serialization format (for communication between machines, not humans). Although the Scala programming language supports textual syntax for XML embedding, the Scala IDE does not check the static semantics of whatever DSL that XML represents.

6.6 Summary

We see many application areas for embedded DSLs, with the discussion about in-place translation, statement-level annotations, and DSL-specific views just showing some of the possibilities. All along we have tried to maintain the main value proposition of well-designed DSLs: offering an easily consumable form of expert knowledge. We think that and embedded DSL is only easier to consume. In particular, the capability to perform in-place translation brings together two seemingly opposite camps: those favoring "abstractions in DSLs" and those promoting design patterns. As we have seen, in-place translation keeps side by side the source DSL statements and their Java translation which exhibits the design patterns captured by the DSL abstractions.

The ASTs we embed with DSL2JDT have all been self-contained: their terminals are compile-time constants. We also skipped on providing any kind of refactoring support for the embedded DSL, as they are necessarily DSL-specific. Similarly, staged compilation, partial evaluation, and weaving (to account for the surrounding Java AST nodes) are all very interesting yet unsupported use cases from the DSL2JDT perspective. Completing the infrastructure put forward in this article is a first step toward enabling the implementation of DSL-aware language processing in the JDT.

Listing 6.3: Fragment of the embedded DSL API for the construct `Region`

```
// start of the method chain for class Region
public static RegionBeingBuilt0 region() {
  return new RegionBeingBuilt(
      miniSC.MiniSCFactory.eINSTANCE.createRegion());
}
// steps of the method chain
public interface RegionBeingBuilt0 {
  public RegionBeingBuilt1 subVertex(miniSC.Vertex... items);
}
public interface RegionBeingBuilt1 {
  public RegionBeingBuilt2 transition(miniSC.Transition... items);
}
public interface RegionBeingBuilt2 {
  public miniSC.Region toAST();
}
// the class holding state between method invocations in a chain
public static class RegionBeingBuilt implements
  RegionBeingBuilt0, RegionBeingBuilt1, RegionBeingBuilt2 {
  private final miniSC.Region myExpr;
  RegionBeingBuilt(miniSC.Region arg) { this.myExpr = arg; }
  public RegionBeingBuilt1 subVertex(miniSC.Vertex... items) {
    this.myExpr.getSubVertex().clear();
    this.myExpr.getSubVertex().addAll( java.util.Arrays.asList(items));
    return this;
  }
  public RegionBeingBuilt2 transition(miniSC.Transition... items) {
    this.myExpr.getTransition().clear();
    this.myExpr.getTransition().addAll( java.util.Arrays.asList(items));
    return this;
  }
  public miniSC.Region toAST() { return this.myExpr; }
}
// ...
```

7 Generation of Authoring Environments from Language Specifications

Contents

Languages are vehicles for abstractions. The active use of such abstractions however goes hand in hand with tooling, whose availability has a decisive impact on productivity, as large as that enabled by DSLs in the first place. This realization has spurred projects aiming at *generating* IDEs from metamodel-based language definitions[1].

There are at least two large problem areas encompassed under IDE generation: *inter-DSL functionality* and *guarantees about generated artifacts*.

Inter-DSL Functionality

An authoring environment is essentially more complex than an *interactive source editor*. That additional complexity has an impact on any declarative formalization one might hope to achieve. An interactive source editor supports intra-DSL functionality, based on awareness of a single DSL. Examples of such functionality include *Content Assist* and visual feedback about breaches of the static semantics of DSL in question. An authoring environment supports the integrated manipulation of software artifacts usually written in a mixture of general-purpose languages and DSLs (e.g., Java + SQL + BPEL), signaling inter-DSL breaches of static semantics [112] and providing navigation mechanisms between artifacts (e.g, type hierarchy view, or navigation between queries and DB schema).

Some of the editors in an authoring environment are diagram based, thus raising the need for bidirectional mappings between (alternative) concrete syntaxes and the abstract syntax for each DSL. In fact, the study of *presentation oriented editors* [188, 133] is a field in itself with dedicated conferences[2].

Guarantees About Generated Artifacts

IDE generation also inherits all the sub-problems that the generation of software components implies. In effect, even in the more limited case of generating an interactive source editor, it is not the case anymore that the generated software will directly run on an operating system. Instead, it will run in an application container (in our case, the Eclipse tool integration platform). Such container is a

---

[1]A note on terminology: in this chapter the terms *integrated development environment* and *authoring environment* are used interchangeably. Same goes for *interactive source editor* and *DSL text editor*.

[2]International Conference on the Theory and Application of Diagrams, http://www.cmis.brighton.ac.uk/diagrams2008/index.php

framework, and therefore imposes a number of interaction protocols that hosted components should abide by. In other words, an IDE generator should, in principle, generate a number of software artifacts (high-level code and configuration files) that simultaneously fulfill all of the following: (a) syntactic conformance; (b) type safety; (c) behavioral compatibility (Lamport's safety properties); (d) realization of the expected functionality of the IDE in question (Lamport's liveness properties); (e) non-functional requirements (e.g., reasonable response time for programs smaller than a certain size).

Structure of this Chapter

As can be concluded from the above, the IDE generation problem in its general form is vast. No spectacular progress around it has been achieved (neither by others in the research community nor in this PhD work). In this chapter, useful contributions toward characterizing the general problem and solutions to specific areas are provided.

After reviewing the state of the art (Sec. 7.1), the main aspects of the generation of DSL text editors are addressed, in terms of components (Sec. 7.2) and functionality (Sec. 7.3). Two case studies are discussed next: the IDEalize generator (Sec. 7.4) and OCL Tools (Sec. 7.5), both developed as part of this PhD work. IDEalize [86] makes use of the OCL compiler presented in Chapter 5: well-formedness rules specified in OCL are checked in the background for the document being edited, providing the user with feedback on breaches of intra-DSL static semantics. Sec. 7.6 reviews related work while Sec. 7.7 charts likely future developments in the field.

7.1 State of the Art in IDE Generation

All prototypes reported in the literature take some form of *language definition* as input. The completeness of such definitions varies: (a) definition of textual syntax; (b) specification of basic well-formedness, for example, "each usage is in scope of its single previous declaration"; (c) specification of type-safety, to avoid runtime executions where a value of type T_2 is assigned to a location declared to hold values of type T_1, with T_2 not a subtype of T_1; and (d) specification of the behavior of programs written in the DSL.

Items (b) and (c) can be captured in a metamodel with OCL invariants. Regarding the definitions of dynamic semantics, existing prototypes [187] usually adopt state transition systems or Petri-nets as semantic domain. The specification of dynamic semantics for arbitrary DSLs is not addressed in this PhD thesis, given the variety of runtime environments targeted by different DSLs. A unified mechanism to specify behavior should be equally applicable to such varied DSLs as BPEL (supporting asynchronous communication, triggers, exception handling); JPQL (query formalisms); and UML2 Statecharts. However, the formalization of static semantics developed for a DSL metamodel can serve as starting point for that of dynamic semantics.

The Eclipse IDE Meta-tooling Platform (Eclipse IMP) [43], started by IBM Research as the SAFARI project, uses an *open compiler* infrastructure [111, 168] to jumpstart the customization of back-end language services. Such services include compilation into an intermediate representation, and control-flow and data-flow analyses. For static program analyses, Eclipse IMP provides building blocks such as pointer analysis, call-graph construction, effects analysis, and type inference. The author of a DSL is expected to write a translator into an internal representation, possibly defining along the way new instruction types. Only if none of the existing constraint handlers can be used as is (which is uncommon, as most DSLs fall in the imperative language category) is it necessary to write a custom constraint handler that takes into account the new instructions.

For illustration, the inter-dependencies between language processing tasks in Eclipse IMP are summarized in Figure 7.1.

7.2 Generation of Parsing Infrastructure

In non greenfield scenarios it is often the case that an existing EBNF grammar is available, most likely with a dedicated text editor. Such scenarios have prompted the development of tools to derive an EMOF model from an EBNF grammar. Is the resulting model a language metamodel? Not really:

- the Concrete Syntax Trees (CSTs) thus built are similar to those prepared

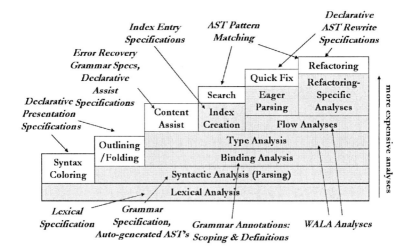

Figure 7.1: Inter-dependencies between language processing tasks in Eclipse IMP (reproduced from [43])

by a parser, before the phase where usages are resolved to declarations (i.e., before their conversion to Abstract Syntax Trees)

- an EMOF model purely generated from an EBNF grammar will lack any constraints to capture static semantics, which are more directly expressed at the AST level rather than at the CST level.

CSTs are ideal for generating structured text (for example, for consumption in a pipes and filters architecture). However, this is not a precondition: unparsing can be performed directly from a (well-formed) AST. Given that no layout information is kept there, pretty-printing has to be specified separately, for example using the Box language [52].

IDEalize reuses a generator of parsing infrastructure for EBNF grammars (Gymnast [49]) and additionally generates infrastructure for:

1. runtime conversion of concrete syntax trees (CSTs) from a Plain Old Java

Object (POJO) representation (returned by the parser) into an EMOF-based one,

2. maintaining at runtime bidirectional maps between CST and AST nodes

3. usability features such as content outline, folding, and syntax highlighting

4. runtime checking of well-formedness

Some of the functionality of an IDEalize-generated text editor is fully realized by superclasses, requiring no customization. For example, navigation history falls in this category. Other interfaces require the generation of custom code, such as those for post-parsing processing, in particular to add problem markers for semantic-level checks.

Besides OCL validation, another practical advantage of EMOF-based CSTs is the possibility to manipulate them using QVT (Chapter 10), which are supported in the Eclipse Modeling Platform.

The steps to transform an EBNF grammar into an Ecore-based model are:

- for the whole grammar a dedicated root `EPackage` in an `.ecore` is created

- for each sequence production (`SeqRule`) a concrete `EClass` is created. The components of a sequence can be either optional subsequences (enclosed in (. . .)?) or subsequences consisting of `SimpleExpr`. A `SimpleExpr` in turn may refer to a token or to any rule. The items in an optional subsequence are mapped to `EStructuralFeature`s with lowerBound = 0, while non-optional ones also get mapped to `EStructuralFeature`s but with lowerBound = 1.

- each alternative production is translated into an interface I, all classes for subcases of the production will have I among its supertypes.

The following optimizations for readability of the resulting `.ecore` constitute heuristics also embodied by the mapping rules above:

- a repetition (`ListRule`) contained in a sequence production is mapped to a field whose multiplicity matches the repetition bounds. The field type is not an artificial container for the `ListRule` but directly the item type.

- user-defined tokens which consist of a fixed number of alternatives are handled as enumerations.

At runtime, an IDEalize-generated CST converter will also maintain a bidirectional map between nodes in their different representations, which allows the generated IDE to support use cases like the following:

1. Clicking on a text region containing a reference to a type, and following the CST-to-AST map, allows obtaining the AST node for the type declaration. With it, all the usages of such type can be obtained from a usages-declarations map. The CST node for each usage (obtained by consulting again the CST-to-AST map, this time in reverse) contains the start and end offsets needed to highlight all usages in the text, thus implementing the *Mark Occurrences* functionality common in IDEs (Sec. 7.5.2).

2. Semantic validations anchored at AST nodes can similarly be used as starting points to create Problem Markers for the corresponding text regions, with these regions being determined again using the automatically maintained CST-to-AST map.

7.3 Functional Categories to Support by DSL Text Editors

It is useful to classify potential functionality of an interactive source editor in terms of its runtime information requirements:

1. Usability features independent from the document being edited

   - templates, including associated preferences page

   - actions on the toolbar and menu bar, in particular retargetable actions (i.e., those actions such as Content Assist whose UI activators are shared between different editors)

   - new file wizard, so that the document does not start empty but in syntactically valid state (thus avoiding spurious parse errors the moment *background parsing* springs into action)

2. Usability features directly working on the document text

   - document partitioning, show range indicator, automatic indentation

   - bracket matching (brace, parenthesis, etc.)

   - AutoEdits (for example, SmartBrace: after typing { in the Java editor, an indented newline and a closing } are added below it). Another example is AutoIndent.

   - Double-click strategy (e.g., double-clicking an opening brace selects all the text up to the matching closing brace)

3. Usability features requiring access to the CST or AST

   - Hover over text fragment, hyperlinks

   - Mark occurrences, Select in Outline

   - Context menu, for example Go to Declaration

   - Hovers over vertical ruler annotations

   - Views, for example Type Hierarchy

   - Content formatting, Content assist

7.4 Case Study: Textual Notation for a Statechart Language

We subscribe to the idea that tools to generate IDEs should support in the ideal case both a human-readable textual notation as well as a visual one (although IDEalize as of now does not generate a graphical editor, leaving for the user the task of manually updating the code to make both editors work together[3]). Given that plenty of visual editors are available for statecharts, we break with that tradition and generate a textual editor. OCL constraints at the CST-level are used to detect badly formed statecharts.

---

[3]Integrating EMF and GMF Generated Editors, http://www.eclipse.org/articles/article.php?file=Article-Integrating-EMF-GMF-Editors/index.html

Statecharts improve on the readability of finite state machines by allowing hierarchy on states and parallelism on transitions. In a nutshell, besides plain states and initial pseudo states, so called *composite* states are allowed. Two kinds of (non-empty) composite states are possible: *or-states* and *and-states*. Each or-state contains a complete statechart and when active one of its contained top states is active. An and-state contains two or more parallel *regions*, each of which can again include a whole statechart.

A transition is labeled with (a) the event it will listen to, with zero or more parameters; (b) a boolean condition (the *guard*) which must hold for the transition to be taken; and (c) an *action* part, i.e. a list of statements. All three parts are optional: a transition without an explicit event implicitly reacts to a *completion event*, and a missing guard is interpreted as true. Finally, more than one outgoing transition can be activated by an event. When one or more of their guards is enabled, the resulting behavior is non-deterministic (any of the the enabled transitions can be taken).

7.4.1 Arguments In Favor of a Textual Notation

The KIEL project [181] aims at simplifying the modeling, analysis and understanding of complex statecharts. One line of activity involves supporting a textual notation, and some of its advantages are conveyed by the example of adding a parallel and-state (which in the text editor just involves typing "—— await C"), as opposed to performing a mouse-keyboard exercise to shift neighbor states and travel from canvas to drawing palette a number of times.

The metamodel of UML2 Statecharts [169, 172] is adopted as a basis for our grammar. An industrial-strength IDE for statecharts (i.e., an ExecutableUML [182] IDE) would also require additional syntax, e.g. to edit class models and the action language. Listing 7.1 on p. 126 depicts a fragment of the grammar for the statechart DSL (the complete version can be found in [86]).

Using the `grammar2ecore` plug-in of IDEalize, an Ecore-based representation of the grammar can be generated (the "CST-level metamodel"). At this level OCL invariants are defined to constrain those that can be converted to ASTs (those ASTs in turn, will be subject to additional checking).

Listing 7.1: Fragment of our Statechart Grammar

```
sequence stateChartDecl : "statechart" name=ID LCURLY vertexDecls
                          (finalStateDecl)? RCURLY ;

abstract vertexDecl : pseudoStateDecl | stateDecl ;

sequence pseudoStateDecl :
    kind=pseudoStateKind name=ID
    (LPAREN outgoing=transitionDecls RPAREN)? SEMI;

sequence stateDecl : "state" name=ID LCURLY inStateDecl
                     (transitionDecls)? RCURLY ;

sequence compositeState : (entry=pseudoStateDecl)? regionDecls
                          (exit=pseudoStateDecl)?;

sequence regionDecl : "region" name=ID LCURLY vertexDecls RCURLY ;

sequence transitionDecl : "transition" kind=transitionKind
    name=ID LCURLY inTransitionDecl SEMI RCURLY ;
```

Several WFRs can be declared, as shown in Listing 7.2, with accompanying explanations for each listed as inlined comments.

7.4.2 An Example: Statechart of Telephone Object

The OMG specification of UML2 contains an example statechart, and we encode it in the generated IDE. For comparison, its *embedded DSL* formulation is discussed in Sec. 6.2.

Listing 7.2: Some OCL-based WFRs

```
context PseudoStateDecl
-- an initial pseudostate may have just one outgoing transition
inv singleOutgoingForInitial:
    self.kind = PseudoStateKind::initial
  implies
    self.outgoing->size() <=1

context RegionDecl
-- there may be at most one initial pseudostate per region
-- (a region is a grouping of states at the same level)
inv singleInitialWithinRegion:
  self.vertexDecls->select (v | v.oclIsKindOf(PseudoStateDecl))
    ->select(v | v.oclAsType(PseudoStateDecl).kind
               = PseudoStateKind::initial)
    ->size() <= 1

context RegionDecl
-- state names must be unique within a region
inv uniqueNameOfStateWithinRegion:
  self.vertexDecls
  ->select(v | v.oclIsKindOf(StateDecl))
  ->isUnique(name)

context CompositeState
-- one or more regions uniquely named
inv uniqueNameOfRegionWithinState:
  self.regionDecls->isUnique(name)
```

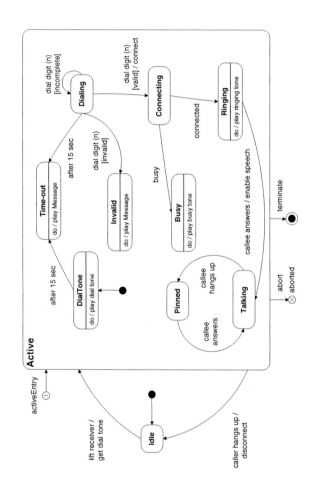

Figure 7.2: Statechart of Simple Telephone Object

7.5 IDE support for OCL

Having made the case for IDEs for DSLs in general, this section focuses on provisioning one such IDE for OCL. *OCL Tools*, developed in the context of this PhD work, has been contributed to the Eclipse Model Development Tools (MDT) Project, with the aim of providing first-class support to modelers working with OCL specifications. Such support includes editing, code generation, execution, and interactive debugging of the OCL constraints given for an underlying Ecore model, thus constituting a natural complement to the compiler described in Chapter 5.

7.5.1 OCL Text Editor

The standard steps when developing a modern text editor using the Eclipse JFace Text framework comprise customizing syntax highlighting, content assistance and content formatting. Underlying all those features, document partitioning is an aspect not directly visible at the UI level but affecting the implementation of the aforementioned functionality. Document partitions are contiguous, non-overlapping regions of text. Each such partition is associated with an specific content type, for which a different behaviour is relevant (for example, comments in a Java source file are one such partition, where *Content Assist* should behave differently from the way it does in non-comment regions). Another useful feature of a text editor is folding [56]. This capability is present in the OCL text editor, shown in Figure 7.6.

The OCL text editor supports in addition other usability features, as described below:

1. **Syntax highlighting** with dedicated colors for keywords, literals, operation invocations of the OCL Standard Library, and comments.

2. **AutoEdit of opening/closing braces**: For example, after typing a left-parenthesis, the corresponding right-parenthesis is added automatically. As expected, this feature is disabled inside the `comment` content type.

3. **AutoEdit for new line**: In the Java editor, the SmartBrace feature places the cursor in a new, indented line after typing an opening curly brace and

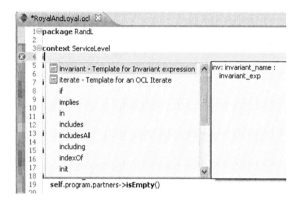

Figure 7.3: Content Assist Example

pressing `Enter`. Additionally, a closing curly brace is placed in yet another new line. Similar functionality in the OCL editor is triggered upon typing a colon and pressing `Enter`.

4. **Content assist** (Figure 7.3). Displays a combo box with a list of choices for syntactically valid completions. Content assist gets activated after typing a dot separator or the → characters. It can also be manually activated by pressing `Ctrl + Space` as a shortcut.

5. **Current line highlighting** and **Show range indicator**. In the Java editor, "Show range" displays a ruler bar to convey the extent of a method body. In the OCL case, similar visual clues are provided for the text regions over which `packages` and `contexts` extend.

6. **Text Folding**. Individual OCL expressions can be folded. In Figure 7.6, to the left of the text fragment "`context transaction`" a folding mark is available to expand that expression.

7. **Templates**. A time saving feature for frequently used constructs in OCL specifications, for example for the `iterate` construct. Additonal templates

can be added, and those available can be reconfigured through a preferences page.

8. **Preference pages**. Through these pages the configuration of Highlight Matching Brackets can be controlled, together with the colors for syntax highlighting and text templates.

9. **Problem and warning markers**. This feature displays at the UI level messages gathered as part of AST building, reacting to updates in the document being edited. Based on the error(s) reported by the parser the editor displays them as problem markers (text underlined with red squigglies) in the Problems View.

10. **Outline view** (top right pane in Figure 7.6). This standard view shows the hierarchy of the defined OCL expressions for the whole document. The root package context is displayed on top. As children, `subPackages` and `contexts` are shown (be it classifier, operation, or property context).

11. **OCL AST View** (lower pane in Figure 7.6). This view saves time in visualizing the types of subexpressions of (long) OCL expressions, also providing feedback about default precedence order in not fully parenthesized expressions.

7.5.2 A Usability Feature in Focus: Mark Occurrences

Figure 7.4 on p. 132 depicts the user view of this feature: upon placing the text cursor on some usage (the association end `transactions` in this case) all other usages for the same declaration are highlighted. This functionality requires querying the CSTs and ASTs that have been built by background processing. We review the necessary queries over CST and AST in this section, as the technique is directly applicable to the editors of other DSLs.

Upon detecting a change in the cursor position, the innermost AST node if any (of the kinds listed below) that encloses such position are found.

1. `PropertyCallExp`. In this case, an association end or an attribute is being referred to.

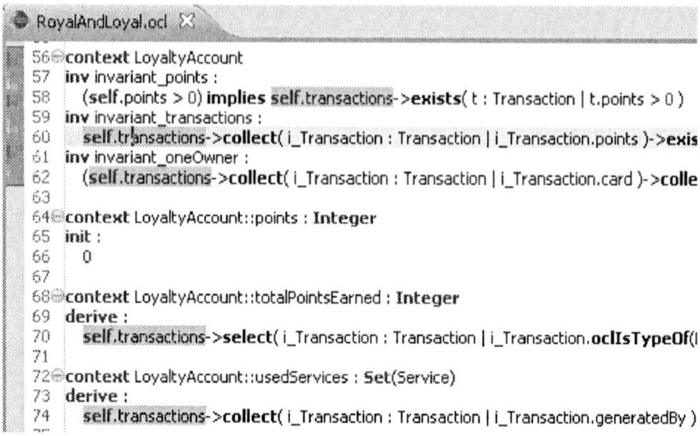

Figure 7.4: Mark Occurrences Example

2. OperationCallExp. For example, if the cursor is placed on isEmpty() then each occurrence of isEmpty() will be marked.

3. Clicking on the declaration of a Variable in a LetExp results in each occurrence of the defined variable being highlighted in the in part. A sample expression of this kind appears in Listing 7.3.

4. Clicking on the usage of a variable (a VariableExp AST node) results in each occurrence of the variable being marked.

Listing 7.3: Example of LetExp

```
let popularTrans : Set(Transaction) =
 result->collect(deliveredServices)
   ->collect(transactions)->asSet()
    in (popularTrans->forAll(date.isAfter(d)))
      and (popularTrans->select(amount>500.00)->size()) > 20000
```

Figure 7.5: A sample `PropertyCallExp` OCL AST View

Having found the innermost enclosing `ASTNode`, the counterparts to highlight can be found by querying or navigating the AST. Navigating from a usage to its declaration can be done in one step, as the AST directly supports it (e.g., a `Variable` has `getInitExpression()` and `getRepresentedParameter()`). As another example, having found a `PropertyCallExp`, its `getReferredProperty()` can be invoked, which returns the property (the `EStructuralFeature` in case of Ecore binding). In Figure 7.5, the highlighted line shows a usage (`self.program`) for which occurences will be marked. The reverse lookup is not directly supported by the AST: once a `EStructuralFeature` is available, custom code has to be written to find other usages in the same context. There are two alternatives for performing this lookup:

- **Using a visitor.** `OCLExpression` is a subtype of `Visitable` and thus may accept custom `Visitors`. A visitor can be created for each kind of `ASTNode` of interest, one such visitor will have just one handler checking whether the visited element is a usage of the declaration passed to its constructor. If so, the usage can be appended to a `List` declared as instance variable of the visitor.

- **Keeping a map.** The second alternative involves keeping a one-to-many `Map` with the declaration as key and usages as values. As for `PropertyCallExp` with Ecore binding, the map is defined as `OneToManyMap<EStructuralFeature,`

PropertyCallExp>.

The algorithm for *Mark Occurrences* comprises the following steps:

1. Find the CST node for the given cursor position.

2. Obtain the corresponding AST node for the selected CST Node.

3. Find the specific part of AST node which is selected by the cursor. The `getStartPosisition()` method of `ASTNode` returns the start position of the full expression. The `getStartOffset()` method of `CSTNode` returns the start offset relative to the editor starting point.

4. Find other usages of the same declaration

5. Obtain their corresponding CST Nodes and mark their occurrences in the text area.

7.5.3 Candidate Extensions

Beyond the "basics" discussed so far, additional features are thinkable to make the OCL text editor more useful.

1. **Content formatting.** Unlike traditional pretty-printing, content formatting takes place interactively and not in a batch manner.

2. **Double click action.** A sensible reaction to double-click is selecting an enclosing fragment, as required later for cut&paste, just like in the Java IDE of Eclipse. Moreover, repeated double-clicks should result in progressively larger fragments being selected, following the composition hierarchy for subexpressions in the OCL AST.

3. **Hyperlinks for variables and types.** For this, besides querying the CST and AST for OCL expression it is also necessary to collect information about declarations available at the AST of the underlying Ecore class model so that usages of a variable or type in OCL can be traced back to their declaration.

4. **Hover over text fragment**. To display hints about usage of the underlying OCL construct (similar to hovers displaying Javadoc comments in the Java editor).

5. **Show in EMF type hierarchy**. Visualizing the Type Hierarchy is necessary when working with but the most basic class models (alternatively, one might rely on a separate graphical view to display it as discussed in Sec. 6.4.4).

6. **Refactorings**. As with their Java counterpart, having tool support for refactorings (and for detecting *code smells*) increases productivity. Several refactorings for OCL have already been documented in the literature (Sec. 5.5). Proposals run the gamut from renaming (a variable or a type), to more complex refactorings such as detecting and removing redundant expressions.

Feedback from the developer community is critical to harvesting real-world and complete OCL specifications. Actually, harvesting such specifications reveals a chicken-and-egg problem: those specifying a system have a reduced incentive to invest effort in preparing OCL specifications if they are to remain paper-only and thus not automatically enforceable. On the other hand, the developers of OCL tooling are reluctant to target a small audience. The OCL Tools component is well positioned to break this cycle, providing immediate benefit to the authors of OCL specifications, and accelerating the synergies of the Eclipse ecosystem.

7.6 Related Work

Alanen and Porres [3] describe in pseudocode algorithms for bidirectional EBNF ↔ MOF transformations. More recently Wimmer and Kramler [207] address the conversion between sentences in the grammar and instances of its MOF-based model. Kunert [137] specifically pays attention to improving the usability of the resulting MOF model (by leveraging the additional expressive power of MOF over EBNF, e.g., inheritance).

Many industrially relevant DSLs (BPEL, XForms) and scientific notations (MathML, several ontology languages) have been defined with an XML notation as preferred exchange representation. While useful for computer interoperability, such notations are nowhere nearly as legible as human-oriented notations (although documents in such languages are always meant to be written by humans). Two interesting lines of activity to overcome the readability problem are: (a) dual syntaxes for DSLs; and (b) verbalization into controlled natural language. It is expected that, in the future, IDE generators will also accept as input, besides metamodel-based language definitions, bidirectional mapping instructions to support human-readable text representations. So far, this functionality is provided by separate prototypes, as described next.

7.6.1 Dual Syntaxes

The main roadblock to supporting XML-based and non-XML grammars for the same DSL is the duplication of effort required to maintain separate grammar, parser, AST manipulation and serialization infrastructure. Brabrand, Møller, and Schwartzbach present in [21] a solution, where a single declarative specification allows generating reversible transformations for both syntaxes:

> Consider the typical situation where an XML language, described by some schema formalism, has been given an alternative syntax. An obvious validation check is that the translations of alternative documents will always result in valid XML documents ... XSugar performs a static analysis that conservatively approximates this check. When the analysis reports success, it is guaranteed that syntactically correct input always results in valid output.

It should be noted that the XSugar algorithm does not allow arbitrary transformations between ASTs, but rather only those which involve reorganization (as opposed to processing) of existing nodes.

7.6.2 Verbalization into Controlled Natural Language

In the context of *ontology engineering*, interest in the verbalization of ontologies has materialized in at least two prototypes for languages in the OWL family: Attempto [127] (whose main application area are Discourse Representation Structures) and

NaturalOWL [48]. Algorithms to paraphrase a formal specification into English have been developed by the (Controlled) Natural Language research community. For example,

$$\forall x. Number(x) \land Prime(x) \land LessThan(x, 3) \Rightarrow Even(x)$$

can be rewritten into *Every prime number less than 3 is even.* These ideas have been realized for OCL in the context of the KeY project, with the tool OCLNL [36]. Admittedly, some paraphrasings sound unnatural, for example:

```
context Copy
inv: Copy.allInstances()->forAll(c1,c2
        not (c1=c2) implies not (c1.barCode=c2.barCode))
```

is translated as

```
for the class Copy the following invariants hold :
  for all copies c2 , c1 in the set of all instances of Copy
        if it is not the case that c1 is equal to c2
        then this implies that it is not the case that
        the bar code of c1 is equal to the bar code of c2
```

However, a big advantage of turning a formal spec into controlled natural language is the larger audience that can review it (and thus find errors).

7.7 Outlook

The declarative formulation of static semantics is nowadays regarded as central for tooling activities. Still, current implementations of mainstream IDEs have yet to embrace this paradigm [186]. There is thus a tension between advanced research prototypes on the one hand (relying on vertical technology stacks) and mainstream IDEs on the other (offering standard frameworks). Two cases in point are *guided model editing* [189] and *framework completion* [199, 185]. In the former, suggestions about valid updates given the current editing state are automatically computed, considering all the artifacts in a software project. In the latter, the steps to realize a unit of functionality when extending a framework are controlled by the IDE.

In order to offer multiple candidate solutions and to allow backtracking to previously consistent states, as required by both guided model and framework completion, a *CLP(FD)* formulation (constraint-logic problem with finite domains) is usually favored. A comparison of different formalisms when querying large code bases [53] reveals that not all logic engines are up to the task. As Jeff Ullmann put it once [198]: *It is not possible for a query language to be seriously logical and seriously object-oriented at the same time.* For example, Ullmann subordinates object-orientation to object-identity: no two tuples instantiated in different ways may be equal, which is at odds with the least-fixpoint semantics of Datalog [198, 53]. While fully agreeing with Prof. Ullmann, we believe to have mitigated some of the identified problems by developing optimizations for querying object graphs using OCL, as reported in Chapter 11 (for the secondary-storage case) and in Chapter 12 (for the main-memory case). Another contribution of this thesis in the context of IDE generation is addressed in Chapter 8, i.e. the conditions guaranteeing bidirectionality in multi-view synchronization.

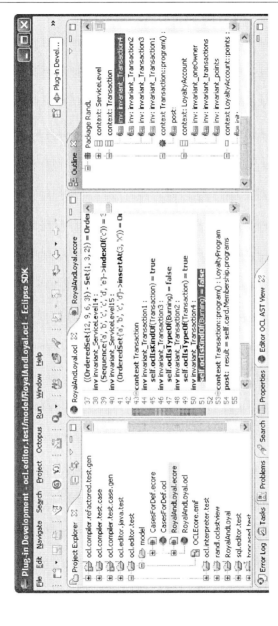

Figure 7.6: OCL Editor Screenshot Caption

8 Bidirectional Synchronization in Multiview IDEs

Contents

Most modeling languages provide different visual notations to highlight different aspects of the System Under Development (SUD). Most notably, UML2 defines a total of thirteen diagram types, grouped into three categories (structure, behavior, and interaction). In general, the same situation arises for Domain-Specific Modeling Languages (DSMLs). There is thus no escape from using several notations when modeling non-trivial software systems, a fact that vendors of modeling tools acknowledge by providing multiview capabilities. At some point in the development process the issue of *inter-view consistency* [64] requires automation due to the complexity of the SUD. For example, determining consistency between a sequence diagram and the statechart for a single traffic-light may be done manually. However, tool support is required for models of realistic complexity (railroad crossings, reservation systems, consumer electronics, etc.)

The definition of a modeling language that introduces views is thus expected to provide an algorithm to determine whether a set of views is consistent. Using meta-modeling terminology, the check for consistency is formulated as follows: (a) for each diagram type a metamodel has been defined, whose instances constitute the views manipulated by the modeler, including geometric information; (b) each such metamodel defines its intra-view Well-Formedness Rules (WFRs); and (c) additional WFRs ensure consistency encompassing several views. Given that WFRs are boolean-valued predicates over an object population, a yes/no answer can be provided about the consistency of the *integrated model*, i.e., the set of all views prepared by the modeler. Unless inter-view consistency is addressed at the level of the language definition itself, disagreement will otherwise ensue. For example, the workshop series *Consistency Problems in UML-based Software Development* was devoted to overcoming such disagreement for UML 1.x.

As useful as they are, yes/no answers about consistency contribute only partially to productivity. In a multiview setting, additional use cases demand automation (*multiview synchronization, model refactoring* [155, 46], and *model completion* [189]). In this chapter, we address the multiview synchronization problem (defined below), leveraging on the lessons learnt from the related problem of inter-view consistency: we rely on a formal technique and address this concern at the language definition level.

Keeping multiple views in-synch requires propagating changes in two directions: (a) change requests validated against the WFRs of the integrated model are to be reflected on views; and (b) user-initiated *view updates* are to be processed in the opposite direction. The algorithm for realizing (a) is fixed once a *view definition* is available: given that the integrated model includes geometric information, updating views amounts to evaluating a function again. The situation is not so simple for (b), where partial information is available. For example, a particular view definition may select only those items at odd-numbered positions in a list. Inserting into the view then raises the question as to where to add an item in the underlying list (which is part of the integrated model).

Such kind of decision problems are not solved by the current best-practices around tool implementation: Model-View-Controller architecture (MVC), runtime evaluation of WFRs expressed in OCL, transparent undo/redo. Rather, the particular realization of (b) is left to the criteria of tool vendors, thus opening the door to non-standard implementations. Our contribution in this chapter improves on this state of affairs, not by building a tool with multiview synchronization capabilities (which is a task for industry) but by disclosing the inner workings of such solution (which industry refrains from doing).

The structure of this chapter is as follows. Competing methodologies around view update are reviewed in Sec. 8.2, followed in Sec. 8.3 by the application of one of them to the multiview synchronization problem, comprising the definition of EMOF-level operators for view specification (Sec. 8.3.1) that are well-behaved from a bidirectionalization point of view (Sec. 8.3.2). Given that any realistic multiview modeling tool will rely on the available MVC frameworks for diagram manipulation, these practical aspects are discussed in Sec. 8.3.3. Sec. 8.4 places the reported techniques in perspective, and Sec. 8.5 examines likely adoption scenarios.

8.1 Benefits of the Proposed Approach

The lack of tool compatibility (and sometimes correctness) around multiview synchronization stems from the fact that the specific policy governing synchronization is encoded manually in the Controller module of MVC (by each tool vendor, usually in an imperative language). In contrast, a declarative formulation, available as part of the language definition itself, allows both generating such implementation as well as statically analyzing the bidirectional transformations at design time. We call this approach DMVC, for Declarative MVC.

The resulting productivity gain is particularly relevant for DSMLs, as the cost of developing tooling for them has to be amortized over a much smaller number of projects than for their general purpose counterparts. The DMVC approach is in line with recent advances in the definition of visual notations, where geometric

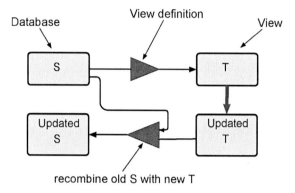

Figure 8.1: A bidirectional transformation, consisting of forward and backward functions [178]

constraints are used at runtime to automate the maintenance of diagram layouts, as discussed in detail by Grundy [152] and exemplified in an Eclipse-based modeling tool generator[1].

Our proposed architecture for DMVC builds upon a bidirectional transformation engine fulfilling formal guarantees. Given a view definition written by the DSML author, the engine can automatically derive its corresponding backward transformation. Importantly, the backward transformations [194] thus obtained can cope with many-to-one mappings (i.e., non-injective functions, where different inputs are mapped to the same output, as for example in $f(x, y) = x + y$). This is achieved with *stateful transformations*, which track the information needed to complement that lost by the mapping (in the example, keeping a copy of either x or y allows handling user updates to $x + y$). Additionally, it is common practice for a backward transformation to take as input, besides the updated view, the original source. The intuition behind this scheme is depicted in Figure 8.1 (reproduced from [178]).

Statefulness and recombination distinguish our problem space from plain function inversion, which is enough in the particular case where each of (source, view) can be fully reconstructed from the other, i.e., whenever there is a one-to-one correspon-

---

[1]Marama meta-tools, https://wiki.auckland.ac.nz/display/csidst/Marama+Tatau

dence (a bijection) between source and target domains. As argued by Stevens [194], such situations constitute the exception rather than the rule in multiview modeling languages. For example, *dual syntaxes* [21] do exhibit this property: a human-oriented syntax is defined for pretty-printing Abstract Syntax Trees (ASTs), while an accompanying XML-based syntax is defined for tool interchange. Both definitions are kept consistent with each other automatically.

An MVC editor displaying a dedicated view for each representation needs no further information than the contents of an updated view in order to refresh the other, as no information is elided in the alternative syntaxes. In terms of our adopted approach, bijections are handled the same as the non-injective case (the latter being the "interesting" one from the point of view of multiview synchronization). In summary, the proposed bidirectional transformation language increases the productivity of the tooling process for DSMLs, as well as the quality of the resulting multiview IDEs.

8.2 Candidate Approaches Distilled

All the approaches reviewed in this section share the common goal of enabling bidirectional transformations between pairs of data structures, with differences spanning the preferred representation (e.g., unordered trees vs. semi-structured data) and the available transformation operators (which may or may not allow user updates to alter the transformation as a side-effect, among other features). Besides highlighting the innovative aspects of each technique, their comparison is necessary to introduce terminology to better characterize the multiview synchronization problem.

For ease of reference, candidate approaches are loosely grouped into (a) general purpose techniques (program inversion, data synchronization, and virtual view update); and (b) techniques aiming at supporting model transformations (graph-grammar based and QVT-Relations). Admittedly, this classification has more to do with the current level of adoption in the model-driven community than with any inherent capability of each approach.

8.2.1 Program Inversion, Data Synchronization, and Virtual View Update

Program Inversion

We discuss this technique first as it constitutes the basis for our proposal. *Program inversion* [157] in the context of functional programming refers to determining, given a function $f(x_1, \ldots x_n)$, its inverse, so as to obtain the arguments given a result. A further insight consists in choosing the building blocks for expressing view definitions such that they fulfill three *bidirectional properties*. Informally, such properties require that (a) unmodified views are transformed back into the same source that gave origin to them (i.e., backward transformations introduce no spurious information); (b) all updates on a source (that affect a view) can be canceled by updates on the view (i.e., the user has means to restore the integrated model to a previous state by just acting on the view); and (c) the backward transformation is oblivious to the order in which updates took place (what counts is the end state). Moreover, any composition of building blocks fulfilling these properties defines again a well-behaved bidirectional transformation. Matsuda [157] provides a Haskell implementation of this algorithm[2].

The principles above have been applied to particular cases: Liu [150] presents a Java library for the bidirectional transformation of XML documents (the transformation operators constituting the BiXJ language). A subset of XQuery is translated into BiXJ in [149], thus allowing using a mainstream language for view definition, again with a prototype realization available[3]. Along the same lines, Xiong [210] translates of a subset of ATL (Atlas Transformation Language), thus achieving bidirectionality[4].

Data Synchronization

Algorithms developed to synchronize intermittently connected data sources (such as file systems or address books between mobile and stationary devices) can also be

---

[2]Generation of backward transformation programs based on derivation of view complement functions, http://www.ipl.t.u-tokyo.ac.jp/~kztk/bidirectionalization/
[3]BiXJ and Bi-CQ, http://www.ipl.t.u-tokyo.ac.jp/~liu/
[4]Bi-ATL, http://www.ipl.t.u-tokyo.ac.jp/~xiong/modelSynchronization.html.

applied to keep complex software artifacts in-synch. An exponent of this approach is the Harmony project [74], whose engine[5] implements Focal, a language with building blocks that allow writing only functions that always behave as *lenses*, i.e., bidirectional transformations. Focal is a low-level language operating on tree-shaped data structures (specifically, edge-labeled unordered trees). Standard encodings for mainstream data structures (lists, XML) are available, as well as libraries of higher-level lenses defined in terms of primitive ones. The design of Focal reflects its theoretical underpinnings in the field of type systems for programming languages, as static assurances can be obtained about the detailed type of inputs and outputs, to avoid runtime checks. In contrast, implementations such as BiXJ resort to returning a default value (e.g., unchanged input) or to throwing an exception whenever a function argument lies outside the function's domain.

The capabilities of EMOF-based modeling infrastructures (in particular undo/redo and evaluation of OCL invariants) grant a large degree of tolerance to inconsistent input, a feature that proves extremely valuable during the initial exploratory phases of DSML language engineering (which comprises the definition of transformations for each view). Moreover, experience shows that modelers frequently perform a series of editing operations which temporarily result in WFRs being broken. We aim at preserving this flexibility, to avoid usability problems similar to those of syntax-directed text editors. In summary, we strike a balance between static assurances and ease of use by relying on runtime checks to capture side conditions not enforceable at design-time. If needed, static assurances beyond those amenable to static type checking can still be obtained by applying the techniques reported in Chapter 9.

Update of Virtual Views in Databases

The view update problem has been studied in the context of databases, where the mechanism to define views is taken as given (relational algebra or calculus) and the kinds of view updates that may be propagated back without loss of information are determined. Recent work focuses on updating virtual and materialized XML views (also incrementally). Most results have been incorporated into the program inversion and data synchronization techniques [157, 74].

---

[5]Harmony Project, http://www.seas.upenn.edu/~harmony.

8.2.2 Graph-grammars and QVT-Relations

Triple Graph Grammars (TGGs)

TGGs [98] build upon directed typed graphs and graph morphisms. Informally, a TGG transformation rule consists of three graphs (left, interface, and right) and two morphisms (from the interface graph to each of left, right) which together describe the correspondence between embeddings of these graphs in source and target. In other words, such rule also states the inter-consistency conditions between source and target, besides specifying a transformation. Figure 8.2 depicts an example, the compilation of `if-then-else` into lower-level constructs (conditional jumps). Before a TGG transformation can be applied, its *positive* and *negative application conditions* are evaluated. These conditions demand a required context (certain nodes or edges must exist) or forbid a context (certain nodes or edges must be absent) connected in a certain topology. An extension of TGG transformations to accommodate N-way relations is offered in [134]. For our purposes, this capability is not necessary as our architecture revolves around a single integrated model (i.e., to synchronize N different view types N bidirectional transformations are defined). Graphical IDE support is available[6], and modularization has been proposed to cope with large-scale transformations. Similar to other rewriting techniques, the control flow aspect of a complex transformation (when to apply which rules) suggests breaking up large transformations into several more focused ones, to be applied sequentially.

As with the data synchronization approach, an encoding of EMOF models is necessary (in this case, into directed typed graphs), as well as expressing transformations in terms of graph morphisms guarded by application conditions. In our setting, some features of the program inversion approach (Sec. 8.2.1) prove beneficial over TGGs: (a) OCL expressions in view definitions can be used directly by Matsuda's bidirectionalization algorithm [157]; and (b) no explicit rules need be declared to delete view elements not supported anymore by source elements. The runtime overhead of encoding EMOF models into graphs can be reduced with the *Adapter* design pattern, at the cost of an indirection level (as with any approach, these design de-

---

[6]Some TGG-based tools: (a) MOFLON, `http://www.moflon.org/`; (b) MoTE/-MoRTEn (as FUJABA plugins), `http://wwwcs.uni-paderborn.de/cs/fujaba/projects/tgg/`; (c) AToM3, `http://atom3.cs.mcgill.ca/`

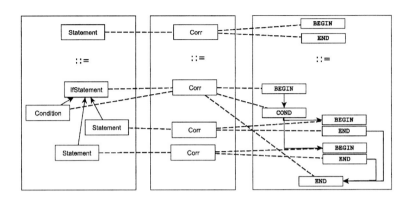

Figure 8.2: Sample TGG-based translation (`if-then-else` into conditional jumps, [146])

cisions would need to be revisited if the modeling infrastructure natively managed models in the format of the transformation engine).

QVT-Relations

QVT-Relations was designed to encode input-output relationships by means of pattern-matching guarded by preconditions. At any given point in time, all but one of the models participating in a transformation are considered as non-updatable, thus constraining the solution space to a well-defined set of (updates, instantiations, deletions) on the *target model*.

Erche et al. [69] point out that metamodel-based language specs do not specify the connection between concrete and abstract syntax and propose QVT-Relations to bridge that gap. Given that such transformations are bidirectional, their architecture aims at solving the same problem space as Declarative MVC. There is no detailed discussion in [69] on whether every QVT-Relations transformation is well-behaved in terms of the conditions defined by Matsuda et al. [157] (Sec. 8.2.1). Irrespective of the particular transformation mechanism adopted, Duboisset [63] recognizes that not all geometric constraints relevant for concrete visual syntaxes can be expressed in

EMOF + OCL metamodels, offering as an example topological constraints in spatial databases. It is clear that QVT-Relations can support roundtripping over one-to-one mappings, however a discussion of its capabilities to back-propagate updates on non-injective views is missing in the literature. Our approach around geometric constraints is covered in Sec. 8.3.3.

Our integration of bidirectionalization for EMOF does not involve QVT-Relations. As a pre-requisite to comparing its expressive power with that of our approach, the formalization of QVT-Relations is addressed in Chapter 10.

8.3 Integration in an EMOF-based Modeling Infrastructure

After settling on the bidirectional program inversion technique [157], the interfacing of its functional inversion algorithm with current metamodeling infrastructure has to be addressed. A canonical approach consists in encoding EMOF models into inductive data types to automatically apply the inversion algorithm to each view definition, expressed as an affine function in treeless form [157]. Alternatively, a *fixed catalog* of bidirectional operators can be defined for EMOF models, fulfilling the three stated bidirectional properties. Both alternatives are explored, in Sec. 8.3.2 and Sec. 8.3.1 resp. Briefly, the advantage of the canonical approach is the open-ended set of base operators that can be defined, while the existing EMOF-based ones can only be recombined. On the other hand, adopting the EMOF-based operators avoids the detour to the inductive-data-types representation. Besides the performance gain, usability is also improved, as modelers are accustomed to conceptualizing transformations in terms of EMOF-level constructs. In any case, the approaches are not mutually exclusive, and any of them can be adopted to define views (injective or not) as part of the Declarative MVC (DMVC) architecture (Sec. 8.3.3).

A possibility consists in finding a subset of QVT-Relations amenable to encoding with bidirectional operators. Given that DSML authors already master the concepts required to understand the building blocks of bidirectionalization, directly using them results in making available their full expressive power. In a next step, subsets

of OCL and QVT-Relations, which are already EMOF-aware, can be recast in terms
of the operators in the next two subsections.

8.3.1 Operators for Two-way Transformations: TwEcore

Each operator consists of a *forward* and a *backward* function. Borrowing notation
from [115], $[\![X]\!]_F(s)$ stands for the application of the (possibly composite) operator
X to the source s in the forward direction, resulting in a view t. The backward
function, $[\![X]\!]_B(s, t')$ takes as argument the *unmodified* source s, the *updated* view
t', and returns a pair (s', X') consisting of an updated source s' as well as a possibly updated operator X', to be used in further invocations. This statefulness is
exemplified by $X = $ twRenameProp(old, new), to rename the property p named
old, where s denotes an EMOF class. In this case $[\![X]\!]_F(s)$ is a clone of s save for
renaming the cloned property p from old to new. In turn, $[\![X]\!]_B(s, t') = (s', X')$
where t' may have user updates, including renaming of property p itself. The backward function returns in s' such changes save for any renaming of p, whose name is
restored to old. An updated property name new' provided by the user on the view
t' is recorded instead in the state of $X' = $ twRenameProp(old, new'). Therefore, a
successive application of X will involve again the latest name entered by the user.

The basic example of a composite transformation is function composition, represented by $X = $ twSeq($X_0 \ldots X_n$), where the simpler transformations $X_0 \ldots X_n$
are applied so that s'_i is the updated source for t_i ($0 \le i \le n - 1$). The definition
for this generic operation is reproduced from [115] (Figure 8.3 on p. 152).

In addition to the operator definitions, an EBNF-based concrete syntax is necessary to facilitate the discussion and exchange of view definitions (an area for future
work in TwEcore). In terms of implementation, such syntax proves useful as it enables the interpretation of ad-hoc, or dynamically generated, view-definition scripts.
In fact, this use case was foreseen by the authors of [157] and is supported in a
Haskell-based bidirectional XML editor where users can update not only sources
and views, but also transformations connecting them.

Regarding correctness, the operators defined in TwEcore are similar to those in
[157, 74] for which formal proofs have been elaborated (proofs about the three bidirectional properties of Sec. 8.2.1). In this sense, and also based on our experiments,

$$
\begin{aligned}
[\![X]\!]_F(s) &= t \\
[\![X]\!]_B(s, t') &= (s', \texttt{twSeq}\ [X_0' \ ... \ X_n']) \\
\text{where } t_0 &= [\![X_0]\!]_F(s) \\
&\ \ ... \\
t &= [\![X_n]\!]_F(t_{n-1}) \\
(s_{n-1}', X_n') &= [\![X_n]\!]_B(t_{n-1}, t') \\
&\ \ ... \\
(s', X_0') &= [\![X_0]\!]_B(s, s_0')
\end{aligned}
$$

Figure 8.3: Definition of twSeq generic operator

the TwEcore operators behave as they should. These assurances could be formalized once and for all (instead of relying on extensive but not exhaustive testing) by building upon the techniques reported in [84, 11].

8.3.2 Encoding of EMOF Models Using Inductive Data Types

This subsection explores the implications (for multiview synchronization) of implementing an EMOF infrastructure using functional programming (FP) instead of Java. The advantages of this approach are: (a) several bidirectionalization algorithms are naturally expressed with FP; (b) functional programs are more amenable to static analysis than their OO counterparts; and (c) most of the proposed new language features for post-Java languages originate in FP[7]. The Declarative MVC architecture does not impose a functional realization, with this subsection serving as outlook for readers sharing an interest in functional programming.

Porting an EMOF infrastructure to the functional paradigm comprises devising encodings for (a) EMOF data structures, and (b) algorithms for views and transformations in EMOF. Regarding (a), given that EMOF models are typed, labelled graphs, the encoding proposed by Erwig is applicable [70]. Regarding (b), the algorithms to port fall into two categories: (b.1) those already formulated in terms of OO concepts (e.g., written in QVT-Relations, ATL[8], or Java); and (b.2) those written

---

[7]Scala programming language, http://www.scala-lang.org/

[8]ATL, ATLAS Transformation Language, http://www.eclipse.org/m2m/atl/

as affine functions in treeless form, as expected by the algorithm for well-behaved bidirectionalization of Matsuda et al. [157]. For (b.1) an encoding style is required that at least preserves the type-checking capabilities of the OO representation. The OOHaskell approach (Kiselyov and Lämmel [130]) fulfills these requirements by exploiting the type checking and type inference mechanisms of Haskell. As a result, Haskell-based processing following an OO style never results in a runtime errors like "method not found" that the OO version would have detected at compile-time.

While the pragmatic approach of TwEcore (and BiXJ, Bi-XQuery, and Bi-ATL) accelerates the construction of proofs of concept for DMVC tools, the same benefits could be achieved in a modeling infrastructure based on functional programming.

8.3.3 Diagrammatic Views and Geometric Constraint Solvers

Besides diagrammatic support, additional infrastructure-level issues must be addressed in the context of existing MVC frameworks, as for example the management of object IDs in source and views. On the one hand, such IDs are necessary for keeping the (source, view) correspondences upon which bidirectionalization will act. However, it is not practical to display in user-level views an ID for each AST node, even if these IDs are kept read-only. This tension is solved by means of a widespread feature in MVC frameworks, *data binding* (for GUI widgets[9], with similar functionality also available for Eclipse Graphical Modeling Framework[10]). Such facility maintains a straightforward one-to-one correspondence between an AST node and its screen real-estate, as part of which updates resulting from UI-level gestures are applied as-is to their data-binding-managed counterpart. As a result, this interaction does not have to cope with injectiveness and remains outside our DMVC framework, but the larger objective of making coexist ASTs (with IDs) and views (without them) is accomplished. The interactions managed by Data Binding are bracketed as (A) in Figure 8.4 on p. 157.

In case an update to the integrated model requires adding figures to a diagram view, default values need to be provided for the figure's position, size, layer, color, etc. While these values cannot be computed by the bidirectional transformation

---

[9]JFace DataBinding, http://wiki.eclipse.org/index.php/JFace_Data_Binding
[10]Eclipse GMF, http://www.eclipse.org/gmf/

engine, they can still be managed declaratively with the help of a *geometric con-straint solver* (e.g., [156]) which assumes the role of a *local Controller* in one of the MVC subsystems depicted in Figure 8.4 (i.e., it processes a subset of the view-level change requests, forwarding the non-filtered ones to the main Controller). Con-straint solvers are responsible for enforcing geometric invariants, such as area inclu-sion or non-overlap between 2D regions.

The constraints on the layout of figures mandated by a *visual syntax* do not usually comprise the heuristics (such as crossings minimization) that distinguish a diagram with a comfortable layout from another which is hard to decipher. After computing a layout that fulfills those cognitive quality measures, small user edits should not cause a full re-arrangement, as becoming familiar with a new layout places a cognitive load on the user. This dynamic aspect is not normally considered in graph layout algorithms [61]. Moreover, capturing all relevant *visual aesthetics* of a given visual notation is nowhere near straightforward, as their relative weight on diagram understanding may be discovered only after extensive use [61, p. 5]:

> *A followup study reveals a visual aesthetic not previously considered by the graph drawing community. This new aesthetic, continuity, is the measure of the angle formed by the incoming and outgoing edges of a vertex. For the task of finding a shortest path between two vertices, con-tinuity can be even more important than edge crossings. This demon-strates how the ultimate goal of maximizing human cognition of graphs can sometimes differ from optimizing well known visual aesthetics.*

Admittedly, geometric constraint solvers are yet to gain acceptance in graphical modeling frameworks. So far they are used in specialized CAD tools and in toolkits for parametric diagramming. Their contribution to declarativeness, and therefore to reducing programming effort, is crucial for an end-to-end Declarative MVC ar-chitecture.

8.4 Related Work

The expression "GUI generation" is commonly equated to mean CRUD (Create-Retrieve-Update-Delete) GUIs, which barely can be used. The problem with gen-

Listing 8.1: Enabling an action in the UI

```
public void selectionChanged(
  IWorkbenchPart part, ISelection incoming) {
  // Selection containing elements
  if (incoming instanceof IStructuredSelection) {
    selection = (IStructuredSelection) incoming;
    setEnabled(selection.size() == 1 &&
    selection.getFirstElement() instanceof ContactsGroup);
  } else { // Other selections, for example containing text
    setEnabled(false);
} }
```

erators of CRUD GUIs is that the only information they consider comes from a class model without OCL. On another extreme, some research prototypes demand an explicit User Task Model to generate GUIs [176], with such Task Model specifying the workflows to support at the GUI level. While the generated GUIs exhibit a distinctly better usability, the price to pay is the cumbersome maintenance of these detailed task models. Somewhere in between approaches such as WebML [23] promote a lightweight notation for workflows that takes into account different user roles, is amenable to refactoring and incremental development, while being platform independent.

A venue worth exploring consists in leveraging OCL and statechart specifications when generating a GUI, by establishing a mapping between GUI gestures on the one hand and statechart events and class methods on the other (saving the OCL and model-compilation aspects, the advantages of a similar approach are documented by Horrocks in [114]). Those events which are not allowed for the current statechart state, as well as those operations whose preconditions are not fulfilled, should be grayed out in the GUI. Letting generators weave this functionality into their output would increase the Return-On-Investment from the effort invested in refining a model spec with statecharts, OCL, and business rules.

The code snippet in Listing 8.1 is typical of GUI programming (for the Eclipse RCP framework [158]) and determines whether a GUI-level action should be enabled, depending on the current selection. A question to ask is: which part of this code *cannot* be generated from information already available in the set of models that our tools process? In fact, all of it can be generated, and in this case, no further customization is necessary. As another example, tutorials on the APIs for GUI programming go long ways to detail how to constrain the targets of a reference offered in a combo box. Without demanding programming, the same can be achieved by an OCL invariant specifying the set of valid items for a structural feature. Similarly, only those actual arguments to an operation which fulfill the precondition (assuming one such precondition constrains them) should be offered for selection. The proposed generator, either targeting a forms-and-menus interface or a diagrammatic-based one, can follow this contract. The proposed architecture opens the door in the future to generation of multi-modal UIs, given the platform-independent nature of an EMOF + OCL + Statecharts model.

8.5 Evaluation

The complexity around keeping views in-synch in multiview authoring environments requires a comprehensive solution. As shown in this chapter, one such solution relies on metamodeling, well-behaved bidirectional transformations, and geometric constraint solvers. Current EMOF infrastructures have paved the way for extensions such as bidirectionalization and geometric constraint solving.

Existing tools for general-purpose modeling have been developed following a traditional (non-declarative) MVC architecture, and are not expected to migrate overnight to a new paradigm. Instead, the primary candidates to benefit from Declarative MVC are Domain-Specific Modeling Languages (DSMLs). More generally, we argue that applying to DSMLs the same (metamodel-based) definition techniques as for UML 1.x will impair their adoption, as such techniques overlook the connection between concrete and abstract syntax, do not handle multiview synchronization, and lack precise semantics for backpropagating updates from non-injective views. The techniques brought together in this chapter address those weaknesses identified in previous efforts around the definition and tooling of DSMLs.

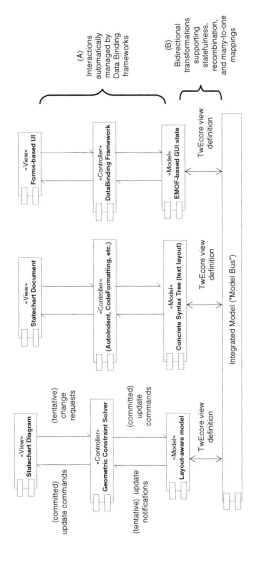

Figure 8.4: Software Architecture for a Multiview Design Environment supporting Bidirectionality, instantiated for a statechart editor supporting three kinds of views: diagram, textual syntax [181], and forms-based

9 Design-time Certification of Transformation Algorithms

Contents

The increasing reliance on model-driven software development calls for model compilers to assume the role of today's compilers, i.e., reliability of these components is of utmost importance. We describe how to certify model transformations in this context by bridging the gap between the languages in which such transformations are specified (Essential MOF, OCL, OO programs) and the decision procedures needed to verify properties expected of such transformations. Two major aspects are investigated in this chapter: (i) valid output is obtained for each valid input, (ii) the output satisfies certain properties. Results from application projects validate our approach, which internally applies model-driven techniques to the certification process itself by mapping transformation specifications into the $^+$CAL model-checking language.

Model-Driven Software Engineering (MDSE) is gaining consensus in the Software Engineering community as a viable technology to improve both productivity and quality. In order for MDSE to deliver on its full potential, commensurate progress is required to increase the quality of emerging model transformers and compilers. In this chapter, a method and its associated tooling are presented to reach that goal for a representative class of model transformations, operating on languages for which an EMOF + OCL metamodel is available. This method involves the automatic translation of the input and output metamodels into a formalism for which a decision procedure is available to answer whether a given procedural transformation exhibits certain properties of interest. Two basic desirable guarantees for such transformations are (a) that all output sentences belong to the target language [116], and (b) that the transformation function covers the whole input language for which it was designed [202]. Experience with current model-driven tooling shows that these basic requirements are not always met. Beyond these general requirements, guarantees specific to a given transformation are also desirable. For example, an optimized implementation should produce the same result as the non-optimized version. Once these analyses have been performed, the follow-up problem is compiler correctness, i.e., ensuring that the transformations are semantics-preserving.

Nowadays, model compilers are in operation for various kinds of application tasks. For instance, transformations into Java Enterprise Edition (Java EE, defined in JSR-220) are very popular and include: DASL [93], SecureUML [31], and WebML [42]. These DSLs allow for the specification of three-tier enterprise systems at a high level of abstraction and have metamodel-based descriptions. Similarly, platform-specific metamodels are available. For example, the persistent query language of Java EE (JPQL) has been metamodeled in [77]: all the normative restrictions formulated in English in Ch. 4 of JSR-220 are recast as OCL invariants. Instantiations of the JPQL metamodel satisfying those invariants are valid abstract syntax trees (ASTs) for particular JPQL queries.

In the current state of the practice, the WFRs on the input and output ASTs are evaluated at transformation-time, for each application of the transformation. We aim instead at certifying transformation algorithms at design-time, to make runtime-checks redundant, but moreover to get model compilers right early on, instead of patching them as new cases are discovered which were overlooked before widespread deployment.

As decision procedure for the task described above we adopt model-checking as described in [142]. A model-checker manipulates execution traces, which can be conceptualized as trees of states (each state also called a system snapshot), with root states derived to cover all initial conditions. Candidate successor states are computed from all actions enabled in the current state.

Once a transformation algorithm has been specified, at algorithm-design time the model-checker can detect situations where the transformation does not terminate, or terminates without establishing the properties of interest. The coverage achieved by the admittedly finite analysis of a model-checker is much higher than testing because (a) states can be manipulated symbolically, and (b) several properties of interest depend on the shape of an object graph rather than on its size or concrete attribute values (the "small scope hypothesis" [120]). For example, the condition "two lines intersect" can be manipulated without considering concrete crossing points. Model-checkers can detect these situations, taking a single state as representative of all those exhibiting such shape.

In summary, the contribution of this chapter is twofold. First, we eliminate the laborious task of preparing a model-checkable specification for nontrivial MDSE transformations by reusing the EMOF + OCL WFRs for the static semantics contained in the metamodels of the languages participating in the transformation. Second, we demonstrate how to support the development of robust transformation algorithms by employing a model-checking engine. In particular, we investigate the language $^+$CAL and use the corresponding model-checker TLC[1]. The significance of the approach is demonstrated using an application scenario concerning a well-known graph transformation problem (Schorr-Waite). This problem involves an in-place transfor-

---

[1]TLC – The TLA$^+$ model checker, http://research.microsoft.com/users/lamport/tla/tlc.html

mation, which are known to be harder to analyze than functional transformations.

The structure of this chapter is as follows. Sec. 9.1 elaborates on static semantics and derives set-theoretic definitions for EMOF + OCL metamodels. Afterwards, it is exemplified how OCL pre- and postconditions are mapped to $^+$CAL. This is followed (in Sec. 9.2) by a discussion of the steps to follow when applying the proposed model-checking-based certification method, including an analysis of a sample transformation (Sec. 9.3). Alternative and complementary approaches to model-based verification are discussed in Sec. 9.4.

9.1 Formalization of Essential MOF + OCL for Model Checking

$^+$CAL [142] is a specification language designed to replace pseudo-code for writing high-level descriptions of algorithms. A $^+$CAL algorithm manipulates mathematical objects in a series of steps. The granularity of a step is chosen by the algorithm designer, ranging from a single built-in statement to a composite step involving several $^+$CAL statements. A step exhibits transaction semantics: intermediate results are not visible to concurrently executing processes and system invariants are required to hold only at step boundaries.

$^+$CAL includes control-flow statements typical from block-structured programming (if-then-else, while-do, sequential composition), as well as constructs for expressing non-deterministic and concurrent algorithms. For the purposes of this work, we focus on the sequential subset of $^+$CAL. Mathematical expressions and logical formulae may appear in $^+$CAL programs whenever a construct calls for a value (e.g., in the condition part of an if-then-else, in an assert statement). In fact, the properties an algorithm should exhibit are routinely expressed as mathematical assertions on the input and output data (in our case: ASTs), with the model-checker being able to compute them for finite system snapshots.

The proposed certification method comprises the following steps:

1. Automatic translation of the definitions contained in the participating EMOF + OCL metamodels into $^+$CAL (these definitions allow the transformation

algorithm to refer to well-formed ASTs).

2. Expressing a model transformation as a $^{+}$CAL algorithm operating on ASTs.

3. If appropriate, annotating the transformation with assumptions about its input, beyond the constraints expressed in the metamodels of input ASTs. The invoker of the transformation is responsible for satisfying these assumptions.

4. Annotating the transformation with assurances about the system state (in particular about the output ASTs) after every successful run of the transformation on valid input (i.e. on well-formed input satisfying the assumptions made in the previous item). The algorithm is responsible for satisfying these assurances.

Following Design-By-Contract [162], the assumptions in (3) are called *transformation preconditions* and the assurances in (4) *transformation postconditions*. This terminology partly overlaps with that of Hoare logic, where a *(precondition, postcondition)* pair fully specifies the transformation between the pre and post states (no procedural statements are necessary). The checks that Design-By-Contract performs at runtime can be carried out at transformation-design time thanks to model-checking. As to the language for pre- and postconditions, besides $^{+}$CAL some or all of them can be expressed in OCL, whose translation into $^{+}$CAL is discussed in the next two subsections. Using $^{+}$CAL directly may however prove beneficial given the growing number of third-party libraries of mathematical theories defined for it.

9.1.1 Translating EMOF into $^{+}$CAL

The translation of a user-specified OO class model (expressed in EMOF) results in definitions of sets, relations, and $^{+}$CAL [142] procedures to allocate instances and manipulate links and attributes, constituting a certified building block that simplifies the expression of the transformation algorithm. Our encoding of EMOF + OCL into $^{+}$CAL leverages previous work on set-theoretic semantics of UML and OCL [18]. In the context of UML, a thorough analysis of the logical consistency of the MOF 2.0 specification is reported in [9]. Our work focuses on the more recent

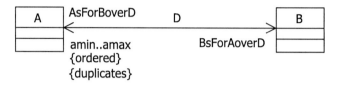

Figure 9.1: Sample EMOF model

EMOF. An example transformation of EMOF language constructs can be found in Figure 9.2, which shows the invariant for the bidirectionality constraint stated in the class model in Figure 9.1

In the example, there are only safety properties (the min-max bounds, lack of duplicates on the BsForAoverD association end, bidirectionality over D) which are trivial yet cumbersome to formalize by hand. In general, the generated specification contains logical predicates (such as *InvariantsDirectionality* in Figure 9.2) to check after every execution trace whether the constraints implicit in EMOF constructs and all OCL invariants are maintained. As a whole, these checks guarantee that the output sentence belongs to the output language, for all possible runs of the MDSE transformation algorithm.

9.1.2 Translating OCL into $^+$CAL

OCL prescribes that, at the end of a transaction, each system snapshot should fulfill the specified invariants. Lacking transaction demarcation, it is generally agreed that invariants in an OO program should hold after object construction and after the execution of each public operation. The concept of transaction boundary is directly supported by $^+$CAL step granularity. The *efficient* evaluation of invariants can be challenging (Chapter 12). Usually an operation involves a small number of updates which leave most invariants unaffected. Being $^+$CAL based on a temporal logic, there is no shortage of expressiveness to encode OCL invariants, with the model-checker evaluating them in the background as execution traces are considered. Model-checkers can take into account the data-flow dependencies of formulae so as to approach non-redundant yet complete evaluation. This shortens the time elapsed

for each instance *b* of *B*, those instances of A
reachable over *D* from it must in turn have *b* among
their instances reachable over *D*

$InvariantBidirectionality\_AtoB \triangleq$
    $\vee AsForBoverD = \langle \rangle$
    $\vee \forall b \in \text{DOMAIN } AsForBoverD :$
        LET $AsReachable \triangleq AsForBoverD[b]$ IN   a sequence
        $\forall i \in \text{DOMAIN } AsReachable :$
            LET $anA \triangleq AsReachable[i]$ IN
            $b \in BsForAoverD[anA]$

counterpart of the above, this time for each a

$InvariantBidirectionality\_BtoA \triangleq$
    $\vee BsForAoverD = \langle \rangle$
    $\vee \forall a \in \text{DOMAIN } BsForAoverD :$
        LET $BsReachable \triangleq BsForAoverD[a]$ IN   a set
        $\forall aB \in BsReachable :$
        $ElemIsInSeq(a, AsForBoverD[aB])$

$InvariantsDirectionality \triangleq \wedge InvariantBidirectionality\_AtoB$
$\wedge InvariantBidirectionality\_BtoA$

Figure 9.2: Bidirectionality expressed in $^+$CAL

from submitting an algorithm till counterexamples are found, thus increasing the productivity of the transformation designer. As already mentioned at the beginning of this section, OCL pre- and postconditions are translated as assertions into $^+$CAL, i.e., they are no substitute for the specification of the input-output transformation, which must be given as imperative statements.

The conversion from OCL to $^+$CAL is performed by visitors over ASTs of OCL expressions, similar to the work of [18]. A metamodel of $^+$CAL was prepared for this purpose. This AST-to-AST conversion could in principle be verified with the techniques described in this chapter. An example of bootstrapping the verification of a transformation is offered by the algorithm to translate from $^+$CAL to TLA$^+$ (Temporal Logic of Actions [141], the logic underlying $^+$CAL), which is itself specified in TLA$^+$.

9.2 Certification Process

Certification of an algorithm is an iterative process. Whenever it can be shown at design time that an algorithm is bound to fail at runtime (i.e., for some inputs does not terminate, breaks metamodel invariants, or does not fulfill its part of the contract in establishing postconditions) the model-checker not only indicates failure but presents an execution trace leading to that situation (a counterexample). The algorithm designer may apply a combination of (i) reformulating the algorithm to handle the situation that caused the failure, (ii) strengthening the preconditions (making the algorithm applicable to a subset smaller than well-formed ASTs), or (iii) weakening the postconditions. The practical limit to postcondition weakening is that the output must still be well-formed, as demanded by metamodel invariants.

9.2.1 Directly Specifying Transformations in Terms of EMOF

As a further means to increase certification productivity, a textual syntax for an object-oriented programming language ("Executable EMOF", or xEMOF for short) could define statements to manipulate instances of metamodels, as a high-level notation to express model transformation algorithms. The rationale for this is the large number of transformations already expressed in terms of the Visitor design pattern [76]. In a green field scenario, a language such as xEMOF would also prove useful by reducing the conceptual distance between a transformation algorithm and its implementation, thus shortening the certification process.

A language such as xEMOF is not just a thin layer of syntactic sugar over $^{+}$CAL. Instead, the translation is non-trivial because (a) method-dispatch in an object-oriented language depends on runtime-types instead of only declared types, (b) method overloading similarly complicates method selection, and (c) the interplay between inheritance and object initialization has to be taken into account. A more realistic modeling of Java, including for examples exceptions (which introduce alternative return paths and require bookkeeping to correctly unfold the activation frames in the call-stack) would not add expressive power yet complicate the translator.

Besides those transformations expressed in terms of visitors, another large group of existing transformations relies on pattern-matching mechanisms followed by in-place transformations (ATL [125], QVT [173], graph-grammars [8]). Provided they manipulate EMOF-based ASTs, their execution engines can similarly be formulated in terms of $^+$CAL reusing the translation performed by our prototype (see Sec. 9.1).

9.3 Certifying a Non-trivial In-place Transformation: Schorr-Waite

9.3.1 A Graph-marking Algorithm for Garbage Collection

The Schorr-Waite [2] algorithm performs a depth-first traversal of a directed graph, starting from a specific node called the root. Given that memory is at a premium during garbage collection, Schorr-Waite offers a constant upper bound on memory usage by avoiding keeping a stack with the nodes in the current path. Instead, as new nodes are visited, the link that was followed last is reversed in place. Upon going back along the current path, the algorithm reconstructs the original topology. Pointer reversal avoids thus the introduction of a stack.

Schorr-Waite is complex enough to serve as a reference case in source code verification [117, 159], as it involves modifying in-place an AST-like pointer-rich data structure, yet intuitive enough that its operation can be explained succinctly. To our knowledge, this is the first account on model-checking Schorr-Waite. Although we manually crafted in $^+$CAL the Schorr-Waite algorithm, the discussion in the previous subsection and also, e.g., the results of [37] indicate that this manual effort can be reduced if not eliminated in the near future.

The correctness and termination of Schorr-Waite have been proved long ago, both as manually written proofs and with assisted theorem provers [159]. These Hoare-style proofs are validation rather than verification, in that not a Java or Java-subset implementation is verified (with, say, JML [35] or Spec# [54]) but instead a formalization of the implementation is made to imply correctness and termination. An exception to this (for the C language) in *Caduceus* is reported by Hubert and

---

[2]An animation of Schorr-Waite appears on slides 15 to 34 of http://www.info. uni-karlsruhe.de/lehre/2005WS/uebau1/folien/06-Speicherbereinigung_v1. pdf

Marché in [117]. Besides an up-to-date review of related work, hints are included as to why JML proved problematic.

Many improvements have been made over the initial Schorr-Waite algorithm. Real-world garbage collection in today's JVMs is quite more elaborate. Therefore model-checking Schorr-Waite is of interest as an exercise only. Besides, not even the guarantee that the implementation will behave as in the checked (finite) concrete worlds can be achieved, because again were dealing with a hand-written formalization of the implementation, i.e. in best case we are doing validation instead of verification.

The practical relevance of model-checking an algorithm is addressed by Daniel Jackson, the author of Alloy [120]:

> The tradeoff is no different in principle from the one you face when deciding whether youve tested a program enough. In practice, though, exhausting a scope of 10 gives more coverage of a model than handwritten test cases ever could. Most flaws in models can be illustrated by small instances, since they arise from some shape being handled incorrectly, and whether the shape belongs to a large or small instance makes no difference. So if the analysis considers all small instances, most flaws will be revealed. This observation, which I call the small scope hypothesis, is the fundamental premise that underlies Alloys analysis.

Alloy [120] is a formalism based on relational logic, designed to simplify modeling the dynamics of software programs. An Alloy model consists of *signatures*, *relations*, *facts* and *predicates*. Signatures are used as templates for the uninterpreted entities of a system (called *atoms*), connected over relations. Analyses are expressed in terms of facts (what can be assumed about atoms and their relations) and predicates (to express constraints on atoms and relations). The Alloy Analyzer is both a *model generator* as well as a *checker*. Typically, both functionalities are used in tandem by letting the tool explore, for all finite concrete worlds structurally conformant to the specification, which assertions in the form of predicates hold. Internally, the Alloy Analyzer formulates an Alloy specification as a SAT problem.

Back to Schorr-Waite. We will define in Alloy an object `Store` as a singleton which contains a root set of references to `Node` which in turn may refer to a set of `Node`.

All instances of `Node` taken together are considered allocated, be they reachable or not from the root set. The root set must be a subset of all the allocated nodes. As in garbage collection, those nodes not (transitively) reachable from the root set should be marked as garbage. The remaining correctness condition after a run of Schorr-Waite is that the topology of the input graph should be preserved (remember that the algorithm temporarily reversed pointers to avoid an explicit stack).

A possible store given as input is depicted on Figure 9.3, where unreachable nodes are signalled with red arrows. To compute them, a declarative definition was made in Alloy, a definition that will be used as yardstick to check the output of the algorithm.

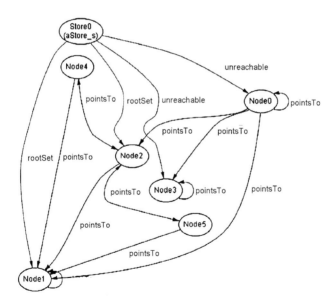

Figure 9.3: A possible initial store

Listing 9.1: Declaration of an object population in Alloy

```
pred aStore ( s : Store ) {
  #s.rootSet = 2
  #allNodes(s) = 6
  #s.unreachable = 2
}
```

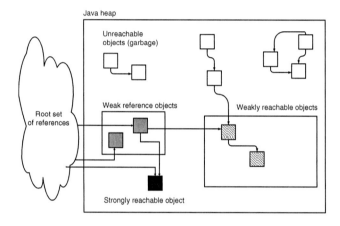

Figure 9.4: Elements in a Java Heap

The data constellation in question was built by declaratively specifying it (Listing 9.1) by requiring a total of six nodes, only two reachable from the root set, and unbounded connectivity between the allocated nodes. The limitations of model checking are known: if only concrete worlds with 5 nodes had been allowed, e.g. by means of `run aStore for 5` then no instances of the predicate `aStore` would have been found.

The memory model above highly abstracts that of Java. Two examples were this is the case are mentioned. First, the JVM defines different degrees of reachability. An intuitive depiction is shown on Figure 9.4 on p. 170. Second, the model does not

Listing 9.2: Additional nodes becoming reachable after an addition to the root set

```
pred addTwo ( s0, s1, s2 : Store) {
    some disj n0 , n1 : Node |
    #(n0.points - s0.reachable - n0 ) > 0 and
    addToRootset (n0, s0, s1) and
    addToRootset (n1, s1, s2) and
    #Node = 6
}
run addTwo for 3 but 6 Node
```

allow reasoning about pointer aliasing. For that, another mapping is needed: from memory addresses to values. With that, references do no point directly to values, but to addresses.

9.3.2 Alloy Formalization of Operations

The main points can be seen in the Alloy formalization in Listing 9.3, for the operation to add a previously allocated but unreachable node to the root set (which may result in other nodes becoming reachable). Notice that pre, post, and frame conditions are specified for the operation.

In order to obtain an "interesting" trace, we will request it to result in additional nodes (other than the one just added to the root set) becoming reachable as a consequence of the first invocation of the operation. This is achieved with the Alloy predicate in Listing 9.2.

With predicate addTwo we request the model checker to find a trace with three snapshots, such that the 2nd and 3rd snapshots result from performing the just defined operation. We can play the snapshots one at a time as in a slide show to better see which unreachable nodes are added to the root set, moreover color-coding the status (root set, reachable, etc.) of nodes in the post-image.

9.3.3 Model Checking with $^+$CAL

As to the readability of $^+$CAL, Listing 9.5 on p. 177 shows the encoding of the Schorr-Waite graph-marking algorithm (the Java formulation appears listed in Listing 9.4 on 176).

The correctness guarantees we expect are: (a) termination, (b) that all nodes reachable from the root (and only those) are marked, and (c) that the algorithm leaves the topology unchanged. These guarantees are encoded as assertions: the results computed by the implementation are compared with those resulting from mathematical definitions which are executable in $^+$CAL. Two assertions are found at the end of Figure 9.5: *Topology(pointsTo)* returns (as a set of edges) the reachability information which was updated in-place, for comparison with the original topology (a discrepancy would result in a counterexample). Similarly, the last *assert* compares the set of reachable nodes (as computed by Schorr-Waite, i.e. those nodes having *markBit* set to true) with the set obtained as the transitive closure of the *g.edge* (mathematical) relationship applied to the root.

We model-checked the $^+$CAL algorithm in Figure 9.5 considering graphs with up to 10 nodes, finding that acceptable runtimes can be achieved (see also [140] for the empirical behavior of TLC). Thus, we conclude that the proposed method is practically significant for MDSE. As mentioned before, due to the small scope hypothesis [120], many, if not all, problems will be found using this problem size.

9.4 Related Work: Alternative and Complementary Approaches

The method reported in this chapter allows for the validation of model transformation algorithms. If implemented carefully, the assertions made for an algorithm carry over to its implementation. This manual coding step in a language such as Java introduces the possibility of a non-conforming implementation. We argue that validation of transformation algorithms is still necessary: a faulty transformation algorithm, however correctly implemented, will not improve quality. In addition, metamodel-based approaches (involving OCL specifications) allow for a high expressiveness of constraints to be validated.

A straightforward solution to the manual implementation problem consists in devising a translator from the language in which the transformation was certified ($^+$CAL) into Java, and certifying this translator. Assuming that verification of a (manually or automatically derived) Java implementation is required, the OCL invariants contained in the metamodel can still be reused by translating them to JML [35] as discussed in [103]. As with all source-code level verification approaches, a larger state space has to be explored, thus reaching practical limits more quickly than for the model-level counterpart as a result of the faithful representation of Java Virtual Machine abstractions. For example, expressions in Java may have side-effects while OCL expressions are guaranteed to be read-only. Adopting EMOF models as the only mechanism to define state allows us to consider only those state evolutions allowed by EMOF, reducing the state space to explore. This is in tune with the principle of reasoning at the highest-level of abstraction possible, because it's more efficient.

The application of TLA$^+$ has been investigated also in other software engineering contexts. In the field of enterprise software architectures, model-checking of web service protocols is reported in [121]. An Eclipse-based text editor to support editing $^+$CAL and TLA$^+$ specifications is described in [99].

Another formalization of OCL with tool support for verification is KeY [17] which targets different verification use cases from the ones addressed in this chapter. Its execution language is JavaCard, with both JML and a dedicated Dynamic Logic as verification backends.

Brucker et al. [33] describe in detail a tool to transform UML+OCL into a formalization processable by a theorem prover. The same team has also mechanized a Hoare-calculus for an idealized object-oriented programming language [32]. In principle, both tools can evolve into an integrated proof environment for object-oriented programs. As of now, verification based on interactive theorem-provers is not fully automatic (that's where the *interactive* comes in), requiring assistance from the user who has to understand the underlying logic and the deduction rules. Once a language-processing algorithm has been formulated in an imperative language amenable for Hoare-analysis, those verification conditions that cannot be automatically derived by the tool have to be specified manually. Proof tactics are then to be applied (automatically or assisted by the user) to discharge the verification conditions and therefore the (Hoare) pre- and postconditions for the algorithm as a whole. $^+$CAL is translated to TLA$^+$, Temporal Logic of Actions [141]. There is as of now no mechanized Hoare-calculus (theorem-prover supported) for $^+$CAL. However, Merz [161] has made progress on mechanizing TLA$^+$ in Isabelle [166].

9.5 Evaluation and Future Work

Given the remarkable progress during the last decade in the areas of model-checking and in anchoring the semantics of metamodeling, there is no reason preventing combining their strengths to increase the reliability of model compilers. Our findings confirm that language metamodeling techniques contribute not only to the productivity of MDSE but also to its quality. Our prototype aims at enabling the interchange of standard metamodels and certified transformations within the software engineering community, reaping the benefits of network effects. Integrated model-driven toolchains for enterprise-scale projects involve metamodels for several languages, whose development costs would be prohibitive if done from scratch and in isolation by separate teams. We foresee the institution of peer-reviewed, public repositories of machine-checked metamodels and transformations in the near future.

Listing 9.3: Alloy predicates allowing symbolic manipulation of Java heaps

```
module mg/schorr_waite
sig Node { points: set Node }
sig Store {
  alloc : set Node ,
  root : set Node ,
  reachable : set Node ,
  unreachable : set Node
} {
 /* invariants of Store (part 1 of 2) */
  Node = alloc
  root in alloc
  reachable = root.*points
  unreachable = alloc - reachable
}
fact {
 /* invariants of Store (part 2 of 2) */
 all s : Store | s.reachable + s.unreachable = s.alloc
   and s.reachable not in s.unreachable
}
pred addToRootset ( n : Node, s, s' : Store) {
   /* precondition */
   n in s.unreachable and n not in s'.unreachable and
   /* postcondition */ s'.root = s.root + n and
   /* frame */ s.alloc = s'.alloc
}
```

Listing 9.4: The Schorr-Waite algorithm in Java

```java
private void schorr_waite(Node r) {
    Node current, prev, next;
    current = r;
    prev = null;
    while (true) {
        while (current != null && !current.markBit) {
            current.markBit = true;
            current.flag = 0;
            if (current.points.length > 0) {
                /* current refers to a non-atomic object */
                next = current.points[current.flag];
                current.points[current.flag] = prev;
                prev = current;
                current.flag++;
                current = next;
            }
        } // end of while current
        // retreat
        while (prev != null && prev.flag == prev.points.length) {
            int lastIndex = prev.points.length - 1;
            next = prev.points[lastIndex];
            prev.points[lastIndex] = current;
            current = prev;
            prev = next;
        } // end of while prev
        if (prev == null) {
            return;
        }
        /* visit subgraph to the right of prev (there's always one,
        otherwise retreat would have occurred ) */
        Node backref = prev.points[prev.flag - 1];
        prev.points[prev.flag - 1] = current;
        next = prev.points[prev.flag];
        prev.points[prev.flag] = backref;
        current = next;
        prev.flag++;
    }
}
```

Listing 9.5: Schorr-Waite expressed in $^+$CAL

```
--algorithm test {
 variables
   g \in VertexGraph; root \in g.node;
   alloc = [ v \in g.node |-> MemnodeForVertex[v] ];
   pointsTo = [ v \in g.node |-> SetToSequence( Targets[v,g] ) ] ;
   current = root; next = Null; prev = Null;
   i = 1; backref = Null; bQuit = FALSE;
   startTime = 0; endTime = 0;
 { while ( ~bQuit ) {
   \* go down the leftmost branch
   while ( ( current /= Null) /\ (alloc[current].markBit = FALSE) ) {
       alloc[current].markBit := TRUE;
       alloc[current].flag := 1;
           if (Len(pointsTo[current]) > 0) {
             \* current points to other objects
             i := alloc[current].flag; next := pointsTo[current][i];
             pointsTo[current][i] := prev; prev := current;
             alloc[current].flag := alloc[current].flag + 1;
             current := next;
           };
       }; \* end of while current
       \* retreat, all objects pointed from current have been visited
   while ( /\ ( prev /= Null )
           /\ ( alloc[prev].flag = Len(pointsTo[prev])+ 1) ) {
         i := Len(pointsTo[prev]); next := pointsTo[prev][i];
         pointsTo[prev][i] := current; current := prev; prev := next;
       }; \* end of while prev
       if (prev = Null) { \* we have retreated back to the starting point
         bQuit := TRUE;
       };
       if (~bQuit) {
     \* visit subgraph to the right of prev (there's always one)
     i := alloc[prev].flag -1; backref := pointsTo[prev][i];
         pointsTo[prev][i] := current;
         next := pointsTo[prev][alloc[prev].flag];
     pointsTo[prev][alloc[prev].flag] := backref;
         current := next; alloc[prev].flag := alloc[prev].flag + 1;
       };
 };
 assert (Topo(pointsTo) = g.edge);
 assert (ReachableFrom[g,root] = { v \in g.node : alloc[v].markBit });
 }
}
```

10 Model Transformation Based on Pattern Matching

Contents

Program transformation is the mechanical manipulation of programs, as performed for example during compilation, refactoring, generative programming, or reverse engineering. Both *term rewriting* [25] and *graph rewriting* [8] have been tried as formalisms for program transformation, with the former outnumbering the latter as reports in the literature are concerned. In principle, model transformations in model-driven software engineering can also benefit from the same theoretical framework. In practice, the design of (industrially relevant) languages for model transformation usually lacks a formal foundation. Approaching an industrial case study with a formal mindset is thus a three-step process: (a) candidate formalisms are reviewed, (b) existing industrially-relevant DSLs are analyzed, and (c) a post-fact formalization is proposed. As Simeon and Wadler argue in *The Essence of XML* [192]:

> ... *there is value in modeling these standards. In particular, such models may: (i) improve our understanding of exactly what is mandated by the standard, (ii) help implementors create conforming implementations, and (iii) suggest how to improve the standards*

The structure of this chapter is as follows. Sections 10.1 and 10.2 provide an overview of term rewriting and our approach toward the formalization of QVT-Relations. In Sec. 10.3, the main constructs of this model transformation language are described: templates for pattern matching, relations for constraining model elements, as well as the update semantics. With that background, the dynamic semantics of QVT-Relations are formalized in Sec. 10.4, which allows uncovering a bug in the UML2RDBMS transformation of the QVT standard. Sec. 10.5 summarizes related work, and Sec. 10.6 evaluates the approach.

10.1 Term Rewriting

A language supporting the abstractions of the domain of declarative transformations facilitates their formulation, by offering constructs reflecting *term rewriting, traversal strategies*, and the possibility to take into account the *context* of a rewriting, a capability supported by *dynamic scoped rules*. These abstractions and the underlying representation of programs as algebraic terms have been applied successfully in a number of case studies both in industry and academia. We focus on the Stratego language [25] as representative of this paradigm. As with any abstractions, they are not a panacea: usability difficulties that Stratego-like DSLs exhibit are reviewed by Lämmel et al. [139].

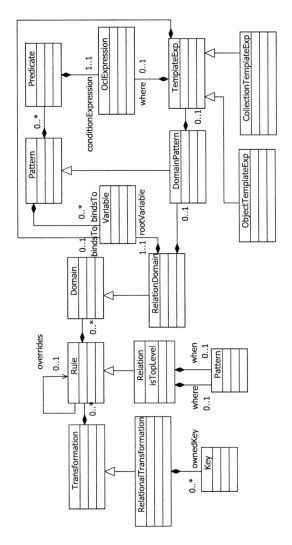

Figure 10.1: Fragment of the QVT-Relations metamodel

The formal operational semantics of Stratego [25] have not been mechanized. A promising approach for its mechanization is Relational Logic, given its successful application to graph transformation systems [16] and algebraic datatypes [136].

Previous work regarding verification of Stratego transformations includes the semi-automatic analyses supported with an interactive theorem prover [209]. Initial considerations toward a Hoare-style logic for Stratego are addressed in [128].

The abstractions for program transformation embodied by Stratego have been expressed as design patterns in other languages (for example, in Haskell[1]). Regarding Java, MatchO [200] is a library encapsulating functionality for object-based pattern matching and for traversal combinators. Although MatchO greatly simplifies strategic rewriting in Java, existing Stratego libraries need to be encoded imperatively and the advanced capabilities of Stratego (such as dynamic scoped rules) have similarly to be encoded manually. The manual steps are error prone, validating an Stratego algorithm may thus be not immediately transferable to its MatchO-based implementation.

Although the matching problem has been throughly addressed for object graphs [180], supporting language constructs are conspicuously missing in modern OO languages. This gap is solved with design patterns (Visitor [76] and the traversal combinators of MatchO). An exception to this state of affairs is the Scala programming language, which essentially makes term rewriting built-in. The design of the pattern matching facilities in Scala are described by Emir in his PhD thesis [34].

10.2 Formalization Approach

In recent years, EMOF + OCL has gained acceptance as the approach of choice to define the structure and static semantics of software artifacts. This consolidation has motivated the need for expressing *model transformations* and *inter-model consistency checking* in a compact manner. Examples include: (a) high-level compilation (e.g., from BPMN into WebML [23]); (b) refinement (e.g., spelling out the possible behaviors sketched in a UML Activity Diagram by means of a set of Statecharts); and (c) round-tripping between alternative notations (e.g., between a

---

[1]Programmable rewriting strategies in Haskell, http://www.cs.vu.nl/Strafunski/

block-structured BPEL process and its tree-based visualization).

In order to address the above scenarios (including the *incremental* and *bi-directional* evaluation of transformations), QVT-Relations [173] was designed to encode input-output relationships with pattern-matching expressions guarded by preconditions.

At any given point in time, all but one of the models participating in a transformation are considered as given (i.e., non-updatable), thus constraining the solution space to a well-defined set of (updates, instantiations, deletions) on the *target model*. To realize round-tripping between two models, upon occurrence of an update on one of them, the transformation is to be evaluated in the direction of the other, thus bringing them back in-synch.

Actually, the well-formedness guarantee for transformations needs to be certified at design-time on a per-transformation basis, in order to avoid runtime exceptions that would disrupt the operation of a model-driven toolchain (in terms of compiler technology, an analogy would be a Java compiler failing to produce valid bytecode for well-formed input, because of an internal exception).

In order to perform such certification in a mechanical way, we enlist the services of Alloy[2], a logic engine developed at MIT by Daniel Jackson [120]. Two capabilities of Alloy prove particularly useful: (a) the expressive power of its formalism, Relational Logic, which extends First-Order Logic with equality and transitive closure; and (b) visualization, which simplifies grasping the *counterexamples* found.

An Eclipse-based plugin for Alloy is available[3], although we intend to keep the operation of counterexample-finding transparent to the author of QVT transformations. Regarding the toolset used, screen captures were obtained from *medini QVT*[4]. Another QVT-Relations tool is *ModelMorf*[5]. Both are as of this writing free of charge for non-commercial use.

---

[2]Alloy, `http://alloy.mit.edu/`

[3]Eclipse plugin for Alloy, `http://code.google.com/p/alloy4eclipse/`

[4]medini QVT, `http://projects.ikv.de/qvt`, open-source (EPL) since early 2008

[5]ModelMorf, `http://www.tcs-trddc.com/ModelMorf/index.htm`

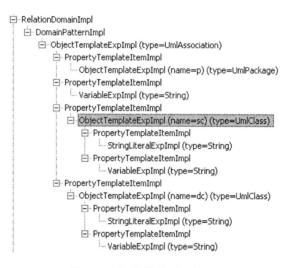

Figure 10.2: QVT AST subtree

10.3 Static semantics, OCL Formulation

The universe of discourse of a transformation is limited to the classifiers defined in one or more metamodels that the transformation expects as *parameters*. A metamodel is defined by means external to the transformation, and groups classifier definitions into packages. Thus, a fully qualified name to uniquely pinpoint a classifier comprises a parameter name (as different parameters may conform to the same metamodel), a fully qualified package name, and a classifier name. Unlike in ordinary OO programs, where variables range over instances of classes like `Employee` and `Car`, the variables of a transformation range over *model elements*, e.g., "all the attributes owned by class C that have primitive type". Although M0-level instances could also be manipulated, this usage is not anticipated by the specification.

Another concept present throughout QVT-Relations is *pattern matching*, which the abstract syntax decomposes into *relation domains* ("domains" for short), *domain patterns* ("patterns"), *templates* (of *object* and *collection* kinds), and *variables*.

```
checkonly domain uml a : SimpleUML::UmlAssociation {
  umlNamespace = p : SimpleUML::UmlPackage {
  },
  umlName = an,
  umlSource = sc : SimpleUML::UmlClass {
    umlKind = 'Persistent',
    umlName = scn
  },
  umlDestination = dc : SimpleUML::UmlClass {
    umlKind = 'Persistent',
    umlName = dcn
  }
};
```

Figure 10.3: Text fragment corresponding to the AST in Figure 10.2

Their main points are covered before presenting well-formedness rules (WFRs) for them. For a transformation to be valid each of its top-level and transitively invoked relations should evaluate to true (which boils down to certain patterns matching). Referring to the metamodel fragment depicted in Figure 10.1 on p. 181, the AST nodes of relations and domains are easy to spot after their concrete syntax representation, which tags them with the keywords `relation` and `domain`. For the other AST nodes, no such mnemonic is available: curly braces may enclose the items in a template and the predicates in a pattern. Figures 10.2 and 10.3 compare an AST subtree with its textual serialization to showcase pattern nesting: variable `a` (an `UmlAssociation`) will bind to an instance whose fields have values as indicated, in particular those for `umlSource` and `umlDestination` being in turn patterns. The pattern for `umlSource` (highlighted) introduces a variable for later use (`sc`). The two equalities required for a binding to succeed (`umlKind = 'Persistent'` and `umlName = scn`) are grouped by an object template (as opposed to a collection template) to denote that a single object will be matched.

Listing 10.1: Properties in an object template must belong to the matching class

```
context QVTTemplate::PropertyTemplateItem
  inv property_part_of_class:
    self.objContainer.referredClass.eAllStructuralFeatures
    →includes(self.referredProperty)
```

10.3.1 WFRs for Templates

As may be concluded from the sample object template highlighted in Figure 10.3, the properties it lists should belong to the class being matched. The corresponding WFR is shown in Listing 10.1. The frame of reference for the WFRs in this subsection is the `QVTTemplate` package, reproduced in Figure 10.4 on p. 187.

After using the term *pattern* in an informal (but not misleading) way, the question arises: what is the counterpart in the concrete syntax of a `Pattern` AST node? Recalling the example in Figure 10.3, no `Pattern` as such is displayed but only one `DomainPattern` whose sole purpose is to own a single `TemplateExp` (and to inherit a collection of `Variable` declarations reachable over `bindsTo`, more on that later). It is templates then that specify matching equalities, and save for primitive domains (as in `primitive domain prefix  :  String;`) we've found no single case of a `DomainPattern` without its (more important) `TemplateExp`, thus raising the question as to why the standard defines such composition as optional [173, p. 33]. Instead of showing another class diagram, this time the same information is presented in Emfatic[6] notation in Listing 10.2. Not shown is the optional composition between a `RelationDomain` (owner) and its single `DomainPattern` (part).

The distinction between (boolean) `Predicate` and the `conditionExpression` it owns can be seen in Listing 10.3, a postcondition for a relation. That fragment has been annotated to reveal the internal structure of a `where` postcondition. Although `Patterns` and `Templates` both look similar in the textual syntax (both appear as curly braces enclosing boolean conditions and boolean equalities, resp.) they serve different purposes: a `Template` not only rules out non-matching object constellations but also specifies how to give initial values to the properties of a new model

---

[6]Emfatic, a text editor for EMF class models, `http://wiki.eclipse.org/Emfatic`

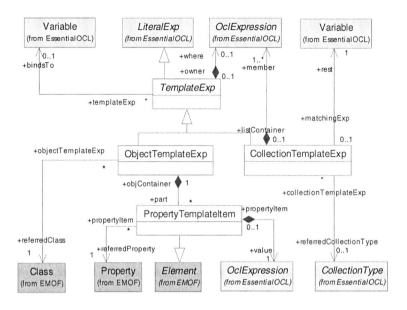

Figure 10.4: Metamodel view of QVT templates [173, Sec. 7.11.2]

element. A `Pattern` instead, fitting to its role as a pre or postcondition, may contain arbitrary boolean expressions in addition to equalities. The well-formedness of these constructs is assured to a large extent by the WFRs of the OCL subexpressions, and thus the QVT-specific WFRs need only check for example that usages of variables occur in visible scopes.

As stated in the QVT metamodel, navigating the `conditionExpression` association end of `Predicate` leads to an `OclExpression`, for example `ClassToKey(c,k)` in Listing 10.3. However, nowhere in the OCL 2.0 standard is `RelationCallExp` to be found as an OCL construct. This is *possible* however because QVT extends the OCL metamodel, as follows: (a) `RelationCallExp` is made a subclass of `OclExpression` [173, p. 33]; and (b) `TemplateExp` a subclass of `LiteralExp` [173, p. 30]. Therefore, whenever QVT states "an OCL expression", a mental translation should be made to consider the new cases. For example, each `PropertyTemplateItem` in a

Listing 10.2: Where do patterns go in the AST?

```
class DomainPattern extends QVTBase.Pattern {
  !ordered val QVTTemplate.TemplateExp templateExpression;
}
class Pattern extends EMOF.Element {
  !ordered ref EssentialOCL.Variable[*] bindsTo;
  !ordered val Predicate[*]#pattern predicate;
}
class Predicate extends EMOF.Element {
  !ordered val EssentialOCL.OclExpression[1] conditionExpression;
  !ordered transient ref Pattern[1]#predicate pattern;
}
```

Listing 10.3: What QVT Patterns are made of

```
where { -- a Pattern owned by a Relation, owning Predicates
  ClassToKey(c,k); -- Predicate with RelationCallExp as condition
  prefix = cn; -- condition is an OperationCallExp: equals()
}-- cn, a variable declared in the relation owning the where
```

`PropertyTemplate` (Figure 10.4) may have as value (as depicted in Figure 10.3) a full-fledged template for nested pattern matching, because of (b).

Just to complete the picture on `TemplateExp`, it should be mentioned that it can have a precondition, as the `where` association end on `OclExpression` shows (Figure 10.4). This name choice constitutes an irregularity in the metamodel, as QVT-Relations reserves the words `when` for preconditions and `where` for postconditions. In any case, the example in Listing 10.4 (reproduced from [173, p. 160]) shows a template followed by its precondition.

The `referredClass` of an `ObjectTemplateExp` should be assignment-compatible to the type of the variable that its instances will bind against, as shown in Listing 10.5. The function `assignmentCompatible(classifierLHS, classifierRHS)` encapsulates the check whether all values of type `classifierRHS` are a subset of those of type `classifierLHS`. In the abscence of parametric polymorphism, such

Listing 10.4: Template with precondition

```
domain relations rp:Pattern
  { predicate = pd:Predicate {
      conditionExpression = re:OclExpression {} } }
  } { not re.oclIsTypeOf(RelationCallExp) };
```

Listing 10.5: Type conformance and Variable agreement

```
context QVTTemplate::ObjectTemplateExp
inv bindingVariableTypeConformance :
  not bindsTo→isEmpty()
  implies assignmentCompatible(bindsTo.eType, referredClass)

context QVTRelation::DomainPattern
inv varOfRootTemplateEqRootVarOfRelDomain :
  not templateExpression→isEmpty()
  implies templateExpression.bindsTo =
        relationDomain.rootVariable
```

check reduces to determining whether they coincide or the former can be found transitively among the **eSuperTypes** ancestors of the latter. In the presence of Generics (as supported by the Eclipse EMF extension of EMOF) additional cases arise, depending on whether `classifierLHS` and `classifierRHS` stand for *type invocations* (all type arguments have been provided) or not (in which case each such type stands for all permissible type invocations, as in Java 5) [79].

An object template that is part of an `enforce` domain may result, when evaluated, in an object being created. Given that the transformation author specifies the type T of the template's variable, T is required *in this case* to be a non-abstract class, otherwise a QVT engine would face a non-deterministic choice among potentially several subclasses of T. On the other hand, although variables passed as actual arguments to a relation invocation may match a freshly instantiated object, they *may be* be abstract: if they do match a new instance, it is only because an `enforce` domain was at play, a situation as that for T above.

[173, Sec. 11.3.4] mandates "*A domain pattern has a distinguished root template expression that is required to be bound to the root variable of the relation domain that owns the domain pattern*". This WFR appears in Listing 10.5 (second invariant) on p. 189. With metamodel classes whose sole purpose is to own another (each `Predicate` owns an `OclExpression`) expressiveness is not increased. Given that the two aspects of pattern matching (guard and slot fillers) are kept separate from each other (as `Predicates` and `Template` resp.), the OCL WFRs that check their agreement must constantly navigate from one to the other. The same difficulty will be addressed by toolsmiths devising algorithms to *process* QVT expressions, for example compilation of QVT instead of interpretation [163].

An area where the concrete syntax of QVT-Relations needs clarification involves the <when> and <where> productions, reproduced below, as they (a) do not generate a `RelationCallExp` (the production <OclExpressionCS> on [173, p. 39] overlooks this case); and (b) they can instead generate arbitrary templates (assuming that <LiteralExpCS> generates any `LiteralExp`, in particular a `TemplateExp`). Allowing a template as part of a pre or postcondition appears problematic, unless interpreted strictly as a side-effects-free query. In any case, it is not crystal clear whether templates are allowed in `when` and `where` clauses:

```
<when> ::= 'when' '{' (<OclExpressionCS> ';')* '}'
<where> ::= 'where' '{' (<OclExpressionCS> ';')* '}'
```

10.3.2 WFRs Around `RelationCallExp`s

Unlike the situation for a transformation, the specification does not include provisions for a relation to specify its list of expected arguments. The actual arguments for an invocation are required by tool vendors to match in order and type the declarations of relation domains. Therefore, as soon as a domain is added or otherwise the lexical order of domain declarations is changed, all existing invocations need to be refactored. Exchanging the declarations of two domains of the same type is a recipe for trouble: while existing invocations remain syntactically valid, the transformation will not behave as before. The situation would be no different in case actual arguments were assigned by name to formal ones: changing the name

Listing 10.6: Conformance between actual and formal args in an invocation

```
context QVTRelation::RelationCallExp
inv actualFormalsConformance :
  argument→size() = referredRelation.domains→size() and
  argument→forAll(arg | let i : Integer =
      self.argument→indexOf(arg) in
    assignmentCompatible(
      referredRelation.domain→at(i).eType, arg.eType))
```

of a domain declaration would again require performing non-local changes in the invocations (Listing 10.6).

The specification states that a top-level relation cannot be invoked (i.e., cannot appear in a `where` clause) [173, p. 164], although it can appear in a `when` clause (an example of the latter can be found in the UML2RDBMS transformation). The corresponding WFR is shown in Listing 10.7. Function `collectRelationInvocations()` receives as single argument a possibly composite `OclExpression`. Its verbose definition requires an `if-then-else-endif` for each branching in the `OclExpression` inheritance tree. A visitor-based formulation is much more compact. The QVT specification authors faced the same problem, as the incomplete definition [173, p. 145] of `getVarsOfExp(OclExpression)` shows, as part of the normative QVT-Relations to QVT-Core transformation. The recurring case distinctions that this tree-walking involves cannot be encapsulated into an OCL utility function because of OCL's inability to pass functions as arguments.

10.3.3 Interplay Between Relation Overriding and the Target Model

For any given transformation, the specification requires only one model parameter to be considered as target at a time. Referring to Figure 10.5 on p. 193 and Listing 10.8 on p. 194, an initial (and wrong) attempt at capturing this WFR would involve finding out, for all `Rules` comprising a `Transformation`, those `Domains` which are marked `isEnforceable`. If more than one model parameter is reachable from them,

Listing 10.7: A top-level relation cannot be invoked

```
context QVTRelation::Relation
inv noInvocationsToTopLevels :
  not self.where→isEmpty()
  implies
  self.where.allRelationInvocations()→forAll( ri |
    ri.referredRelation.isTopLevel = false)


context QVTRelation::DomainPattern
 def allRelationInvocations() : Set(RelationCallExp) =
   self.oclAsType(Pattern).allRelationInvocations()→union(
     collectRelationInvocations(templateExpression.where))


context QVTBase::Pattern
  def allRelationInvocations() : Set(RelationCallExp) =
    predicate.conditionExpression
    →select(c | c.oclIsKindOf(RelationCallExp) )
              .oclAsType(Set(RelationCallExp))
```

the WFR would have been broken. This formulation is actually overrestrictive, as QVT-Relations allows a `Relation` (subclass of `Rule`) to override another. What counts, then, are the domains of the *applicable* relations. The specification states [173, p. 27]: "*The overriding rule is executed in place of the overridden rule when the overriding conditions are satisfied. The exact semantics of overriding are subclass specific*". Problem is, the specification is silent on the customization of this criterion for `Relation`. But a reasonable assumption is that a more specific (i.e., subclassing) relation takes precedence, provided its `when` guard is fulfilled. The resulting partial-order may still return in the general case two or more non-comparable relations (e.g., two enabled relations directly overriding a third one). This runtime non-determinism about which rule to apply requires clarification from the specification authors. In terms of an Alloy-based analysis, non-determinism can be detected at design time.

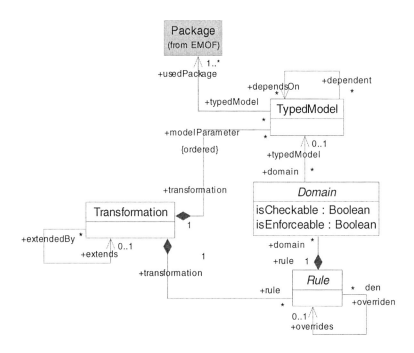

Figure 10.5: Metaclass QVTBase::Transformation

10.3.4 Types of Members of a `CollectionTemplateExp`

Collection templates allow matching against a set, ordered set, bag, or sequence; using a notation inspired in that for function parameters in Haskell. For example, to match against a set-valued attribute, expected to contain at least three strings including "ab", a preamble with three fillers is specified followed by the concat operator: `col:Set(String) { 'ab', s, _ ++ remainingElems }`. In general, the preamble lists a *fixed number* of elements, which may include, besides literal constants and nested templates, variables (`s` in the example) and the special wildcard _ which matches against anything (that we don't care to reference later). Different occurrences of _ need not refer to the same element, unlike multiple occurrences

Listing 10.8: An over-restrictive formulation of the one-target-model constraint

```
context QVTBase::Transformation
inv onlyOneTargetModel :
  rule.domain→select(isEnforceable)→collect(typedModel)→size() <= 1
```

Listing 10.9: Concrete syntax for collection templates

```
<collectionTemplate> ::= [<identifier>] ':' <CollTypeIdentCS>
  '(' <TypeCS> ')' '{' [<memberSelection>] '}'

<memberSelection> ::= (<identifier> | <template> | '_')
  (',' (<identifier> | <template> | '_'))*
  '++' (<identifier> | '_')
```

of the same named variable. A new set containing all of the original elements other than those matched by the preamble will be bound to the variable after ++ (remainingElems in the example, _ would also have been allowed). The concrete syntax for CollectionTemplateExp appears in Listing 10.9 (it is not clear how an arbitrary OCL expression can be generated from the alternative <identifier> | <template>, but the spec intends to allow such expressions).

As shown in Figure 10.4 on p. 187, a CollectionTemplateExp owns one or more OCL expressions to denote elements in the preamble. However, unless further constrained by a WFR, such expressions do not necessarily result in a type-conformant element. The OCL invariant in Listing 10.10 performs this type-check.

Listing 10.10: Type conformance of members in a CollectionTemplateExp

```
context QVTTemplate::CollectionTemplateExp
inv typeConformingMembers :
 member→isEmpty() or member→forAll( m |
  isUnderscoreWildcard(m) or
  assignmentCompatible(bindsTo.getItemType(), m.getType())))
```

10.3.5 A Sidenote on Terminology

The choice of terms and abbreviations favored by the standard can easily lead to misunderstandings. Some choices appear to stem from the desire to achieve consensus between the QVT-Core and QVT-Relations camps (both using for example the term *pattern*) which also resulted in creating a sense of agreement by sharing abstract superclasses, e.g., `Domain` (in the `QVTBase` package) is extended by both `RelationDomain` (in `QVTRelation`) and `CoreDomain` (in `QVTCore`). Same situation arises between `Rule`, `Relation`, and `Mapping`. Besides the name overcrowding, some logical connections end up being split across packages. For example, the fact that a `Relation` owns `RelationDomains` can only be found by inspecting `QVTBase`, where a `Rule` owns `Domains`. Not incorrect, but arguably counterintuitive: with that decision, a dedicated WFR is now needed for `Relation` (namely, domain→size() >= 2). On the other hand, it is not clear why certain facilities are *not* shared between QVT languages. For example, QVT-Operational allows adding new operations to classes [173, Sec. 8.1.8], even to primitive types, as in: `query String::withUnderscore():String = "_".concat(self)`. There appears to be no principle obstacle to supporting this concept of *open classes* in QVT-Relations too.

10.4 Dynamic Semantics, Alloy Formulation

An Alloy specification [120] declares concrete worlds, each consisting of set-theoretic relations connecting atomic symbols ("atoms"), for analysis in different snapshots of interest. Three kinds of analyses are possible [120, p. 150]:

- With *model finding*, visual depictions of all the finite concrete worlds that satisfy the specified constraints can be obtained (an analysis triggered with `run predicate`). Finding no concrete worlds is a strong indicator that the specification is inconsistent, i.e., all constraints cannot be satisfied simultaneously (however, some predicates could have been fulfilled in a larger finite *scope*).

- For unsatisfiable predicates, *Unsat Core* can be used to highlight the relevant portions of the Alloy specification that contributed to unsatisfiability.

Listing 10.11: A more detailed abstraction for Strings in Alloy

```
abstract sig Character{}
one sig A, B, C, D, E extends Character{} -- etc.
one sig CharacterOrd {
  First, Last: set Character,
  Next: Character -> Character
}{ -- some facts about this single linear order on Character
  Character in First.*Next -- every elem is in the total order
  no First.(~Next) -- first element has no predecessor
  no Last.Next -- last element has no successor
  (all e: Character | {
    (e = Last || one e.Next) -- each except last has one succ
    (e = First || one e.(~Next)) -- one pred except first
    (e !in e.^Next) -- there are no cycles
  }) -- enumeration of (prev, next) pairs elided
}
```

- Assertions can be given, which are claimed to follow from the rest of the specification. *Counterexample finding*, triggered with check *assertion*, reveals finite concrete worlds that are conformant save for the broken assertion. *Regression testing* is similar in spirit to this analysis, only that not as encompassing.

As to Alloy's expressiveness about state evolutions over time, no dedicated syntax is provided (in contrast to imperative-style transformations [84]). Instead, Hoare-style pre and postconditions are preferred, where values in the pre and post snapshots are denoted by different variables, e.g., p and p'. Internally, Alloy encodes analyses as boolean satisfiability (SAT) problems. SAT solvers have experienced dramatic performance improvements during the last decade. With the arrival of multicore processors and novel optimizations [196] further gains are expected. Moreover, Alloy offers a Java API for integration, used for example by its Eclipse plugin. Therefore, an integration in a QVT tool is feasible, with QVT-Core and QVT-Operational also standing to benefit from formal analysis.

The lack of dedicated Alloy syntax for EMOF's String and numeric types has been pointed out as a disadvantage, as well as a missing counterpart for the OCL Standard Library, which is reused by QVT-Relations. These difficulties can be overcome by automating the encoding of the appropriate Alloy abstractions. For example[7], if all a transformation T requires from Strings is comparison for equality, then the following Alloy definition will do: `sig String{}`. If, additionally, string comparison appears in T, then a more detailed abstraction (a linear ordering over the `Character` type, shown in Listing 10.11) should be generated *by the encoding algorithm.* Together with the definition `sig String{content : seq Character}`, the OCL condition `a = b.concat(c)` can then be represented as in `sig Example{ a, b, c : String }{ a.content=b.content.append[c.content]}`.

10.4.1 Methodology

Given that a transformation implicitly manages correspondences between model elements some notion of identity is necessary to warrant modification or deletion of the "right" counterpart from those available in the target model, or the creation of a genuine counterpart instead of a duplicate. QVT-Relations adopts the concept of *keys* from relational databases, in the form of per-class sets of fields. Actually, a metamodel definition has by itself no provision to enforce keys, and tools are expected at transformation-application time to detect key duplicates. In terms of the Alloy formulation (Listing 10.14 on p. 200), keys are rephrased as constraints, and only duplicates-free models are considered during certification, thus contributing to scalability: the more constrained the input, the more pruning of the search space that a symbolic engine such as Alloy can perform early on (for a naïve generate-and-test methodology the opposite is the case, as significant effort is invested in the generation phase before the test phase can discard cases).

The basic steps to encode the definitions of OO classes and associations into some formalism are similar, as a comparison of the encodings into First-Order Logic [18], Relational Logic [10], Description Logic [39], and Constraint Satisfaction [39] shows: classes are formalized as sets of atoms (paying attention to disjointness and coverage) with additional predicates to capture the semantics of the specified relationships (in-

---

[7]http://tech.groups.yahoo.com/group/alloy-discuss/message/1266

Listing 10.12: Predicates to enforce deletion of a part upon deletion of its owner

```
pred enforceDeletionOfParts[
  wholes : set univ,
  parts : set univ,
  owningRel : wholes -> parts,
  deletedOwners : set univ /* for enforce mode */ ] {
    // if owner has been deleted, so must have been part too
    all p : parts | let owner = owningRel.p |
      ( (owner in deletedOwners) => (p in deleted[]) )
}

// when the owner has been deleted so must have been its parts
fact { enforceDeletionOfParts[this/Package, PackageElement,
          elements, (SimpleUML/Package - this/Package) ]
       enforceDeletionOfParts[this/Class, this/Attribute,
          attributes, (SimpleUML/Class - this/Class) ]
     }
```

heritance being captured as subset, composition by ruling out multiple simultaneous owners as well as lack of owner, and multiplicities as restrictions on the number of links between atoms related by an association). Given that a transformation may result in deletions, the effects on parts owned over composition have to be included in postconditions (Listing 10.12).

The encoding of QVT-Relations into Alloy starts with the *model type parameters* of a transformation T, i.e., the metamodels whose instances are passed as arguments to T. Given that different arguments may conform to the same model type, a separate population is required for each argument: pairwise disjoint subsets are defined. After that translation, Alloy can generate conforming arguments for T, to automatically explore the input space. In case the analyses should be limited to certain inputs, the pertinent definitions are declared *abstract* with a number of singletons populating them, thus preventing *model finding* from stipulating additional atoms. For checkonly domains a similar strategy is followed: without extra concrete definitions extending the abstract sets, the given populations are constant.

Listing 10.13: Class encoded in Alloy with WFRs for transformation compliance

```
abstract sig ForeignKey extends RModelElement {
  fkColumns : some Column, -- at least one Column required
  refersTo : one Key
}{-- an FK in table T cannot contain columns not in T
  all c:fkColumns | owningTable[this] = owningTable[c]
  -- column types should match those of the PK being referred
  fkColumns.type = refersTo.keyColumns.type
}
```

Listing 10.13 depicts the Alloy declaration for class `ForeignKey`, with two WFRs for transformations.

At this point, functions can be encoded for (a) the templates in `checkonly` domains; and (b) `querys` defined alongside `relations` in T. Although such definitions may in turn involve pattern matching, the need to encode a particular search order is circumvented by letting Alloy bind variables to valid values: a predicate is specified parameterized with the variables and matching conditions that show up in the template of interest. Behind syntax, a set comprehension is at work. In Alloy, $\{x_1:e_1, \ x_2:e_2, \ \ldots, \ x_n:e_n \ | \ F\}$ denotes a set-theoretic relation with all tuples of the form $(x_1, x_2, \ldots, x_n)$ for which the constraint F holds, and where the value of x_i is drawn from the value of the bounding set expression e_i. The translation so far allows detecting whether some QVT-Relations variable is predestined never to be bound, as a result of the interplay between metamodel constraints and matching conditions. This kind of conclusion cannot be arrived at with testing alone, unless prohibitively exhaustive.

10.4.2 Case Study

In order to facilitate methodological comparison, we formalize the running example of the QVT specification (UML2RDBMS, transforming class models to relational database schemas, [173, Annex A.1]) to later analyze whether well-formed output is obtained for each well-formed input. A counterexample is depicted in Figures 10.6 and 10.7, exhibiting duplicate column names in an output `Table`. The in-

Listing 10.14: Formulating QVT-R keys as exemplified by `Table(schema, name)`

```
/*
Keys are unique within each model parameter, not metamodel wide
(i.e., instances in different model parameters may have the
same values for their key attributes, those instances are
still considered different). That is why declarations
like the ones below should also be present in the declarations
for other domains (of type SimpleRDBMS) in case
they were also input to the transformation.
*/

fact {
  all t1,t2:this/Table |
    ( t1.name=t2.name and
      SimpleRDBMS/owningSchema[t1] = SimpleRDBMS/owningSchema[t2]
    ) implies (t1 = t2)
}
```

put shown involves two superclasses declaring primitive attributes with the same name, which are mapped as-is by `SupperAttributeToColumn`. The transformation can be fixed by assigning a different attribute-prefix for each such superclass (`SupperAttributeToColumn` had already the means to do this, but the prefix being passed was empty). The Alloy specs used to debug the transformation are available for download[8].

For example, the relation `ClassToTable` is mapped to all `c:umlDomain/Class`, `t:rdbmsDomain/Table` | *guardClause[c,t]* implies *postCond[c,t]*. After identifying its essential features, the uncluttered visualization in Figures 10.6 and 10.7 was obtained. Subsequently, a commercial QVT-Relations tool was used to run the transformation for the reported input, obtaining the predicted malformed output but no warnings. The Alloy response times remained below one minute for most analyses performed.

---

[8]Alloy formulation of UML2RDBMS, http://www.sts.tu-harburg.de/~mi.garcia/pubs/2008/qvtr/

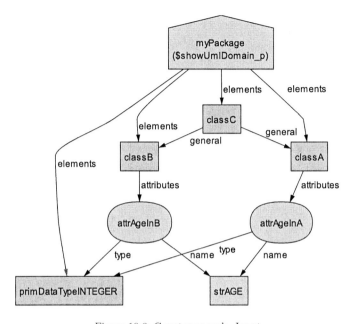

Figure 10.6: Counterexample, Input

10.5 Related Work

Anastasakis developed a translation from UML class models and an OCL subset into
Alloy [10], with details on OCL coverage provided in the tool documentation[9]. In
follow-up work, a transformation between workflow notations was manually encoded
in Alloy to certify output well-formedness [11]. Dingel [57] uses Alloy to rectify the
definition of the UML2 package merge operation.

The ideas of *programs as proofs* and *verifying compilers* are still today holy grails
in Computer Science. Although the mechanization of such theories is not explored
in this PhD thesis, an introduction and a summary of current progress is offered
for the interested reader. Another recent review can be found in Sec. 1.2 ("The
Verification Landscape") of [45].

---

[9]UML2Alloy, http://www.cs.bham.ac.uk/~bxb/UML2Alloy/index.php

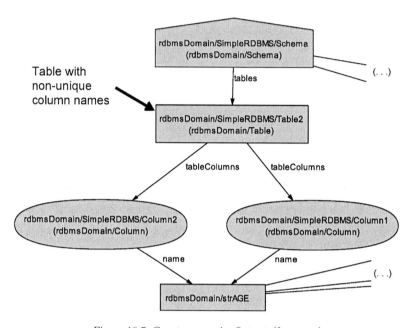

Figure 10.7: Counterexample, Output (fragment)

In essence, any attempt at proving properties about programs relies on proof techniques (e.g., well-founded induction) which are independent from any particular domain. A readable introduction to such techniques, with case studies drawn from the field of programming languages is Winskel's classic *The Formal Semantics of Programming Languages* [208]. Additionally, paper proofs from that book can be compared with their HOL mechanization, discussed by Nipkow in [165]. Another very complete introduction offering context to proof techniques is the lecture *Computer Supported Modeling and Reasoning* by Basin, Wolff, and Brucker, whose materials have been made available by the authors[10].

Part of the ground rules for verification of OO programs with theorem-prover is typed lambda calculus [104], as it has strongly influenced the formalizations of OO

---

[10]http://www.infsec.ethz.ch/education/ws0405/csmr/material

languages for reasoning about typing (heralded by Abadi and Cardelli's *A Theory of Objects* [1]). Regarding Isabelle/HOL implementations, a proof of Church-Rosser is elaborated by Nipkow in [164]. An extension to the concurrent case has been developed by Caromel and Henrio in [41], but no mechanization for their work is as of now available. Regarding the syntactic device of Isabelle's built-in meta-logic, most results are brought together by Baader and Nipkow in the book *Term Rewriting and all That* [14].

The general approach to mechanizing a Hoare-logic in the Higher-Order Logic (HOL) is explained by Gordon [94] (Harrison [109] covers the same topic). Mechanizations of large subsets of the Java programming language have been achieved by von Oheimb [174], Klein [131], and Hanbing Liu [151]. Brucker and Wolff follow a different approach: rather than starting with an already defined language, object-oriented concepts are refined into checkable implementations. The resulting toolset [32] allows sequential program verification. An integration with the HOL-OCL mechanization [33] is planned. The faithful formalization of an existing language as opposed to an abstraction is alone in terms of raw size a difficult problem. For example, a *shallow embedding* of expressions from an object language into an underlying logic allows reusing the proof techniques for the logic in question. However, a more faithful approach consists in formalizing the object language itself, including for example arithmetic. The IEEE-based arithmetic of Java has been mechanized by Rauch and Wolff [183], being an example of a *deep embedding*.

A theorem-prover-based validation of transformations (expressed as rules of a Triple Graph Grammar) has been accomplished by Leitner [146].

Although some researchers believe that program verification will never be fully automated for unrestricted programming languages, efforts in this field are expected to continue expanding the application area of these techniques.

10.6 Evaluation

The notation in Annex B of the QVT specification is not suitable as semantic anchor (unlike Relational Logic) because it only exhibits a vague resemblance to First-Order Logic (FOL) and cannot be mechanically checked.

The UML2RDBMS transformation does not aim at encoding all the rules required for realistic Object-Relational Mapping[11] (for example, no provision is made to handle many-to-many associations). Therefore, a minimal criteria was adopted (the aforementioned well-formedness) as it suffices to demonstrate the methodology. An industrial-strength transformation should additionally be certified to preserve the "semantics" in terms of the languages for input and output (thus guaranteeing *compiler correctness* [91]). In the example, we do not check whether the resulting database schemas have the same expressive power as the input class models. As it turns out they don't: although foreign keys are generated for many-to-one associations, such foreign keys are not included in the tables for subclasses, unlike the columns for inherited attributes. QVT-Relations cannot be expected to be aware about the semantics of all the languages whose sentences it may transform. As a consequence, compiler correctness has to be validated separately, by manually specifying verification conditions that cannot be extracted mechanically from the transformation under study.

Ideally, the translation from QVT-Relations into Alloy should be tool supported, as well as the subsequent analyses (coverage of input language, and well-formedness of output sentences), for example by building upon our Eclipse-based OCL compiler [87, 78] and the metamodel of QVT-Relations.

Given the progress experienced by logic engines in terms of efficiency, portability, and componentization, we believe the time is right for adopting the best-practice of anchoring the semantics of software modeling standards in decidable formalisms, as demonstrated in this chapter for QVT-Relations.

---

[11]Scott Ambler on ORM, http://www.agiledata.org/essays/mappingObjects.html

11 Efficient Run-time Integrity Checking: Software Repositories

Contents

The efficient detection of run-time violations of integrity constraints (or their avoidance in the first place) has not been satisfactorily addressed for the combination of object model and constraint definition language most widely accepted in industry, namely OMG's Essential MOF and Object Constraint Language (OCL). We identify the dimensions relevant to this problem, and classify existing proposals by their position in the solution space. After this comparative survey, we propose a solution for the efficient integrity checking of invariants expressed in OCL over the Essential MOF data model, and describe the software architecture of its implementation using object-relational mapping technology.

As MDSE techniques are applied to development processes of ever increasing complexity, additional demands are placed on the infrastructure supporting those processes. Software repositories [58] play a vital role in the management of software artifacts conforming to an EMOF data model, checking the integrity constraints given as OCL invariants. The task of runtime integrity checking has proven non-scalable if performed without regard for optimization techniques, yet many EMOF software repositories in use today do not adequately address this concern. Solving this industrially relevant problem requires identifying a calculus expressive enough to handle OCL yet tractable enough that optimizations of collection operations are feasible. Moreover, an empirical evaluation of the proposed approach should validate the findings before real-world deployment.

Integrity checking is an instance of the model-checking problem, i.e., determining whether a concrete world satisfies predicates. In turn, query evaluation is an area thoroughly studied in the academic literature. We follow the engineering approach of coherently combining existing scientific knowledge to solve an industrial problem. Our work falls just short of building a concrete product based on the technology choices made (because that's a task for industry). Rather, we disclose the detailed reasoning behind our approach (which industry refrains from doing).

The structure of this chapter is as follows. Sec. 11.1 reviews the strategies for integrity checking available to repository designers. Sec. 11.2 covers the often over-looked interplay between expressiveness of the constraint language and runtime cost of integrity checking. Sec. 11.3 presents a technology choice that balances these conflicting requirements. A review of the difficulties associated to checking computationally-complete OCL can be found in Sec. 11.4, followed by the translation rules into the chosen calculus (Sec. 11.5) and a sample of the optimization techniques thus enabled (Sec. 11.6). Related work (Sec. 11.7) includes pointers to the main-memory case and to recent progress on integrity checking in the SQL/relational setting. Sec. 11.8 discusses the insights gained as a result of the presented formalization.

11.1 Integrity Checking in Software Repositories

Given the ubiquity of EMOF and OCL in MDSE, it comes as no surprise that software repositories are required to manage artifacts conformant to EMOF + OCL metamodels [184]. Infrastructural functionality expected of such repositories includes scalability, concurrent access, integrity checking and enforcement, versioning [135], and view maintenance. These capabilities in turn are needed to support higher-level use cases such as: traceability between requirement specifications and implementation artifacts, impact analysis, refactoring, and avoidance of architectural erosion [185].

The implementers of some EMOF + OCL software repositories in use today have not paid enough attention to the formal foundation of those languages, with the end result that it cannot be determined anymore whether some tool behaviors are correct or not. Analyses of ambiguities in past revisions of the MOF and OCL specification can be found in [9] and [33]. A formalism that offers rigorous precision is a good start, yet Fegaras and Maier define in [71] additional criteria for a calculus to be suitable for a query language:

- *Coverage*: whether the calculus has enough expressive power to represent all concepts of the query language. In the case of OCL, these concepts include aggregation, duplicate values, sort orders, several collection types (sets, bags, ordered sets, lists), negation, and user-defined (potentially recursive) functions.

- *Ease of manipulation*: expressions in the calculus should lend themselves to uniform matching and rewriting, such as in type-checking or optimization.

- *Evaluation fitness*: whether all valid query plans can be derived from an expression in the calculus. A formalism that expresses queries at too low a level of abstraction acts as a barrier to effective evaluation.

By relying on a formal calculus that is suitable with respect to OCL, precise definitions for the problems of query optimization, integrity checking, and view maintenance become possible, and correctness of their solutions can be examined. Efficient implementations are the next step. Before discussing a calculus that fulfills the above criteria, we elaborate on the alternative approach of directly anchoring the semantics of EMOF + OCL in terms of the Relational Data Model, turning OCL into a surface syntax. This would acknowledge the fact that results from the object-oriented and deductive database communities have become mainstream in SQL3 and are thus likely to be efficiently supported by conformant DBMSs. We see however some disadvantages with this approach:

- Pre-SQL3 relational formalisms do not fulfill the coverage criteria as defined above. Queries involving aggregation or sort orders have to be formulated as a mixture of relational algebra interspersed with control structures. Only those fragments bracketed between control structures are amenable to optimization.

- Post-SQL3 extended-relational formalisms strongly resemble the calculus adopted in our approach. Algorithms for incremental view maintenance based on these formalisms can thus serve as a foundation for our solution architecture.

- It is more efficient to manipulate query plans at the highest level of abstraction possible. Once optimized, object-level queries can be cast in terms of relational algebra thus opening the way for further potential optimizations.

- EMOF concepts cannot be mapped one-to-one to relational "counterparts", thus making a direct relational anchoring non-trivial in itself. For example, a relational view may contain the primary keys of its base relations, while each object in an object view has a globally unique object-ID.

11.2 Expressiveness and Runtime Cost of Integrity Checking

There is a mutual dependency between the expressiveness of a constraint language and the computational complexity of evaluating integrity constraints upon updates to database state. Three categories can be distinguished:

1. *Design-time avoidance of integrity violations*: By carefully limiting the expressive power of the data model and constraint language, it is possible to

determine at database schema design time whether some ordering of update transactions may violate the integrity constraints. After this proof has been carried out (e.g., based on algorithm model-checking as shown by Lamport in [142]) no run-time checks are needed. An example of this approach for a variant of the F-Logic language is presented in [143]. Actually there is still a run-time overhead in that each transaction is augmented with its generated weakest precondition. Those fragments of the precondition which cannot be proved to be implied by the database invariants have to be checked at runtime.

2. *Run-time integrity checking with efficient evaluation*: For more expressive constraint languages, not all integrity checks can be skipped at runtime. Nevertheless, the evaluation of those remaining checks can be made more efficient than that for arbitrary formulas in first-order predicate logic (PSPACE-complete in the worst-case for finite object graphs [195]). We aim at identifying the subset of OCL whose expressive power fits in this category. An algorithm for incremental view maintenance [5] optimizes integrity checking, as discussed in Sec. 11.3.

3. *Run-time integrity checking with best-effort evaluation*: For some specific combinations of database schemas and full-OCL invariants, custom checks are derived whose efficiency is comparable to that of category 2 above, sometimes using heuristics. For the remaining cases, large data sets have to be scanned. This approach is followed in [38] and [7] where the non-declarative subset of OCL is also adopted (including control structures and negation).

The chosen complexity of integrity checking (second item above) does not preclude ad-hoc queries from using full-OCL (and require full scans of entity extents in some cases). It seems questionable, however, for the formulation of an integrity constraint to require computational completeness, as the constraint is rendered non-declarative. Those constraints, if really needed, are best enforced by the business logic that manipulates the software repository, e.g., following Design-By-Contract [162], as recommended by best practices evolved over the years for the architecture of multi-tier information systems.

11.3 Incremental Integrity Checking for OCL

Integrity enforcement comprises two runtime phases: (a) *violation detection* and (b) *consistency restoration*. For each OCL invariant, a view to hold the object-IDs of those instances not fulfilling it is defined (a *denial view*). At transaction commit time, all such views should be empty, otherwise a consistency restoration policy is to be applied (rollback, compensating action, or postponing consistency restoration altogether). Policies for consistency restoration are outside the scope of this chapter. Given that most transactions leave the majority of invariants unaffected, full recomputation of views after each update is impractical. Instead, *incremental maintenance* is preferred, a process comprising design and runtime activities:

1. At database design time, each view definition is mechanically analyzed to determine which update operations (when performed on certain data elements) affect the resultset.

2. For such events, actions are generated to react to them, taking as input the delta caused by the update and using it to bring the materialized view into an up-to-date state (a *self-maintenance* strategy as opposed to querying the base extents).

3. At runtime, the planned actions are executed upon being triggered by the updates being monitored, performing *change propagation*.

An efficient algorithm for incremental view maintenance in an EMOF + OCL context is not as concise as the above summary might suggest because:

- Update operations on an object model are richer than their relational counterpart, given the additional collection types available (lists, ordered sets, bags).

- Method overriding is an issue in that a subclass may redeclare a side-effects-free operation (an OCL defined one), with that operation being used in an invariant. Instances of the subtype should have the overriding definition evaluated in place of the overridden one.

210

- Updates may have side effects, which in turn may affect invariants. These side effects result from inverse relationships maintained automatically in EMOF between two entities (its closest counterpart in relational databases is referential integrity). For example, upon deleting an instance which is bidirectionally linked to another, this second instance will have its reference cleared.

A concrete realization of the above ideas, satisfying the complexity requirements introduced in Sec. 11.2, is provided by the MOVIE algorithm for incremental view maintenance [5], explained in detail by Akhtar Ali in his PhD thesis [4]. A thorough performance evaluation [6] confirms its practical usefulness. The MOVIE algorithm is based on the translation of queries into the monoid calculus and their subsequent optimization, as discussed in [72] and [101]. The monoid calculus embodies the relational calculus, and has proven versatile enough to support both traditional as well as innovative optimizations. The software architecture of the solution proposed in this chapter comprises:

1. The design time mapping of a model expressed in EMOF into a relational database schema (performed by a ready made component [68]). Data manipulation occurs at runtime only as EMOF-level update operations that are intercepted and matched against event patterns derived by MOVIE from view definitions for invariants.

2. The design time translation of OCL invariants into monoid calculus expressions. The resulting event patterns (derived by MOVIE for runtime interception) correspond to EMOF-level update operations. The accompanying actions generated by MOVIE to effect view maintenance are also EMOF-level updates.

The data definition, manipulation, and query languages (DDL, DML, DQL) of our solution are: EMOF, EMOF-level update operations, and full-OCL. The (incrementally maintainable) constraint language is the subset of OCL translatable into monoid calculus, and moreover valid as input for MOVIE (as defined in Sec. 4.1.2.2 of [4]). Although full-OCL is our standard DQL, nothing prevents the user from expressing read-only queries directly in SQL or in the ORM-level query language,

JPQL [66] (Java Persistence Query Language, sometimes referred to as EJB3QL). Writing these "pass-through queries" in SQL requires knowledge of the mapping decisions encapsulated in item 1 above.

The barriers to efficient evaluation introduced by full-OCL are covered next, followed by an in-depth discussion of the translation of OCL into monoid calculus as a prerequisite to applying the MOVIE algorithm.

11.4 Computationally Complete Constraint Language

Proposals using full-OCL for integrity constraints [38, 7] involve re-evaluating candidate broken invariants on a set of instances collected at runtime. The applied strategy consists in minimizing the amount of relevant instances, instead of avoiding re-computing subexpressions whose value has not changed (e.g., by caching their values). This is a major difference with incremental view maintenance. The essential aspects of the full-OCL approaches are illustrated with two examples, including the difficulties introduced by recursion. For a more detailed presentation see Sec. 4 in [7].

A core aspect of [38] and [7] is the observation that for each data element on which an OCL invariant depends, it is possible to derive a navigation-based query in the direction from the data element back to the instance where the invariant is evaluated. On the wake of an update on some data element, these navigation paths lead to a set of instances relevant for re-evaluating the invariant in question. For example, in an scenario where Departments may have good and bad Employees (Figure 11.1 on p. 213), an integrity constraint may require the union of two sets (all bad employees and those good employees over forty) not to contain a hobbyist:

```
context Department
inv    noHobbyist : badEmps->union(goodEmps->select(age > 40))
                    ->select(hasHobby)->isEmpty()
```

Given a Department d, adding or removing employees (good or bad), as well as changing their hobby status may affect the invariant noHobbyist when evaluated for d. However, for this particular invariant, age updates are relevant only for

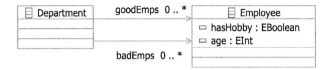

Figure 11.1: The noHobbyist example: Departments and Employees

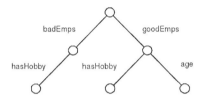

Figure 11.2: Reachability for noHobbyist

good employees. This intuition is reflected in the reachability paths shown as a tree in Figure 11.2. Thanks to bidirectional associations, upon an update to a node in that tree, the fixed-length path to the root can be followed to find the Department instance (i.e., d) on which invariant noHobbyist should be re-evaluated at transaction-commit time.

Special care is required for recursive functions ranging over dynamic data structures, as illustrated by the forward-only list of Figure 11.3. In that example, the invariant lastWagonHasLightsOn is fulfilled for a Wagon w in a train as long its last wagon has the lights on. In this case, a statically fixed back-navigation path will not achieve the desired result, as the required number of links to traverse changes at runtime. A conservative approach consists in re-evaluating recursive invariants for all instances of their contexts, thus achieving completeness at the expense of efficient evaluation. It is not clear from [38, 7] how recursion over dynamic data structures is dealt with.

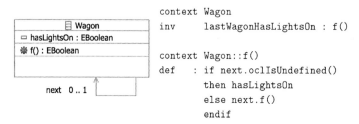

```
context Wagon
inv      lastWagonHasLightsOn : f()

context Wagon::f()
def    : if next.oclIsUndefined()
         then hasLightsOn
         else next.f()
         endif
```

Figure 11.3: The `lastWagonHasLightsOn` example

11.5 Translation of OCL into Monoid Calculus

Queries translated into the monoid calculus refer to the same object-oriented schema as their OCL counterparts. No schema mapping is needed because most EMOF constructs have a direct counterpart in the monoid calculus, with the following exceptions: (a) EMOF-level ordered sets (no duplicates, insertion order preserved) are represented as monoid lists; (b) EMOF *dictionaries* (Maps in Java) are represented as sets of *(key, value)* pairs, where pairs are monoid lists. Under these conventions, for the purposes of side-effect-free queries, the result of evaluating the monoid translation agrees with its original OCL formulation. For update purposes instead, these conventions would not be consistent, as for example monoid lists do not capture the semantics of EMOF ordered sets (which require membership testing before insertion). We do not claim to optimize updates, whose semantics are enforced by the ORM engine. The fact that the same data schema is shared by both OCL and monoid expressions makes possible to optimize the monoid formulation without the additional complication of data mapping. No schema changes are introduced during rewriting for optimization. Finally, the optimized version is semantics preserving with respect to its original formulation.

An internal node in the AST of an OCL class invariant stands for a function application, with each subnode providing actual arguments. Some OCL constructs (e.g., `let v = ...  in  ...`) add identifiers to the scope visible in subtrees. Such syntax can be removed by expanding definitions, thus achieving the shape of "function application only" mentioned before. This rewriting does not alter meaning as OCL has call-by-value evaluation semantics. Terminal nodes are not tagged with function applications but with any of: (a) a literal constant; (b) the predefined OCL variable `self`; (c) entity extents of the form *ClassName*`.allInstances()`. The variable `self` ranges over an entity extent, namely that for the class where the invariant was defined. Unlike UML, there are no class-scoped attributes or associations in EMOF. We assume furthermore that invocations of user-defined, non-recursive functions have been replaced with their definitions (this may involve substituting usages of formal arguments by their corresponding actual arguments). To account for late binding (choosing a function definition based on the actual type of a usage instead of its declared type) a potentially verbose case distinction is needed. This is no principle obstacle with *whole-model analysis*: all possible actual types are known at translation time and the actual type of an object can be queried with `oclIsTypeOf()`. After this preprocessing step, each internal node stands for the invocation of either an OCL predefined function or a user-defined (directly or indirectly) recursive function.

11.5.1 The Monoid Calculus

The monoid calculus provides a uniform notation for collections such as lists, bags and sets, based on the observation that the operations of set and bag union and list concatenation are monoid operations (that is, they are associative and have an identity element). Monoids for collection types are known as *collection monoids*. Operations like conjunctions and disjunctions on booleans and integer addition are instead *primitive monoids*. Borrowing notation from [72], a monoid of type T is a pair $(\oplus, \mathcal{Z}_\oplus)$ where $\oplus$ is an associative function of type $T \times T \to T$ and $\mathcal{Z}_\oplus$ is the left and right identity of $\oplus$. A monoid may be commutative (i.e., when $\oplus$ is commutative), idempotent (i.e., when $\forall x : x \oplus x = x$), or both. For example, $(+, 0)$ is a commutative and anti-idempotent monoid, while $(\cup, \{\})$ is both commutative and idempotent.

An expression of the form $\oplus[\![e \mid e_1 \ldots e_n]\!]$ is a *comprehension over monoid* $\oplus$. Unlike the prominent role granted in functional programming languages to *list* comprehensions, the notation above uniformly captures collection operations, whose kind is revealed by the outermost braces ($[\!]$ for lists, $\{\!\{\ \}\!\}$ for bags, $\{\}$ for sets). Each e_i is a qualifier, which can either be a generator of the form $v \leftarrow E$, where v

is a variable and E is a collection-valued expression, or a filter p (a boolean valued predicate). Informally, each generator $v \leftarrow E$ sequentially binds variable v to the elements of expression E's value, making it visible in successive qualifiers. A filter evaluating to *true* results in successive qualifiers (if any) being evaluated under the current bindings, otherwise "backtracking" takes place. The *head* expression e is evaluated for those bindings that satisfy all the filters, and taken together these values constitute the resulting collection. For example, the following SQL-like nested query:

```
select distinct e(x)
from ( select d(y) from E as y where q(y) ) as x
where p(x)
```

is translated as $\{\, e(x) \mid x \leftarrow \{\!\{ d(y) \mid y \leftarrow E\, , q(y) \}\!\} \,, p(x) \,\}$

Applying a function f to each element in a collection (`map f xs` in Haskell) is thus expressed as $[\![\, f(x) \mid x \leftarrow xs \,]\!]$, while `filter p xs` becomes $[\![\, x \mid x \leftarrow xs,\, p(x) \,]\!]$. Comprehensions in turn are syntactic sugar for *monoid homomorphisms*, which express structural recursion on the collection constructor (++ for lists, $\cup$ for sets, $\uplus$ for bags), as shown pictorially in Figure 11.4 [100]. For example, taking $\otimes$ to be `max(x,y) = case x<y of true` $\to$ `y | false` $\to$ `x` makes $(\!\mid\!-\infty; max]\, C$ find the maximum of collection C.

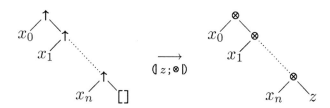

Figure 11.4: Graphical representation of the homomorphism from monoid $(\uparrow, [])$ to $(z, \otimes)$ (the latter not necessarily a collection monoid)

11.5.2 Translation Rules

Transformations for languages with a number of syntactic constructs (such as OCL) take the form of $LHS \rightarrow RHS$ pattern-based substitutions, where each OCL construct is matched by only one LHS. The transformation algorithm can be shown to correctly preserve meaning if each rewrite transformation is proved meaning-preserving. This follows case by case from definitions (in the respective semantic domains of OCL and monoid calculus). The rewrite rules are terminating because they decrease the number of occurrences of OCL constructs available for matching, and are confluent given that the LHSs partition the set of shapes that OCL constructs may take (each OCL construct being matched by one rewrite rule). Translation operates bottom-up from the leaves of the AST. For each node all required information is available locally due to pre-processing: no lookup of the correct binding for an OCL variable is needed as no such usages are left except for `self`.

Regarding the possible OCL constructs, Figure 5.1 on page 69 depicts the relevant fragment of the OCL metamodel [171], i.e. the classes whose instances are nodes in an AST. As part of preprocessing, some constructs have been desugared (`LetExp`, `VariableExp`), while others do not appear in invariants (`MessageExp`). Occurrences of `UnspecifiedValueExp`, `InvalidLiteralExp`, and `NullLiteralExp` stand for the result of applying a partial function outside its domain. `StateExp` and `TypeExp` are functions that access instance-level data (the current state, given an associated statechart) and the actual type (which remains constant throughout the lifetime of the instance, as EMOF lacks dynamic reclassification). Related to this, the boolean operation `oclIsKindOf()` reports whether a pair of types belongs to the transitive closure of the direct subtype relationship $\leq_1$ of EMOF + OCL [79].

OCL constructs of the form `LiteralExp` are translated as follows: (a) a literal of the primitive types (integer, real, string, or boolean) has a corresponding monoid constant, the same goes for literals of a user-defined enumerations; (b) a collection literal of type ordered set or list is translated as a monoid list, while set and bag collections have direct counterparts; (c) a tuple literal is translated as a set of pairs $(tag, value)$.

The iterator expressions (`LoopExp`) comprise non-recursive subcases (Table 11.1). The remaining subcases are first desugared to their `iterate()` form as defined in the OCL standard ([171], Sec. 11.9 and A.3.1.3). `iterate()` in turn can be expressed as a left-fold. To capture this primitive recursive function, the *function composition monoid* $(\circ, \lambda x.x)$ is needed [72] where the function composition, $\circ$, defined as $(f \circ g)\,x = f(g(x))$, is associative but neither commutative nor idempotent. Even though the type of this monoid, $T_\circ(\alpha) = \alpha \to \alpha$, is parametric, it is still a primitive monoid. For a list $L = [a_1, a_2, \ldots, a_n]$, applying $\circ[\lambda x.f(x,a) \mid a \leftarrow L]$ to z expands to $(\lambda x.f(x,a_1)) \circ \ldots \circ (\lambda x.f(x,a_n))(z)$ which computes the left-fold $f(\ldots(f(f(z,a_n),a_{n-1}),\ldots a_1)$. The formulation of OCL's `c→iterate(a ; acc=init | expr(acc,a))` is thus the comprehension $\circ[\lambda\,acc.expr \mid a \leftarrow c](init)$. The expressive power of comprehensions involving $\circ$ lies in their ability to compose functions that propagate a state during list iteration. For example, the reverse of list L is $\circ[\lambda x.x +\!+ [a] \mid a \leftarrow L]([])$. Actually, the OCL standard defines the semantics of all `LoopExp` in terms of `iterate()`, but as can be seen from Table 11.1 the additional expressive power is not necessary, and may complicate optimization by hiding properties that $\otimes$ may exhibit (commutativity, idempotence).

In EMOF terminology, a *class feature* is either (a) an instance field or association end; or (b) a method. Accessing the value of (a) is represented by `PropertyCallExp`, and invoking an (OCL-defined, side-effect free) method by `OperationCallExp`. Occurrences of these constructs are translated as function application in monoid expressions. The sibling of `PropertyCallExp` (`AssociationClassCallExp`) is not relevant for EMOF, as class-scoped structural features are not allowed. The pending cases of `OperationCallExp` not translated so far comprise: (a) operations on the primitive types boolean, integer, real, and string; and (b) collection operations (not to be con-

OCL	Monoid calculus
`c→select(e	boolExpr(e))`	$[\![\, e \mid e \leftarrow c ,\ \mathrm{boolExpr}(e)\,]\!]$
`c→reject(e	boolExpr(e))`	$[\![\, e \mid e \leftarrow c ,\ \mathrm{boolExpr}(e) = \mathrm{false}\,]\!]$
`c→exists(e	boolExpr(e))`	$\vee\{\,\mathrm{boolExpr}(e) \mid e \leftarrow c\,\}$
`c→forAll(e	boolExpr(e))`	$\wedge\{\,\mathrm{boolExpr}(e) \mid e \leftarrow c\,\}$
`c→collect(e	expr(e))`	$[\![\,\mathrm{expr}(e) \mid e \leftarrow c\,]\!]$
`c→one(e	boolExpr(e))`	$1 = \mathrm{length}(\,[\, e \mid e \leftarrow c ,\ \mathrm{boolExpr}(e)]\,)$ where $\mathrm{length}(x) \equiv +[1 \mid e \leftarrow x]$

Table 11.1: Non-recursive subcases of `LoopExp`

OCL	Monoid calculus
c→count(m)	$+[1 \mid e \leftarrow c, e = m]$
c→excludes(m)	$\wedge\{e \neq m \mid e \leftarrow c\}$
c1→excludesAll(c2)	$\wedge\{\wedge\{e \neq m \mid e \leftarrow c_1\} \mid m \leftarrow c_2\}$
c→includes(m)	$\vee\{e = m \mid e \leftarrow c\}$
c1→includesAll(c2)	$\wedge\{\vee\{e = m \mid e \leftarrow c_1\} \mid m \leftarrow c_2\}$
c→isEmpty()	$c = [\![\,]\!]$
c→sum()	$+[e \mid e \leftarrow c]$
c→size()	$+[1 \mid e \leftarrow c]$
c1→product(c2)	$\{(x, y) \mid x \leftarrow c_1, y \leftarrow c_2\}$

Table 11.2: Standard OCL operations on all collection types

fused with iterator operations). The first group can be translated as-is given that all storage engines implement them natively. From the point of view of optimization, they are handled as black-boxes. Translation rules for collection operations appear in Tables 11.2 to 11.4, classified by computational complexity, complexity which is not apparent from the uniform OCL syntax.

The implementation of OCL AST transformations is discussed in [78], including techniques such as the encapsulation of walker code, instantiation of type-parametric visitors with type substitutions, and tracking the input-output relationship between AST nodes along a chain of visitors.

11.6 Optimizations with Monoid Calculus

The invariant noHobbyist (Figure 1 in Sec. 11.4) is amenable to a basic optimization, pushing selections below joins (the predicate hasHobby = true appears only after building partial results, performing it earlier increases selectivity). The vast body of query optimization algorithms is not applicable to the surface syntax of OCL: the same concept can be expressed in so many different ways that *ease of manipulation* (Sec. 11.1) is impracticable.

We claim that query optimization is required for two purposes in an EMOF + OCL setting: (a) for ad-hoc queries, and (b) to optimize expressions obtained from OCL invariants before their *maintenance plans* are derived by MOVIE. The case for

OCL	Monoid calculus
`c1`→`excluding(c2)`	$[\![e \mid e \leftarrow c_1, \wedge\{d \neq e \mid d \leftarrow c_2\}]\!]$
`c`→`append(m)`	$c \mathbin{+\!\!+} [m]$
`c`→`asBag()`	$\{\!\{e \mid e \leftarrow c\}\!\}$
`c`→`asOrderedSet()` `c`→`asSequence()`	$[e \mid e \leftarrow c]$
`c`→`asSet()`	$\{e \mid e \leftarrow c\}$
`c`→`flatten()`	$\oplus[\![e \mid s \leftarrow c, e \leftarrow s]\!]$
`c`→`including(m)`	$c \oplus [\![m]\!]$
`c1`→`intersection(c2)`	$\oplus[\![e \mid e \leftarrow c_1, \vee\{e = d \mid d \leftarrow c_2\}]\!]$
`c`→`prepend(m)`	$[\![m]\!] \oplus c$
`c1`→`union(c2)`	$c_1 \cup c_2$
`c1`→`symmetricDifference(c2)`	same translation as for (`c1`→`union(c2)`)→ `excluding((c1`→`intersection(c2)))`

Table 11.3: Overloaded collection operators ($\oplus$ stands for the merge operator of the resulting collection monoid)

(a) should be evident. As for (b), the authors of [7] observe that invariant rewriting may disconcert users, who would be faced with integrity violation errors based on expressions they have never seen before. As a consequence, rewriting in general (and optimization in particular) is explicitly avoided. The usability concern in question can be addressed in that error messages can be produced by evaluating the original OCL invariant once it is known (by optimized evaluation) that it has been broken. Actually, re-evaluation is inherent to the approach in [7], thus incurring no additional overhead.

The primitive operations supported by storage managers or query engines correspond to query algebra operators (*semi-joins*, selection supported by indexes, etc.) The monoid calculus takes advantage of this fact by offering a uniform framework for query translation, rewriting for optimization, and execution plan generation: query optimization can be made aware of the physical schema (table partitioning applied as part of ORM), saving I/O costs. To illustrate this kind of optimization, we show an end-to-end example of translation, optimization, and plan generation aware of physical schema, adapted to the EMOF + OCL setting from [101].

c→at(i)	$(\circ[\![\lambda(x,k).(\text{if } k = i \text{ then } a \text{ else } x, k-1) \mid a \leftarrow c]\!]$ $(\text{NULL}, \text{length}(x))).\text{fst}$
c→first()	$\circ[\![\lambda x.a \mid a \leftarrow c]\!]$
c→last()	same translation as for c→at(c→size())
c→indexOf(m)	$(\circ[\![\lambda(x,k).(\text{if } a = m \text{ then } k \text{ else} -1, k-1) \mid a \leftarrow c]\!]$ $(-1, \text{length}(x))).\text{fst}$
c→subOrderedSet(j,k) c→subSequence(j,k)	$(\circ[\![\lambda(x,i).\text{if } j \leq i \leq k \text{ then } ([a]\!+\!\!+x, i-1)$ $\text{else } (x, i-1)]\!](\text{[]}, \text{length}(c))).\text{fst}$
c→insertAt(k,m)	$(\circ[\![\lambda(x,k).\text{if } i = k \text{ then } ([m]\!+\!\!+[a]\!+\!\!+x, i-1)$ $\text{else } ([a]\!+\!\!+x, i-1) \mid a \leftarrow c]\!](\text{[]}, \text{length}(c))).\text{fst}$

Table 11.4: Collection operations involving comprehensions of function composition

Consider a database of Films and the actors appearing in them (recording in how many scenes, scenes), together with the films' directors, as shown in Figure 11.5.

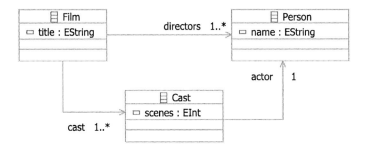

Figure 11.5: EMOF logical schema for the films, actors, and directors database

Assuming that most queries access either actors or directors, it makes sense to *vertically decompose* the logical schema into four tables (see Figure 11.6). Clustering table columns that are frequently accessed together avoids unnecessary I/O, as its elements are stored physically contiguous.

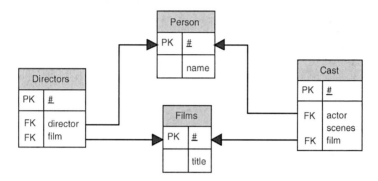

Figure 11.6: Physical schema for the films, actors, and directors database

The OCL query below (in terms of the logical schema in Figure 11.5 on p. 221) returns the titles of Hitchcock-style films: the director appears as an actor in exactly one scene.

```
Film.allInstances()->select( f |
    f.directors->exists( d |
        f.cast->exists( c | c.scenes = 1 and c.actor = d ) ) )
->collect( f | f.title )
```

Its translation as a monoid comprehension is as readable as the OCL version:

$$\{f.\text{title} \mid f \leftarrow \text{film},$$
$$some\{some\{d = c.\text{actor} \mid c \leftarrow f.\text{cast}, c.\text{scenes} = 1\} \mid$$
$$d \leftarrow f.\text{directors}\}$$
$$\}$$

Before optimization can start, the connection to the physical schema is established by replacing *film* by its definition in terms of the vertically decomposed tables, using the *nest* operator to reconstruct the owned collections of actors and directors for each film. With that, the monoid comprehension can be normalized: all variables ranging over collections (i.e., f, d, c) appear first followed by a predicate in conjunctive normal form. This not yet optimized formulation has a direct counterpart in query algebra (Figure 11.7 on p. 223), a tree of cartesian products. In principle, relational optimizations could start from there, thus guaranteeing that monoid-based optimizations do not end up in execution plans worse than relational optimization (e.g., exchanging two generators results in join reordering).

$$\pi_{f_p.\text{title}}((\text{Films}_{f_p} \underset{f_p.\#=d_p.\text{film}}{\bowtie} \text{Directors}_{d_p}) \underset{f_p.\#=c_p.\text{film} \wedge d_p.\text{director}=c_p.\text{actor}}{\bowtie} (\sigma_{c_p.\text{scenes}=1}(\text{Cast}_{c_p})))$$

Figure 11.7: Query algebra formulation, non-optimized stage

The semijoin $E_1 \ltimes_p E_2$ is a join variant that delivers only those left operand objects having at least one join partner with respect to the join predicate p. Its implementation is efficient because as soon as a join partner is found for an E_1 object, then it is known to belong to the result and no further E_2 objects need be accessed. The monoid comprehension formulation allows detecting those access patterns that correspond to semijoins. In the example, after partial flattening of subqueries (not shown), the shaded subexpression in Figure 11.8 on p. 223 is one such case.

$$\{f.\text{title} \mid f \leftarrow \text{films}, \ d \leftarrow f.\text{directors},$$
$$some\{d = c.\text{actor} \mid c \leftarrow f.\text{cast}, c.\text{scenes} = 1\} \}$$

Figure 11.8: Semi-join access pattern

The resulting optimized formulation appears in Figure 11.9 on p. 224.

The resulting query plan expressed in relational algebra has a straightforward translation into JPQL [66], the ORM-level query language. Further potential relational optimizations may be performed by the RDBMS. In keeping with MDSE

$$\text{Films}_{f_p} \underset{f_p.\#=d_p.\text{film}}{\bowtie} (\text{Directors}_{d_p} \underset{c_p.\text{actor}=d_p.\text{director}\wedge d_p.\text{film}=c_p.\text{film}}{\bowtie} (\sigma_{c_p.\text{scenes}=1}(\text{Cast}_{c_p})))$$

Figure 11.9: Query algebra formulation, optimized stage

principles, this translation is not implemented as string manipulations but as an AST-to-AST transformation [77]. Well-formedness is thus ensured before delivering output for further processing.

Without the conceptual framework of the monoid calculus, applying similar rewritings directly on OCL ASTs would not have been feasible. This is further evidence to the claim that integrity checking for EMOF + OCL should follow the approach proposed here.

11.7 Related Work

Database-centered Approaches

The influence of the Object Query Language (OQL) defined in the 1990s by the Object Data Management Group (ODMG) cannot be understated, reaching to JPQL today. Trigoni [197] formalizes type inference for OQL queries. Additionally, algorithms are provided for applying two semantic optimization heuristics: constraint introduction and constraint elimination. These refined heuristics take into consideration *association rules* discovered with data mining, which are not as strong as integrity constraints (they may have exceptions in fact). Given that these "rules" statistically hold most of the time, it pays off to monitor their validity at runtime. Unless they become invalid, they can be used during optimization to increase selectivity and to skip evaluations, thus improving performance. As with other heuristic techniques, safety measures are built in to prevent the cost of analysis to exceed optimization speed-up.

Ritter et al. [184] also aim at integrity checking by translating OCL into a view definition language, this time SQL'92. However, no systematic performance analysis is made. The Dresden OCL Toolkit [55] compiles full-OCL into RDBMS stored procedures including control structures, thus compromising query optimization in the general case.

A recent book on the subject of database integrity is [60]. Most contributions focus on the relational case. The book [102] is devoted to view materialization.

Declarative Integrity Constraints for EJB

The EJB component model [66] is a major player in the field of Enterprise Software Architectures. Due to the resulting ecosystem around it, EJB has been explored as candidate architecture for (transaction-oriented) software repositories. However, no general methodology has been found to generate EJB systems having throughput and performance levels comparable to those manually built by experts.

Different approaches have been put forward to encode the behavior required for integrity enforcement. An approach favored by industry involves *business rules*, i.e. sets of Event-Condition-Action (ECA) statements such as:

- a time-triggered ECA rule: for example, "whenever a customer has a payment overdue more than five working days stop receiving orders from that customer"

- a query-triggered rule: for example, "whenever a customer surpasses the limit of three bad credit histories downgrade the customer's status one level"

Moreover, these rules should ideally be updatable at runtime (*runtime adaptability*), with *rule engines* in charge of applying them to an object population. Object orientation brings with it the expected issues of polymorphism and reference aliasing, which complicates two analyses required for ECA-based specifications of behavior:

- Termination: to avoid keeping applying rules rules forever.

- Confluence: a property of term rewriting systems (and active rule systems), describing that terms in this system always yield the same result, even if rewriting may take place in more than one way.

Runtime adaptability may be required in case the metamodels evolve (similar to schema evolution in database management). If the integrity constraints has been hardcoded in running applications, the following seems unavoidable: (a) refactor the system to accomodate the new constraints; (b) refactor the data schemas; (c) perform regression tests around constraints not affected by the change; (d) perform data migration; (e) redeploy.

All in all, the business layer of an EJB system is responsible for enforcing liveness conditions (by applying ECA-style rules) as well as safety conditions expressed in OCL invariants. A model compiler could assume thus the responsibility of generating code enforcing the declarative specification. Addressing EJB as target platform is not an easy fit for rule engines, whose algorithms were designed for the main-memory case. If left unchanged, hitting the database becomes the dominant cost factor for such algorithms, as rules get activated and the objects they refer to are retrieved through ORM (Object Relational Mapping).

Early on it was recognized that naïve implementations of rule matching and firing are not scalable, as they iterate over all objects and all rules at each working memory change. For 100 rules and 10,000 objects the naïve approach results in 1,000,000 tests at every change. Some common heuristics were identified (most restrictive test first, detect shared tests across rules) and were systematized in the Rete algorithm [73]. Queries defined with OCL can participate in the matching condition of an ECA rule, as outlined in Sec. 12.7.

Assuming that a model compiler for integrity constraints targeting EJB is aimed at, what resources can be leveraged? Design patterns to handle ECA rules have been proposed for the EJB case [204] and some products include components realizing variations of the Rete algorithm. However, no comprehensive solution to the proposed translation task has been found in the literature.

11.8 Evaluation

We have addressed an industrially relevant problem by going back to first principles, leveraging research results from object databases to improve the efficiency of software repositories for EMOF + OCL. Our choice of integrity checking mechanism does not require for the database to be in a consistent state before an update can take place, yet reporting of integrity violations is sound and complete (no false positives, no missed violations). This is deemed vital to account for the realities of collaborative design environments.

Incremental view maintenance adds a measure of reactivity to the monitoring of invariants. Unlike the more powerful Event Condition Action rules (ECA) of an active DBMS, view definitions based on OCL invariants cannot make statements about events external to the database state, nor range over several snapshots as in versioned data models [135] (values in pre- and poststates can only be referred from OCL postconditions, not from class invariants). OCL-based views are however sufficient to support a variety of use cases in software repositories, such as monitoring the conformance of artifacts to coding and modeling conventions [185]. Moreover, not all views need be maintained incrementally (as required for integrity constraints): in some cases results are only periodically needed (e.g., after an integration build, or on a daily or weekly basis). Examples include: (a) detecting opportunities for applying refactorings; (b) checking mutual consistency between artifacts and documentation; and (c) deriving software metrics.

As usual, irrespective of whether an OCL-based view is tagged for incremental or batch evaluation, it makes for concise composite queries. Materialized views naturally support OCL's `derive` statement, which is used to specify values for attributes or association ends. Looking into the future, the proposed infrastructure can serve as a basis for supporting ECA and versioning functionality through extensions to the OCL language.

12 Efficient Run-time Integrity Checking: Main-memory

Contents

The combined expressive power of Essential MOF (EMOF) [170] and the Object Constraint Language (OCL) [203] has proved satisfactory in Model-Driven Software Engineering (MDSE) to define the abstract syntax and static semantics of custom Domain Specific Languages (DSLs).

Given a DSL metamodel as input, a modeling infrastructure (such as Eclipse EMF) allows generating components which are ready for integration into a Model-View-Controller architecture. However, these generated components fall just short of supporting two increasingly important runtime scenarios: transparent concurrency and efficient evaluation of invariants. To support them out-of-the-box, we describe extensions to the OCL compilation algorithm of Chapter 5 to support shared-memory transactions [113] and incrementalization [191]. The first technique allows for a programming style where ACID properties are enforced for a block of statements, yet no coding of locking operations is required. In effect, the runtime system keeps rollback logs and detects interactions which lead to failure of memory transactions. To address the second concern (efficient evaluation of invariants), a similar interception mechanism is used to detect those data locations that have been updated. Invariants dependent on them are candidates for re-evaluation as their cached values may have become stale. Other invariants are not affected, and their evaluation can be skipped.

As motivating example, consider a multi-user editor of statecharts. Such an editor allows manipulating a single shared instance of the statechart metamodel. The runtime infrastructure should enforce transaction bracketing to avoid those interleavings of read-write accesses by distinct threads that corrupt the shared data structure. Additionally, the runtime engine should report those pairs *(instance, invariant ID)* for invariants not evaluating to `true` on certain instances at transaction commit. The need for concurrency management is not limited to the multi-user case: a single-user tool may run background tasks, or a single user may perform multi-step updates on different views of the same model (e.g., during *round-tripping* between textual and visual views).

Relational databases also manage concurrency and support incrementalization (the latter via incrementally maintained, materialized views [102]). In Chapter 11 the incrementalization for software repositories is addressed. However, the techniques reported next are also necessary: between repository check-ins, an editing session works on a local copy. We spare editing sessions from hitting the database inside transactions, improving usability for small datasets by reducing latency and offloading the server.

Our incrementalization technique makes viable for EMOF an algorithm (DITTO, [191]) originally formulated to incrementalize a Java subset. By exploiting the semantics of EMOF + OCL additional improvements are realized: (a) incrementalizing collection operations required tracking each item as an implicit argument in [191], our formulation instead tracks the involved collection objects, not their items. (b) Intermediate results are not cached in full, updates to their base data are intercepted instead. (c) Certain cases of infinite recursion can be detected. (d) Finally, only those mutator methods on collections that influence the outcome of an evaluation trigger re-evaluation. The proposed memoization algorithm is applicable to any EMOF realization, for example the Eclipse EMF implementation.

The structure of this chapter is as follows. Sec. 12.1 provides background, with Sec. 12.2 giving an overview of OCL incrementalization and an analysis of the termination behavior of OCL. Sec. 12.3 details the compile-time aspects of our solution, while Sec. 12.4 covers the runtime aspects, followed by a review in Sec. 12.5 of the design choices made. Sec. 12.6 addresses planned support for shared-memory transactions, with Sec. 12.7 discussing related work and Sec. 12.8 concluding.

12.1 Preconditions for Incrementalization

12.1.1 Overlapping Subproblems

Techniques that allow reusing results already computed have been identified as beneficial long before their application to computing. For example, in Dynamic Programming the properties of *overlapping subproblems* and *optimal substructure* allow minimizing the number of computation steps, by basing the optimal decision for a given formulation of the problem in terms of the optimal decisions for previously solved formulations. For example, the shortest path to a goal from a vertex in a graph can be found by first computing the shortest path to the goal from all adjacent vertices, and then using these optimal solutions to pick the best overall path.

The solution process is not only recursive, but moreover solving the same subproblem is required more than once (thus the term *overlapping*). As another example, whenever two successive Fibonacci numbers are computed, their previous Fibonacci number is required. A naïve approach would waste time recomputing optimal solutions to subproblems already solved. The term given in computer science to avoiding recomputing from scratch is *memoization*, on which the next section expands. However, it can already be seen that just storing solutions for subproblems in a cache may get out of hand if they are not going to be needed anymore (i.e., a *cache eviction* policy is required).

12.1.2 Referential Transparency

Reusing the cached result of a function in a computer program (for another invocation with the same inputs) is warranted provided that *referential transparency* holds. An expression is said to be referentially transparent if it can be replaced with its value without changing the meaning of the program. Given that referential transparency requires the same results for a given set of inputs at any point in time, a referentially transparent expression must be deterministic [205]. Examples of *referentially opaque* functions are those depending on a mutable global variable (which may be modified from another thread if not from the current one), or depending on an external source of events (e.g., an input device). In summary:

> "*The importance of referential transparency is that it allows a programmer (or compiler) to reason about program behavior. This can help in proving correctness, finding bugs that could not be found through testing, simplifying an algorithm, assisting in modifying code without breaking it, or optimizing code by means of memoization, common subexpression elimination or parallelization*" [205].

Our proposed incrementalization technique must thus cope with functions that depend on mutable data, with such data not being explicitly listed among the function's arguments. The functions of interest will themselves be side-effects free, as all expressions defined in OCL are.

12.2 Incrementalization

An incremental algorithm computes anew only those intermediate results that have been affected by changed input, reusing cached results for non-affected subcomputations. Manual incrementalization is error prone, thus motivating automation. Given a finite object population, every no-args (i.e., parameterless) side-effects free method on it is amenable to incrementalization. In terms of OCL this comprises: (a) class invariants, (b) derived object attributes, and (c) derived no-args operations. The result of such parameterless methods are not constant, given that they usually navigate the object structure (starting from `self`) when computing their result, thus reading *implicit arguments*.

OCL invariants are beneficial both at debug time (as they combine the advantages of continuous testing and "declarative data-breakpoints") as well as during production. Their main disadvantage is the runtime slowdown (100x are not uncommon) when re-evaluated from scratch, as they may involve traversing an entire data structure. An incremental algorithm, instead, reuses the cached results of subcomputations whose inputs have not changed. This fits the typical runtime behavior of OCL invariants: they aggregate further invariant checks on fragments of a data structure, with those subcomputations usually returning "the same previous value" (i.e., the *success value*) even for modified inputs, as most updates preserve consistency. As a result, upstream computations do not become stale, and their evaluation can be skipped. Pointer aliasing complicates keeping track of all program locations that may mutate a given data location, with interception techniques coming to the rescue, as all updates to data locations are only possible through well-known methods in EMOF (setters and their counterparts to mutate collections).

Two candidate techniques to incrementalize OCL invariants are: (a) memoization [191] and (b) view materialization [5]. A spreadsheet analogy can be used to explain the operation of materialization: the availability of changed inputs triggers the recomputation of dependent values, avoiding redundant recomputations by leveraging a *dynamic dependency graph* (DDG). Because of object instantiation, updates, and garbage collection, the topology of the DDG changes at runtime and has to be kept in-synch with the underlying object population. Memoization happens instead on-demand: whenever a function is invoked, the cached values for its inputs are compared to those in the current *system snapshot*. If they match, the cached ("memoized") return value can be reused. A big pitfall of unoptimized memoization involves subcomputations (a special case of input): in order to compare their cached and updated values, a subcomputation need in principle be invoked, which in turn may need to invoke its own subcomputations (if any) to decide whether to reuse memoized returns value or not. For example, assume the usual recursive formulation of the `height()` function on trees:

```
context Node
def : height() : Integer =
  if children->isEmpty()
    then 1
    else 1 + children->collect(c | c.height() )->max()
  endif
```

Given a node n and cached evaluations of `height()` for each of its children, knowing that such set has not changed does not entitle to reusing the cached return value of n.`height()`, as the topology downstream may have been updated. In terms of memoization, knowing that the implicit arguments have not changed (the children of n in this case) does not preclude the subcomputations (another kind of input) from having changed. Implicit arguments comprise those data locations accessed directly by a function evaluation, not by its callees.

Optimistic memoization [191] instead assumes such subcomputations will behave as in the typical case, thus skipping their invocation. This may lead to mispredictions, which are detected in all cases, as will be seen in Secs. 12.3 and 12.4 (incrementalization is sound and complete, i.e. neither false-positives are reported nor broken invariants are overlooked). The next subsection presents an example of

the DITTO algorithm in action, followed in Sec. 12.2.2 by the considerations that
lead to our incrementalization algorithm for OCL.

12.2.1 The DITTO Instrumentation Algorithm

Code Instrumentation is a technique to (automatically) perform program transformations. The most common scenario for instrumentation is *profiling*, i.e., gathering
information about the performance of the instrumented program at execution time.
Instrumentation can be classified according to the time where the program transformation takes place into:

- at compile time

    - performed manually, by following programming conventions, as in the
      Java JMX API [177]

    - compiler assisted, as some compilers provide switches to generate the
      additional instructions

- at deployment time, in the case of Java at class load time, using a library for
  bytecode manipulation (e.g., TOM [15])

- at runtime, where either: (a) the code is executed by a modified runtime environment, (b) code is morphed as instructions are fetched, or (c) the whole
  interaction between program and runtime environment is simulated in a simulator.

DITTO follows the bytecode instrumentation approach, while our proposal relies
instead on an automatic compile-time transformation.

In essence, DITTO caches a *function evaluation* by collecting additional information at runtime besides computing its result. In particular, the actual arguments are
recorded, with such bookkeeping information being kept across invocations. Reading an object-field during a function evaluation also results in the pair *(instance,
field ID)* being tracked as an *implicit argument*. During the update phase of a transaction, all setters are intercepted and thus a mapping can support the lookup (using
(instance, field ID) as key) of those function evaluations that require re-evaluation

235

Listing 12.1: A method to check whether a binary tree is locally sorted

```
boolean isSorted(Tree t) {
    if (t == null) return true;
    if (t.left != null && t.left.value >= t.value) return false;
    if (t.right != null && t.right.value <= t.value) return false;
    return isSorted(t.left) && isSorted(t.right);
}
```

(also called "refreshing the cached return value"). Another event that forces re-computation is garbage collection of an implicit argument, a situation detected by tracking instances with *weak references*[1]. At the time a weak reference is created or a `WeakHashMap` entry is made, a listener is registered to be notified upon the referenced object becoming unreachable.

In order to introduce terminology, a method to check whether a binary tree is locally sorted (Listing 12.1) will be discussed next, reproduced with modifications from a DITTO presentation[2].

For the fragment of the binary tree displayed in Figure 12.1(a), method `isSorted()` is invoked for each of the nodes marked with an arrow, to compare the values (letters in this case) displayed inside each node.

A visualization of the invocations for `isSorted()` appears in Figure 12.1(b). This unrolling of the call stack is purely conceptual, as (without memoization) no record is kept of invocations once they have terminated. Moreover, the arguments shown in the ovals (the contents of the node passed as argument) have been chosen for ease of reference, the nodes as such are not named on the heap. This will cause no confusion as we'll avoid the case of two different nodes having the same value.

As depicted in Figure 12.2, a particular update on a tree consists in adding nodes L, N (the second out-of-order) and removing node C, as part of a single transaction

---

[1] An introduction to weak references is `http://weblogs.java.net/blog/enicholas/archive/2006/05/understanding_w.html`. A longer but slightly out-of-date discussion appears in `http://java.sun.com/developer/technicalArticles/ALT/RefObj/`

[2] AJ Shankar, presentation at PLDI'07, `http://ditto-java.sourceforge.net/ditto.ppt`

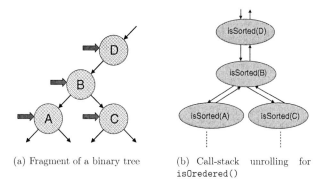

(a) Fragment of a binary tree   (b) Call-stack unrolling for isOredered()

Figure 12.1: Visualization of the invocations for isSorted()

which should fail. During such transaction, at least one field in each of M, L, and B has been updated (i.e., fields that are read by isSorted(), for some invocations). This example is introductory in that there is a one-to-one correspondence between nodes in the tree and nodes in the call stack unrolling, thus simplifying deciding which memoized invocations need to be refreshed (after one or more of its implicit inputs have been updated).

The *Dynamic Dependency Graph* (DDG) contains thus *stale* information (although L is lexicographically smaller than M, N does not come in the alphabet before B). DITTO introduces an optimization to minimize the cost of refreshing, once the invocations with modified inputs have been identified. First, the invocation for M is replayed, which in turn activates for the first time an invocation for node L (resulting in a node being added to the DDG). The problem with evaluating isSorted(L) is that it depends recursively on isSorted(B), whose cached result is not only stale but also wrong. However, DITTO assumes (for now) that downstream invocations need not be replayed (thus *optimistic*). This decision is suspect until replaying isSorted(B) reveals a wrong assumption was made. In that case, a propagation from callees to callers as depicted in Figure 12.3 will be performed.

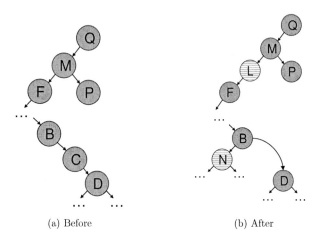

(a) Before   (b) After

Figure 12.2: Before and after update

12.2.2 Design Considerations

EMOF collections may act as both explicit and implicit arguments in an OCL expression, with the former being possibly an intermediate result (computed as an OCL expression at the invoker's call site). In order to qualify as an implicit argument, a read-access must happen on a field of an application-level instance, as opposed to being performed upon an intermediate result, which stays on the heap only during a call stack activation. Intermediate results do influence the outcome of a function, however they can change only if their base data (implicit arguments, subcomputations) has changed. Therefore, tracking updates to base data is enough to signal the need for refreshing a cached computation.

Given that collection operations are quite common in OCL specifications, it pays off to devise dedicated optimizations beyond those in DITTO, considering their distinguishing features: (a) mutating a collection does not affect its object identity; (b) collection mutators are invoked on the collection object itself, instead of on some object holding the collection in one of its fields; (c) after passing a collection c as argument to a setter in a different instance, the same collection c can be ob-

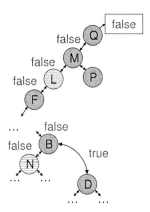

Figure 12.3: Upstream propagation

tained through getters in different instances; (d) internally, collections are realized as binary trees, linked lists, or some other data structure with fields having at-most-one multiplicity. Instead of instrumenting at this low level we adopt a dedicated mechanism other than *(instance, field ID)* to track collection arguments.

Our mechanism of choice to achieve incrementalization is thus *collection-aware optimistic memoization,* to be activated on-demand at transaction-commit time achieving the same effect as naïve evaluation of all invariants on all instances. Read accesses take place within a transaction and thus do not observe partial results. The interaction with the mechanism for shared-memory transactions (Sec. 12.6) is safe, as it can cope with both read and write accesses. In effect, the incrementalization concern is orthogonal to memory atomicity, with the former being layered upon the latter. Before presenting in detail our incrementalization algorithm (Secs. 12.3 and 12.4), the next two subsections cover (a) an overview of the proposed incrementalization technique in terms of an example, which allows introducing terminology; and (b) the termination behavior of OCL expressions.

Listing 12.2: Requiring two sets be disjoint

```
context Department
inv noOverlap :
  self.goodEmps->intersection(self.badEmps)->size() = 0
```

12.2.3 A First Example of OCL Incrementalization

The object models of Java and EMOF mostly overlap but neither of them is a proper subset of the other. An EMOF implementation (such as Eclipse EMF) enforces the semantics of EMOF by mediating the manipulation of Java objects through generated methods. For example, besides assigning a new value, setters also take care of performing "reference handshaking" for the participants in a bidirectional association. Reflecting the distinction between value and object types, a "field" in an EMOF class can be either an *attribute* or a *reference* (with the term *structural feature* covering both). Besides setters, a multiplicity-many structural feature has additional methods used at runtime to update a collection *c*. Intuitively, not all of these mutators will impact an OCL function taking *c* as argument. For example, adding an element impacts `c.size()` while changing the position of an item does not. In terms of EMF, method `c.add(newElem)` (for the collection in question) should be instrumented, while `c.move(fromPos, toPos)` may be left as is. We exploit this fact by analyzing at compile-time the ASTs of OCL expressions and by extending the EMF code generation process, applying techniques reported in [78] and [87] resp.

The runtime behavior of incrementalization is illustrated on Listing 12.2 with the invariant `noOverlap` (involving `Department`s for which two sets are kept, those of good and bad employees). Its non-instrumented translation into Java appears on Listing 12.3 on p. 258, while the AST available at compile-time is depicted in Figure 12.4.

As in DITTO we collect additional information during a function invocation, associating it to a node in the *Dynamic Dependency Graph* (a "DDG node" from now on). Such nodes can be regarded as 5-tuples consisting of: (a) the unique identifier for the evaluated function, this ID is obtained by reflection; (b) the *self* reference to

```
<OperationCallExp> resultType: [ Boolean ] name: [ = ] is: [ Infix ] has: [ one arg ]
⊟ <source>
  ⊟ <OperationCallExp> resultType: [ Integer ] name: [ size ] is: [ Prefix ] has: [ zero args ]
    ⊟ <source>
      ⊟ <OperationCallExp> resultType: [ Set(Employee) ] name: [ intersection ]
        ⊟ <source>
          ⊟ <PropertyCallExp> name: [ goodEmps ] type: [ Set(Employee) ]
            ⊟ <source>
              └ <VariableExp> name: [ self ] type: [ Department ]
        ⊟ <arg>
          ⊟ <PropertyCallExp> name: [ badEmps ] type: [ Set(Employee) ]
            ⊟ <source>
              └ <VariableExp> name: [ self ] type: [ Department ]
└ <IntegerLiteralExp> symbol: [ 0 ] type: [ Integer ]
```

Figure 12.4: Visual depiction using OCLASTView [78] of the AST for the invariant noOverlap

the target instance; (c) the *explicit arguments* passed by the invoker; (d) the data locations of *implicit arguments*, resulting from read accesses to structural features performed during an execution of the instrumented function (but not by its callees); and (e) *subcomputations*, represented as references to DDG nodes. Which particular inputs of kinds (d) and (e) are accessed during a given activation can be traced back ultimately to (b) and (c) values, as dictated by the logic of the invoked function. The same implicit argument may show up in different DDG nodes, therefore mappings are used to point from them into DDG nodes, thus speeding lookup (C_{map} and F_{map}, for collection and non-collection arguments resp.).

Reasoning about the way DITTO builds DDG nodes for noOverlap requires breaking the encapsulation of the Department's goodEmps and badEmps collections, instrumenting the accesses to single-valued fields to add the *(instance, field ID)* pairs to the list of implicit arguments in the current DDG node. Whenever a subcomputation is invoked, the DDG is searched using as key the triple *(self, function ID, explicit arguments)*. Collections acting as explicit arguments introduce a large overhead, as DDG lookups now involve testing for value-equality the actual and recorded arguments. We avoid this penalty by instantiating a new DDG node only for OCL functions with no collection arguments. The instrumented versions of these functions still track accesses to structural features and subcomputations, only that they add them to the DDG node at the top of a thread-local stack (D_{stack}). Such node stands for the caller of the current function (there is always one caller, as all incrementalizable OCL constraints have no arguments at all).

The described design decision (not having dedicated DDG nodes for some functions) is a departure from traditional memoization, grounded on the observation that DDG nodes serve two different purposes: (a) making readily available a return value, thus saving time; and (b) tracking dependencies, as needed to detect when refreshing should be performed (thus assuring correctness). Our scheme still achieves (b), as implicit arguments and subcomputations *are* collected (in the DDG node for the invoker). On the downside, *some* function invocations that *could* have been found in the DDG (those for OCL-defined operations with coll-args) will result in recomputation instead of memoization. We believe this tradeoff is balanced in our favor.

Similarly, *collection-valued* functions also involve a time-space tradeoff. Of the OCL incrementalizable functions, only derived attributes and operations may return collections, unlike invariants. Given that the lookup of DDG nodes for this kind of functions will be fast (as they lack collection arguments) we adopt the decision to have their instrumented version *create* a new DDG node, caching their result using strong references. Without memoization, the lifetime of some of these results would have been limited to single call-stack activations (i.e., strictly temporary results). Our design makes them outlive such invocations, thus increasing the memory footprint. In the particular case of derived attributes and no-args operations, the chosen scheme was the only sensible, as these OCL constraints are interpreted as defining *materialized views*. Additionally, caching a collection return value results in an equality test between collections, after the DDG node had been marked dirty and recomputed (the test determines whether the new value should percolate up the invocation hierarchy). However, this expensive comparison occurs less frequently, as compared to DDG lookup. For these reasons, we believe the pros of memoizing coll-valued functions outweigh on average the cons, although contrived cases can be construed where the opposite is the case.

12.2.4 Termination Behavior of OCL Expressions

The evaluation of OCL expressions containing recursive function invocations is not guaranteed to terminate in a finite number of steps (in the general case). However, the special case of non-recursive expressions over a finite object population is relevant for our incrementalization technique. For them, termination can be shown by case analysis on the structure of OCL language constructs, as discussed next.

Applying a function outside its domain (e.g., requesting the first element in an empty list or dividing by zero) results in `OclInvalid`: unlike in Java, no exception is thrown. A finite population is obtained when applying `allInstances()` to a class (in contrast, the expression `Integer.allInstances()` is not well-formed). OCL is a function-based rather than a functional programming language: functions are not first-class-citizens, in that lambda abstractions cannot be built with the available language constructs and thus cannot be passed as arguments or returned as values. Regarding collection operations, the non-recursive subcases of `LoopExp` amount to linear iteration (`select`, `reject`, `exists`, `forAll`, `collect`, `one`). The remaining subcases can be desugared to their `iterate` form as defined in the OCL standard ([171], Sec. 11.9 and A.3.1.3). `iterate()` in turn can be expressed as left-fold, a primitive recursive function with a finite-depth tree expansion (under the stated assumptions of finite object population and non-recursive invocation).

12.3 Incrementalization: Compile-time Tasks

The OCL-defined functions subject to instrumentation are determined by transitive closure over the caller-callee relationship, taking as starting point the union of (a) class invariants, (b) derived attributes, (c) and derived no-args operations. Whenever an operation is added to this set, all its override-compatible operations in subclasses are also added. We call the resulting set *Instr*. The declaration of each function in *Instr* can be uniquely identified at runtime, as EMOF reflection assigns compile-time IDs that can be woven into the generated instrumentation code (e.g., into the code to look up DDG nodes).

12.3.1 DDG Lookup

The first Java statements generated for an OCL function f in *Instr* assign to the local variable cDN the current DDG node, if any. This lookup is performed differently depending on whether f has one or more collection arguments or not:

1. f has one or more coll-args. As no dedicated DDG nodes are kept for f, the return result must be computed afresh (however, calls performed by f may be resolved in the DDG). The current DDG node is peeked from D_{stack} (i.e. read but not popped).

2. otherwise, a lookup using *(self, f's ID, explicit arguments)* is performed against the globally-shared DDG, with one of two outcomes:

    a) if found, and the node is not dirty, the cached return value is returned to the caller. Otherwise the function will be re-evaluated, which implies clearing the dirty bit, the implicit arguments, and the subcomputations in the found node.

    b) if not found, this is the first invocation for the triple in question. A new DDG node $newDN$ is instantiated, assigned to cDN, with its sets of implicit arguments and subcomputations initially empty. Before adding $newDN$ to the set of subcomputations of the caller node (i.e., the node, if any, at the top of D_{stack}), an optional check can be made whether doing so would establish a cycle in the DDG, thus preventing some cases of stack overflow (but not *runaway recursion* where explicit arguments are different for all invocations), a safety measure not present in from-scratch recomputation nor in DITTO.

Finally, for functions in *Instr* lacking collection arguments (cases 2.a and 2.b), the generated code pushes cDN into the thread-local stack D_{stack}, and pops it just before returning.

12.3.2 Implicit Arguments and Their Setters

Executions of the generated code having reached thus far can rely on a current DDG node, reachable via the non-null cDN. The instrumentation code must abide by the evaluation semantics of OCL constructs. For example, the condition part of an `if-then-else-endif` is evaluated first, depending on which one of the two other branches will *not* be evaluated. Correspondingly, only the inputs (implicit arguments and subcomputations) for the evaluated branch are to be added to *cDN*. This is achieved by choosing the order to visit subnodes of an AST subtree according to the OCL construct in question. In the `if-then-else-endif` example, a visitor for code generation will visit first the condition part, generating code that at runtime will leave the result in a temporary local variable `condPartResult`. A Java "if (condPartResult) $\{s_1\}$ else $\{s_2\}$" is generated next, with the statement blocks resulting from visiting the `then` and `else` subnodes of the OCL `if` subtree. Each of s_1, s_2 assigns to yet another temporary variable wich will hold the result for the OCL `if` expression as a whole (as needed for example for subsequent computation). Further details on OCL $\rightarrow$ Java translation can be found in [87].

The above code generation scheme accommodates the injection of statements to store references to implicit arguments and to subcomputations just before they are accessed. For example, when visiting an OCL `PropertyCallExp` AST node (which stands for a field read-access) code to capture the target instance and the field declaration is generated. Such code will add at runtime an entry with that key to F_{map} (one of the two *implicit args* $\rightarrow$ *DDG nodes* maps, the other being C_{map} for collection mutators). The receiver of the getter indicated by the `PropertyCallExp` will never be a temporary object: no OCL construct result in objects being instantiated by generated Java code, and thus must be application-level, possibly referenced through a local variable or an explicit argument (in contrast, temporary collections are instantiated, as can be seen in Listing 12.3 on p. 258). Moreover, the receiver object is not a collection, as only method calls can be performed on OCL collections (represented by `OperationCallExp` AST nodes). The accessed field may have multiplicity > 1. What code (if any) is generated to instrument collection mutators other than setters is the topic of the next subsection. The general rule that no derived results are tracked, but instead updates to their base data, can thus be seen at play for field accesses. After all functions in *Instr* have been visited, the set of structural features that may influence their results is known, and their setters look up DDG nodes at runtime as described in Sec. 12.4.1.

12.3.3 Operations on Collections and their Mutators

DITTO considers no mutators other than field setters. If left uninstrumented, changes performed through collection mutators (`add(newElem)`, `setItem(pos, elem)`, etc.) will go unnoticed to the incrementalization infrastructure (intercepting these mutators is the counterpart to the reduction in implicit arguments achieved by tracking collection objects instead of their items). Instead of flatly instrumenting *all* collection mutators, the generated code will be qualified to monitor *certain* mutators, depending on the function taking the collection as argument. This function must be one in the OCL Standard Library, as all user-defined functions fall under the "subcomputations" category (Sec. 12.3.4), in particular those with one or more coll-args.

For incrementalization purposes, the OCL built-in functions taking (one or more) collection arguments can be classified into: (a) those accessing each item in the collection; and (b) those aggregating a result. All iterator constructs (for example, *source*→`forAll`(*boolCond*) and *source*→`select`(*boolCond*), in general all subtypes of `LoopExp` in the OCL metamodel) fall into the first category, while *source* → `isEmpty()`, and *source*→`first()` are examples of the second category. The *source* fragment stands for a collection-typed subexpression providing an argument for the function following the → (such *source expressions* are not limited to providing collection arguments, as the AST in Figure 12.4 shows for the subtrees rooted at + and =).

The analysis to determine the subset of collection mutators that triggers re-evaluation also takes into account the most specific type of the source collection. For example, *source*→`collect(` e | *exprOnE*) maps *exprOnE* to each e item in *source*. Given that OCL is strongly typed, it can in general be known at compile time whether *source* is (a) set or bag, or (b) sequence or ordered set. In the first case, the result of the `collect()` is invariant under reorderings of *source*. Therefore, `move(from, to)` is *not* among the mutators to watch for when visiting the subtree for *source* in the AST. Once a field access is reached in the course of that visit (i.e., a `PropertyCallExp` subtree is reached), the generated instrumentation code will *not* trigger a false-positive upon invocation of `move(from, to)` on the source of the `PropertyCallExp`, which may itself be an ordered collection, as for example the field holding chronologically ordered `publications` in class `Researcher` in the expression `self.publications`→`asSet()`→`collect(p | p.authors`→`size()` `)`→`max()` that finds the largest number of co-authors.

12.3.4 Subcomputations

After generating instrumentation code for operations on collections (as per the previous subsection) the only `OperationCallExp` subtrees not yet translated are those standing for invocations to operations defined by the user using OCL. No special code is needed at the caller site other than the usual invocation, as the current DDG node has already been pushed onto D_{stack}, and the lookup of a DDG node for the callee (if any) is performed by the callee itself.

An error scenario to avoid is for a function f_1 in *Instr* to invoke a non-instrumented function f_2, as f_2's execution would not leave a trail of its dependencies, with the incrementalization infrastructure later not being able to properly react to changes in f_2's inputs. This failure scenario is ruled out by the construction procedure of *Instr* (transitive closure over the static caller-callee relationship, including override-compatible methods in subclasses).

Moreover, there are no "volatile" functions in OCL (i.e. functions that return a fresh value on each invocation, such as `System.currentTimeMillis()` or `RAND()`), thus reducing the amount of dirty DDG nodes otherwise requiring recomputation.

12.4 Incrementalization: Runtime Tasks

12.4.1 Update Phase of a Transaction

During the compile-time phase described in Sec. 12.3.2, all setters potentially affecting a function in *Instr* have been instrumented. At runtime, each such setter looks up in the globally-shared F_{map} zero or more DDG nodes, using *(instance, field ID)* as key, and marks each found node as dirty. This step is no different from DITTO's, save the implementation technique (code generation in EMOF vs. Java bytecode instrumentation in DITTO). The callers of the found DDG nodes are not yet marked as stale, because the assumption that their return values will prevail is going to be validated at the time mispredictions are detected and resolved. The previous value of a field was not stored in the F_{map} entry, therefore any setter invocation (even those leaving the same value as-is) results in one or more DDG nodes being marked dirty. Again, a time-space tradeoff.

The code generated for collection mutators uses as key *(collection, mutator ID)* to look up zero or more DDG nodes in the globally-shared C_{map}. This map is populated by the code generated as per Sec. 12.3.3. Both F_{map} and C_{map} are implemented with Java's `WeakHashMaps`, so as not to interfere with the normal garbage collection of application-level objects when becoming unreachable from other application-level objects.

12.4.2 Commit Phase Activities

Transaction commit involves four phases: (c.1) pruning DDG nodes with any garbage collected input; (c.2) invoking computation of incrementalizable functions for new objects; (c.3) refreshing dirty DDG nodes; and (c.4) handling mispredictions.

Phase (c.1) Pruning

As updates are performed by application-level code, application-level objects being tracked as (explicit or implicit) arguments may be garbage collected. Removing their entries from F_{map} and C_{map} is taken care of by the `WeakHashMap` infrastructure, but the DDG nodes these entries target must be explicitly pruned (they might be referenced from caller DDG nodes, thus GC alone will not do the trick). Pruning a node also results in flagging as dirty all nodes directly depending on it. Transitively dependent nodes however are not yet considered as stale because the assumption that their return values will prevail is going to be validated at the time mispredictions are detected and resolved. Pruning a node may leave some of its callees unreachable over the subcomputations relation (this may also happen as a consequence of refreshing in phase c.3). Such nodes may be kept in a dedicated, DDG-owned set to prevent their GC (with the expectation of later use) or traded for memory right away. In the latter case, recomputation of dirty nodes will repopulate the DDG with those subcomputations not found by memoization.

Phase (c.2) Incrementalizing functions for new objects

OCL's `allInstances()` are tracked using the AspectJ-based mechanism of [206], which reports the instantiations made after the last run of commit-phase. On those instances, their instrumented invariants, derived attributes, and derived no-args operations are invoked for the first time.

Phase (c.3) Refreshing dirty nodes

The optimal ordering to refresh dirty nodes is breadth-first over the subcomputations relation as shown in [191]: assume $f(x)$ and $g(y)$ need refreshing, with $g(y)$ a transitive callee of $f(x)$. Upon replaying $f(x)$ it may well be the case that $g(y)$ is not invoked anymore (neither directly nor transitively through $f(x)$'s callees). Breadth-first search will thus not reach $g(y)$. As with previous callees not used anymore as subcomputations (as determined in the pruning phase), if $g(x)$ is not a top-level invariant, its unreachable DDG node may be left unpruned to survive a number of incrementalization rounds, or traded for memory right away.

Phase (c.4) Handling mispredictions

After the refresh phase, some nodes are marked as having a return value different from that previously cached. The callers of such nodes are then suspect, as their own return values need to be corroborated. Bottom-up refreshing (from callees to callers) proceeds until (a) a node is reached where the cached and newly computed return values match; or (b) a root node is reached (a node for a top-level invariant, derived attribute, or derived no-args operation). Bottom-up walking always terminates (there may be several callers for the same DDG node, but the DDG is acyclic).

By now, all of the incrementalizable functions have up-to-date values for all application-level, not garbage collected objects.

12.5 Consequences of the Design Choices Made

The original description of optimistic memoization [191] restricts the usage of return values from subcomputations by forbidding passing them as explicit arguments in further subcomputations or using them in loop conditionals (both written in a Java subset). This conservative measure is motivated by the real danger that a mispredicted return value could lead to infinite recursion or an exception being thrown in the memoized version, while from-scratch recomputation would have terminated normally. The termination behavior of OCL expressions (Sec. 12.2.4) allows relaxing this restriction, by forbidding only recursive invocations from taking as explicit arguments the results of previous subcomputations (all other callees terminate, in particular all functions in the OCL Standard Library). If this less restrictive ban is also lifted, only those OCL-defined functions that would have looped forever in from-scratch recomputation will not terminate when evaluated by optimistic memoization (even with cycle detection in the DDG). In this sense, the chosen incrementalization technique is as robust as the base case.

Incrementalization is oblivious to the particular way a function is computed, thus providing leeway at compile time in choosing a particular implementation. For example, OCL provides no dedicated syntax for expressing equijoins, with a custom function being usually defined to encapsulate the rather awkward building of cartesian product and selection. In the long run, OCL should be extended with query constructs as found in LINQ (*Language INtegrated Query*, [19]). In the meantime, the product-selection pattern can be detected at compile-time, to generate instead an instrumented version using indexes as described in [206]. Another optimization involves "small functions", e.g., functions having only explicit arguments and lacking both implicit arguments and callees: their DDG nodes are terminal and computing them anew is faster than memoizing them. A visitor can be used to determine the average complexity of an OCL expression [78] to choose these functions. Incidentally, the Java implementation of some functions in the OCL Standard Library (e.g., `size()`) already incrementalize their computation.

12.6 Future Work: Shared-memory Transactions

12.6.1 Motivation

As of now, the compilation algorithm presented in Chapter 5 generates Java code following the patterns of the EMF Framework, which assume the invoker to be responsible for achieving synchronization in the multi-threaded case. An active research area, *software transactional memory* (STM) [113] aims instead at devising translations from OO programs extended with transaction bracketing, so as to relieve the programmer from explicitly specifying synchronization. A concise description of the technique is provided by Hindman and Grossman [113]:

> *To make shared-memory multithreaded programming easier, many researchers have argued for atomicity, also known as software transactions. Atomicity can complement or replace existing synchronization mechanisms with the statement form* `atomic { s }` *where s is a statement. Semantically, it means s must execute as though there is no interleaved computation, i.e., no other threads are running. (The implementation, of course, need not actually stop other threads provided it preserves the semantics.) Furthermore, a language should also ensure fair scheduling: Long transactions must not starve other threads.*

In Java, synchronization mechanisms include *intrinsic locking* and the facilities added in Java 5 as part of the `java.util.concurrent` package [92]. [3]

Atomicity in the context of transactional memory implies that, within an atomic block of statements: (a) no partial results from other threads are seen, whether those threads are executing an atomic block or not; and (b) in case a transaction fails, its memory updates are rolled back, so as to preserve property (a) for other threads. A transaction may fail for a variety of reasons: an exception is thrown in its block, or the required locks cannot be acquired. In general, the set of locks required for a transaction is not known statically and depends on the branching and looping logic of the atomic block.

---

[3]For a bibliography on transactional memory see `http://www.cs.wisc.edu/trans-memory/biblio/index.html`

Design patterns for transactions are well known ([144], §. 3.6), and usually include:

- elaborate protocols to establish an ordering for lock acquisition and release (for resources accessed by the transaction), as well as

- a logging mechanism to track the old and new value pairs for *(instance, field)* pairs accessed.

Manually applying those patterns is inherently error-prone, thus calling for automation in the form of compilation. Grossman [97] establishes an analogy between transactional memory and garbage collection: If history repeats itself, transactional memory is posed to follow the same evolutionary path as garbage collection, i.e. it is to become mainstream, albeit later than predicted by researchers.

Simon Peyton Jones reviews in [122] the perils associated to the explicit-locking programming model: (a) taking too few locks opens the door to data structure corruption; (b) taking too many locks may inhibit concurrency or cause deadlock; (c) the language does not preclude taking the wrong locks, as the connection "which data is guarded by which locks for which operations" exists only in the mind of the programmer; (d) taking locks in a wrong order eventually causes deadlock; (e) performing error recovery once data structure corruption has taken place is extremely tricky; among others. Another shortcoming is the requirement to know the internals of individually atomic operations, if they are to be bracketed into a composite transaction: the set of required locks may be data-dependent and thus known only at runtime. The fact that one can "glue" operations into a larger transaction without detailed knowledge of the internal locking protocol is another advantage of `atomic { s }`.

As useful as it is, translation of Ecore + OCL into transactions-aware code is not the only desirable feature that the resulting code may exhibit: automatic checking of OCL invariants can also be woven in. In a nutshell, while transactional memory guarantees atomicity and isolation (A and I in ACID), automatic checking of OCL invariants caters for Consistency [108]:

> *We propose a simple but powerful new operation, `check E`, where E*
> *is an expression that must run without raising an exception after every*

transaction. Using atomic blocks provides us with a key benefit over existing work on dynamically-checked invariants: the boundaries of atomic blocks indicate precisely where invariants must hold. They may, and often must, be broken within transactions, something that causes trouble in other systems.

Besides communication through locations in shared-memory, another mechanism useful in distributed algorithms is synchronous communication over message channels. Donnelly and Fluet [59] elaborate on the adaptation of transactionality to cover channel-based communication (also building upon Concurrent Haskell, as STM Haskell did for transactional memory). The reduction in complexity in expressing distributed algorithm (e.g., three-way rendezvous) is significant.

12.6.2 Runtime Detection of Data Races

Supporting shared-memory transactions effectively solves synchronization problems when manipulating EMOF-based models, however at the cost incurred by runtime instrumentation. It is instructive to see what tradeoffs were made around these aspects for Java, and how their design decisions might evolve in the near future.

The integration of concurrency constructs and object oriented programming received a lot of attention at the end of the 1980s. Still, the first versions of Java went through a number of improvements (e.g., regarding interruptability between threads, de-emphasis of thread groups) until a stable design was reached with Java 5, including a formal Java Memory Model and multi-threading enabled data structures in `java.util.concurrent`. A driving force along the whole design effort was increasing the raw performance of (correctly synchronized or not) concurrent programs, to the point that JVMs are not required to detect data races at runtime. Two accesses to the same data variable form a *data race* in an execution of a program if they conflict (i.e., at least one of them is a write), they are done from different threads, and they are not ordered by *happens-before* ([95, §17]).

Given the non-trivial definition of *happens-before*, a number of approaches have tried to alleviate the ensuing complexity, ranging from subsets of Java whose programs can be statically shown not to result in deadlock or data races [2, 96], to

runtime monitoring to detect when a data race is about to happen, in order to throw
a `DataRaceException` [67], thus assuring that only correct computations may continue. Implementing the latter approach exhibits a number of similarities with the
techniques required in EMOF for shared-memroy transactions. In particular, optimizations applicable to the JVM case can also be included in the (managed) runtime
for EMOF models. One such optimization is the compile-time determination of assignments that *cannot possibly* result in a data race. Thus, their instrumentation
can be skipped. This kind of analysis is conducted by `rccjava`.

12.6.3 Initial Assessment

Composite transactions enable *integrated refactorings*, which span instances from
different metamodels and correspondingly require additional consistency checks (in
the form of pre and postconditions) beyond those of the transactions they compose.
For example, the *Rename Attribute* refactoring may be individually correct when
only the namespace for an EMOF class model is considered, however the existence of
OCL constraints referring to that attribute requires additionally checking whether a
variable declaration with the same name already occurs in a shared naming scope (to
avoid an unintended *name capture*). Another scenario for composite transactions is
round-tripping, with a formal analysis of the conditions under which bidirectional
transformations are possible provided in [74] (see also Chapter 8).

We aim to adapt and integrate into our compilation algorithm the techniques for
shared-memory transactions presented in [113]. The adaptations involve subsetting
(as the EMOF object model lacks arrays, native code, built-in classes, and static
fields, methods, and initializers) as well as new developments.

We believe incrementalization can coexist as-is with memory transactions. For example, a rollback never turns objects made unreachable back into reachable (instead,
the log prevents them being garbage collected until successful commit). Therefore,
pruning of DDG nodes need not be undone. A rollback may however restore implicit arguments back to their values at transaction start. In between, transaction
progress marked DDG nodes dirty, which is not undone as the ensuing redundant
recomputation will not deliver a wrong result.

Grossman [97] establishes an analogy between mechanisms for shared-memory

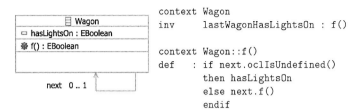

```
context Wagon
inv     lastWagonHasLightsOn : f()

context Wagon::f()
def    : if next.oclIsUndefined()
         then hasLightsOn
         else next.f()
         endif
```

Figure 12.5: The `lastWagonHasLightsOn` example: data accesses traverse links known only at runtime

transactions and those for garbage collection: both began being manually applied, later compiled as source-to-source translations, to finally become part of the runtime system (JVM for garbage collection, with memory transactions still waiting to reach that stage).

12.7 Related Work

The efficient evaluation of OCL invariants is also the goal of [7], where a methodology is presented to determine at compile-time the navigation paths from an updated *(instance, field ID)* back to objects with one ore more invariants depending on it. This analysis is only possible for non-recursive OCL expressions, as illustrated in Figure 12.5: a forward-only list of `Wagons` is constrained by invariant `lastWagonHasLightsOn`, which is fulfilled for a train as long its last wagon has the lights on. Our incrementalization mechanism can handle the addition, deletion, or update of `Wagons` anywhere in the list, by updating the topology of the DDG. Computing a reverse navigation path from the last to the first element in the list would instead require unwinding the call hierarchy for a particular execution trace, which is known only at runtime. Besides providing a detailed account of our algorithm and a termination analysis, our work also differs from [7] in that we reduce the number of DDG nodes marked dirty by instrumented collection mutators. Once an invariant is recomputed as per [7], it is done from-scratch: there's no memoization cache to hit, and therefore no materialized views can be maintained.

Discrimination networks [105] have been proposed for active databases as a generalization of the original Rete algorithm [73]. Broadly speaking, there is a correspondence between the distinguishing feature of Rete networks (storing materializations of partial rule bodies, which are shared among all the activation conditions where they appear) and the sharing of subcomputations in optimistic memoization (which also skips recomputation for successful DDG lookups). Our implementation does not yet detect duplicate OCL fragments as in Rete: two invariants with the same body but different names result in duplicate DDG nodes. This is an area for improvement, made difficult by the fact that OCL expressions are many-form (different syntactical expressions for the same function). Other than that, we believe that a derivative of the Rete algorithm handling full EMOF + OCL would strongly resemble our proposal, modulo terminology.

Rete-based rule-engines employ a proprietary query language to express the activation conditions of production rules, and force the programmer to specify a subset of the object population to monitor for updates (the *working set*). The semantics of OCL class invariants call instead for tracking all instances. A compile-time analysis of the ASTs of such expressions limits runtime instrumentation overhead to only those object-fields participating in *some* OCL incrementalized expression. The alternative (monitoring all updates) has the potential advantage of allowing incrementalizing ad-hoc expressions at runtime. As for invariants (an important use case), this is not reasonable: invariants do not come and go. The best of both worlds (low monitoring overhead and incrementalization of ad-hoc expressions) could be achieved with instrumentation techniques that allow for (un-)deploying interceptors at runtime, such as the debug API (the Java Virtual Machine Tool Interface, JVMTI). We cast instead our solution in the MDSE field by extending a compilation algorithm for EMOF + OCL, using Eclipse technologies.

Algorithms for efficient recalculation of spreadsheets are reviewed in [190]. Automatically checking invariants at transaction boundaries (moreover, in the concurrent case) is addressed for Concurrent Haskell in [108].

12.8 Evaluation

The acceptance of EMOF as the mainstream approach to metamodeling has spurred a number of innovations in the tooling for authoring DSLs, most of them leveraging the Eclipse EMF implementation of EMOF. The well-defined semantics of EMOF allows adding orthogonal capabilities to EMOF-enabled runtime environments (e.g, transparent persistence, change notification, versioning, refactoring support), thus increasing the appeal of the EMOF object model. The open nature of the EMF compiler enables integration efforts like ours. We expect support for incrementalization, tracking of invariants, and shared-memory transactions to be generally usable across a variety of vertical domains. Some of these extra capabilities may find their way into future virtual machines, with the openness of EMF lowering the entry barrier to prototypical realizations that foster competition and innovation.

More fundamentally, one might ask: Why are dedicated runtimes needed at all for modeling infrastructures? Don't existing runtimes (the Java Virtual Machine, Database Management Systems) provide all necessary features? They support only partially some features critical to reduce the cost of DSL tooling. For example, the JVM does support concurrency, and data races can be avoided by careful programming — the required case-by-case reasoning results from a trade-off where raw performance has been favored over a simplified programming model. The runtimes used for MDSE restore the balance toward increased developer productivity. In terms of consistency checking, given that no declarative specification is possible in Java to make explicit what constitutes *shared state* (the state to be kept consistent across execution interleavings), there is no automatic, fail-safe way to detect incorrect interleavings. The default definition of data race in the JVM is agnostic toward application semantics: it precludes an individual data location from being accessed without synchronization. In the general case, this is neither a necessary nor sufficient condition for transactional semantics, and an inadequate condition for MDSE runtimes, where software models exhibit shared state spanning multiple objects.

Listing 12.3: Non-instrumented version of the noOverlap invariant of Listing 12.2

```java
public boolean noOverlap() {
  Collection<Employee> intersection1 = null;
  int size1 = this.getGoodEmps().size();
  int size2 = this.getBadEmps().size();
  // if either collection is empty, so is the result
  if (size1 == 0)
    intersection1 = CollectionUtil.createNewSet(this.getBadEmps());
  else if (size2 == 0)
    intersection1 = CollectionUtil.createNewSet(this.getGoodEmps());

  if (intersection1 == null) {
    intersection1 = CollectionUtil.createNewSet();
    // loop over the smaller collection and add only shared elems
    if (size1 > size2) {
      for (Employee e : this.getBadEmps())
        if (this.getGoodEmps().contains(e))
          intersection1.add(e);
    } else {
      for (Employee e : this.getGoodEmps())
        if (this.getBadEmps().contains(e))
          intersection1.add(e);
    }
  }
  boolean equal2 = intersection1.size() == 0;
  return equal2;
}
```

13 Conclusions

The research hypothesis stated in Chapter 1 called for the application of formal techniques in the design of (a) domain-specific languages, (b) their translation procedures, and (c) their runtime systems. In this chapter we evaluate the evidence supporting the research hypothesis, i.e., the contributions of this PhD work.

13.1 Evaluation of the Research Hypothesis

Well-formed ASTs are the focal point of runtime activities in a model-driven toolchain. We say "activities" and not just "transformations" to encompass *model authoring* (guided editing, visualization, navigation) and *model analysis* (consistency checking and restoration, as well as DSL-specific analyses). The authoring and analysis of software artifacts expressed in different DSLs distinguishes MDSE from compiler engineering. The enlarged set of problems addressed in MDSE impacts the way DSLs are specified: (a) guided editing can be supported if the DSL specifications can be formulated in terms of constraint logic programming, (b) consistency checking in software repositories can scale if the employed constraint language falls in a tractable complexity class. The list of examples can be extended: (c) multi-view authoring environments exhibit correct behavior only if the view definitions are well-behaved for inversion. These examples have been drawn from the contributions of this PhD work, thus backing the argument that the design of DSL specifications should be formally founded.

Given that most model transformations are expressed (a) in a computationally complete language, (b) following an imperative style with destructive updates; and operate on (c) structure-rich graphs, it is then unavoidable for their formal verification to be complex. To a certain extent, concurrency issues are also present, if not in individual transformations (which are formulated as sequential algorithms) but in the interaction of multiple tools against a single model repository. Without a formal approach, the resulting complexity is unmanageable. There is an additional element of "needless complexity" introduced by industry standards lacking a formal foundation. For the reasons discussed in Chapter 10 there is value in formalizing such standards, beyond being a prerequisite to applying formal techniques when analyzing model transformations. The contributions in this PhD thesis addressing translation procedures support the argument that their verification is both feasible and advantageous, given that the boundary conditions chosen (regarding data model, transformation language, and verification conditions) are representative of those in software engineering practice. In other words, complexity has not been defined away.

For the purpose of this PhD work, the runtime systems of interest are those manipulating ASTs, i.e., tools in a model-driven toolchain. These runtime systems were classified following the main-memory vs. secondary storage divide. In both cases, the significance of the automatic consistency checking at transaction boundaries was highlighted from the beginning, and ways were described to allow mainstream modeling infrastructures to support consistency checking. Efficiency was achieved only through optimization techniques, and these in turn were made possible by a proper formalization. Therefore, the argument that formalization is necessary as part of the design of runtime systems has been confirmed.

13.2 Closing Remarks

Having tried a number of approaches to balance quality and cost (from agile processes to offshoring to service-orientation), the software industry has embarked recently on a large scale effort to embrace model-driven techniques. The resources being devoted to training and tooling attest to the high expectations placed on these techniques, fueled by the perception that they represent a "disruptive technology," a phrase reserved for outstanding inventions. As we have seen, there is nothing like magic behind model-driven techniques but rather incremental advances made possible by building upon solid previous work. After following developments around MDSE tools for some years, one might be left with the impression that decision makers in industry have a tendency to underestimate the benefits (for the customer) resulting from going back to first principles when designing such tools, and of applying existing theoretical results to problem areas emerging in MDSE. In particular, few works leverage the experience accumulated in compiler technology to flesh out the architecture of model compilers. As another example, laborious non-automated encodings of a software solution into formalisms amenable for verification are still the norm rather than the exception, although such workflows are ideally suited to model-based techniques. As the market for model-driven tools matures, i.e., as tool consumers demand better engineered products, the adoption of formal methodologies in MDSE will increase. A vendor-initiated push is not likely, as the necessary investments are justified only in terms of financial indicators after the market need is there.

The good news is that the engineering of model-driven tools has no lack of theoretical foundations on which to thrive, with recent activities in academia making a conscious effort to include case studies and prototypes materializing proposed concepts, a strategy that has been followed during this research. Such approach establishes a healthy feedback from industry to academia, motivating further progress in the several fields that contribute to the software sciences.

Bibliography

[1] Martín Abadi and Luca Cardelli. *A Theory of Objects*. Springer-Verlag New York, Inc., Secaucus, NJ, USA, 1996.

[2] Martín Abadi, Cormac Flanagan, and Stephen N. Freund. Types for Safe Locking: Static Race Detection for Java. *ACM Trans. Program. Lang. Syst.*, 28(2):207–255, 2006.

[3] Marcus Alanen and Ivan Porres. A relation between context-free grammars and meta object facility metamodels. Technical Report 606, Turku Centre for Computer Science, Åbo Akademi University, Finland, March 2003.

[4] M. Akhtar Ali. *Incremental Maintenance of Materialized Views in Object-Oriented Databases*. PhD thesis, University of Manchester, UK, September 2002.

[5] M. Akhtar Ali, Alvaro A. A. Fernandes, and Norman W. Paton. MOVIE: an incremental maintenance system for materialized object views. *Data Knowl. Eng.*, 47(2):131–166, 2003.

[6] M. Akhtar Ali, Norman W. Paton, and Alvaro A. A. Fernandes. An Experimental Performance Evaluation of Incremental Materialized View Maintenance in Object Databases. In Yahiko Kambayashi, Werner Winiwarter, and Masatoshi Arikawa, editors, *DaWaK*, volume 2114 of *LNCS*, pages 240–253. Springer, 2001.

[7] Michael Altenhofen, Thomas Hettel, and Stefan Kusterer. OCL Support in an Industrial Environment. In Birgith Demuth, Dan Chiorean, Martin Gogolla, and Jos Warmer, editors, *OCL for (Meta-)Models in Multiple Application Domains*, pages 126–139, Dresden, 2006. University Dresden.

[8] C. Amelunxen, A. Königs, T. Rötschke, and A. Schürr. MOFLON: A Standard-Compliant Metamodeling Framework with Graph Transformations. In A. Rensink and J. Warmer, editors, *Model Driven Architecture - Foundations and Applications: Second European Conf.*, volume 4066 of *LNCS*, pages 361–375, Heidelberg, 2006. Springer Verlag, Springer Verlag.

[9] C. Amelunxen and A. Schürr. On OCL as part of the Metamodeling Framework MOFLON. In *6th OCL Workshop at the UML/MoDELS Conference*, 2006.

[10] Kyriakos Anastasakis, Behzad Bordbar, Geri Georg, and Indrakshi Ray. UML2Alloy: A Challenging Model Transformation. In *MoDELS*, pages 436–450, 2007.

[11] Kyriakos Anastasakis, Behzad Bordbar, and Jochen M. Küster. Analysis of model transformations via Alloy. In Benoit Baudry, Alain Faivre, Sudipto Ghosh, and Alexander Pretschner, editors, *4th MoDeVVa workshop Model-Driven Engineering, Verification and Validation*, pages 47–56, In conjunction with MoDELS07, Nashville, TN, USA, 2007.

[12] Andrew W. Appel and Jens Palsberg. *Modern Compiler Implementation in Java*. Cambridge University Press, New York, NY, USA, 2003.

[13] Franz Baader, Diego Calvanese, Deborah L. McGuinness, Daniele Nardi, and Peter F. Patel-Schneider, editors. *The Description Logic Handbook: Theory, Implementation, and Applications*. Cambridge University Press, New York, NY, USA, 2003.

[14] Franz Baader and Tobias Nipkow. *Term rewriting and all that*. Cambridge University Press, New York, NY, USA, 1998.

[15] Emilie Balland, Pierre-Etienne Moreau, and Antoine Reilles. Bytecode Rewriting in TOM. *Electron. Notes Theor. Comput. Sci.*, 190(1):19–33, 2007.

[16] Luciano Baresi and Paola Spoletini. On the use of Alloy to Analyze Graph Transformation Systems. In Andrea Corradini, Hartmut Ehrig, Ugo Montanari, Leila Ribeiro, and Grzegorz Rozenberg, editors, *ICGT*, volume 4178 of *LNCS*, pages 306–320. Springer, 2006.

[17] Bernhard Beckert, Reiner Hähnle, and Peter H. Schmitt, editors. *Verification of Object-Oriented Software: The KeY Approach*. LNCS 4334. Springer-Verlag, 2007.

[18] Bernhard Beckert, Uwe Keller, and Peter H. Schmitt. Translating the Object Constraint Language into First-order Predicate Logic. In Serge Autexier and Heiko Mantel, editors, *Proceedings VERIFY Workshop at Federated Logic Conferences (FLoC), Copenhagen, Denmark*, pages 113–123, 2002. DIKU Technical Report 02-07.

[19] Gavin M. Bierman, Erik Meijer, and Mads Torgersen. Lost in Translation: Formalizing proposed extensions to C#. *SIGPLAN Not.*, 42(10):479–498, 2007.

[20] E. Borger and Robert F. Stark. *Abstract State Machines: A Method for High-Level System Design and Analysis*. Springer-Verlag New York, Inc., Secaucus, NJ, USA, 2003.

[21] Claus Brabrand, Anders Møller, and Michael I. Schwartzbach. Dual syntax for XML languages. *Information Systems*, 33(4–5):385–406, 2007.

[22] Aaron Bradley and Zohar Manna. *The Calculus of Computation: Decision Procedures with Applications to Verification*. Springer, 2007. ISBN 978-3-540-74112-1.

[23] Marco Brambilla. Generation of WebML Web Application Models from Business Process Specifications. In *ICWE '06 Proc 6th Intnl Conf on Web Engineering*, pages 85–86, New York, NY, USA, 2006. ACM Press.

[24] Martin Bravenboer. Connecting XML Processing and Term Rewriting with Tree Grammars. Master's thesis, Institute of Information and Computing Sciences, Utrecht University, Delft, The Netherlands, Nov 2003. `http://www.cs.uu.nl/people/martin/docs/master-thesis.pdf`.

[25] Martin Bravenboer, Arthur van Dam, Karina Olmos, and Eelco Visser. Program Transformation with Scoped Dynamic Rewrite Rules. *Fundam. Inf.*, 69(1-2):123–178, 2006.

[26] Martin Bravenboer and Eelco Visser. Designing Syntax Embeddings and As-similations for Language Libraries. In Holger Giese, editor, *Workshop on Language Engineering (ATEM'07)*, Nashville, USA, October 2007. ISBN 978-3-540-69069-6.

[27] L. C. Briand, W. J. Dzidek, and Y. Labiche. Instrumenting Contracts with Aspect-Oriented Programming to Increase Observability and Support Debug-ging. In IEEE Computer Society, editor, *21st IEEE Intnl. Conf. on Software Maintenance (ICSM), Budapest, Hungary, September 25-30*, pages 687–690. IEEE, 2005.

[28] Lionel C. Briand and Clay Williams, editors. *Model Driven Engineering Languages and Systems, 8th International Conference, MoDELS 2005, Mon-tego Bay, Jamaica, October 2-7, 2005, Proceedings*, volume 3713 of *LNCS*. Springer, 2005.

[29] Björn Bringert, Anders Höckersten, Conny Andersson, Martin Andersson, Mary Bergman, Victor Blomqvist, and Torbjörn Martin. HaskellDB improved. In *Haskell '04: Proc. of the 2004 ACM SIGPLAN workshop on Haskell*, pages 108–115, New York, NY, USA, 2004. ACM Press.

[30] Kim B. Bruce. *Foundations of Object-Oriented Languages: Types and Seman-tics*. MIT Press, Cambridge, MA, USA, 2002.

[31] Achim D. Brucker, Jürgen Doser, and Burkhart Wolff. A Model Transforma-tion Semantics and Analysis Methodology for SecureUML. Technical Report 524, ETH Zürich, 2006.

[32] Achim D. Brucker and Burkhart Wolff. A Package for Extensible Object-Oriented Data Models with an Application to IMP++. In Abhik Roychoud-hury and Zijiang Yang, editors, *International Workshop on Software Verifi-cation and Validation (SVV 2006)*, Computing Research Repository (CoRR). Computing Research Repository (CoRR), Seattle, USA, August 2006.

[33] Achim D. Brucker and Burkhart Wolff. The HOL-OCL Book. Technical Report 525, ETH Zürich, 2006.

[34] Emir Burak. *Object-oriented pattern matching*. PhD thesis, EPFL, 2007. `http://biblion.epfl.ch/EPFL/theses/2007/3899/3899_abs.pdf`.

[35] Lilian Burdy, Yoonsik Cheon, David Cok, Michael D. Ernst, Joe Kiniry, Gary T. Leavens, K. Rustan M. Leino, and Erik Poll. An Overview of JML Tools and Applications. *Software Tools for Technology Transfer*, 7(3):212–232, June 2005.

[36] D. A. Burke and K. Johanisson. Translating Formal Software Specifications to Natural Language. In *Proc. Logical Aspects of Computational Linguistics*, pages 51–66, 2005.

[37] Fabian Büttner and Hanna Bauerdick. Realizing UML Model Transformations with USE. In Dan Chiorean, Birgit Demuth, Martin Gogolla, and Jos Warmer, editors, *UML/MoDELS Workshop on OCL (OCLApps'2006)*, pages 96–110. Technical University of Dresden, Technical Report TUD-FI06, 2006.

[38] Jordi Cabot and Ernest Teniente. Incremental Evaluation of OCL Constraints. In Eric Dubois and Klaus Pohl, editors, *CAiSE*, volume 4001 of *LNCS*, pages 81–95. Springer, 2006.

[39] Marco Cadoli, Diego Calvanese, Giuseppe De Giacomo, and Toni Mancini. Finite Model Reasoning on UML Class Diagrams via Constraint Programming. In Roberto Basili and Maria Teresa Pazienza, editors, *AI*IA*, volume 4733 of *LNCS*, pages 36–47. Springer, 2007.

[40] Diego Calvanese and Giuseppe De Giacomo. Lecture notes on Description Logics for Conceptual Data Modeling in UML, August 2003. http://www.dis.uniroma1.it/~degiacom/didattica/esslli03/.

[41] Denis Caromel and Ludovic Henrio. *A Theory of Distributed Objects*. Springer-Verlag, 2005.

[42] Stefano Ceri. Process Modeling in Web Applications. In Robert Meersman, Zahir Tari, Mohand-Said Hacid, John Mylopoulos, Barbara Pernici, Özalp Babaoglu, Hans-Arno Jacobsen, Joseph P. Loyall, Michael Kifer, and Stefano Spaccapietra, editors, *OTM Conferences (1)*, volume 3760 of *LNCS*, page 20. Springer, 2005.

[43] Philippe Charles, Julian Dolby, Robert M. Fuhrer, Jr. Stanley M. Sutton, and Mandana Vaziri. SAFARI: a Meta-tooling Framework for Generating

Language-specific IDEs. In *Companion to the 21st ACM SIGPLAN OOPSLA '06 conference*, pages 722–723, New York, NY, USA, 2006. ACM Press.

[44] Kai Chen, Janos Sztipanovits, and Sandeep Neema. Toward a Semantic Anchoring Infrastructure for Domain-Specific Modeling Languages. In *EMSOFT '05: Proc. of the 5th ACM Intnl Conf on Embedded Software*, pages 35–43, New York, NY, USA, 2005. ACM Press.

[45] Adam Chlipala. *Implementing Certified Programming Language Tools in Dependent Type Theory*. PhD thesis, University of California at Berkeley, 2007. `http://www.cs.berkeley.edu/~adamc/papers/ChlipalaPhD/ChlipalaPhD.pdf`.

[46] Alexandre Correa and Cláudia Werner. Refactoring Object Constraint Language Specifications. *Software and Systems Modeling*, 6:113–138, 2007.

[47] Michelle L. Crane and Jürgen Dingel. UML vs. Classical vs. Rhapsody Statecharts: Not All Models are Created Equal. In Briand and Williams [28], pages 97–112.

[48] D. Galanis and I. Androutsopoulos. Generating Multilingual Descriptions from Linguistically Annotated OWL Ontologies: the NaturalOWL System. Proc. of the 11th European Workshop on Natural Language Generation (ENLG 2007), Schloss Dagstuhl, Germany, 2007.

[49] Christopher J. Daly. AST Framework Generation with Gymnast. In *Tech Exchange Panel: Language Toolkits*. EclipseCON 2005, 2005. Available at `http://www.sts.tu-harburg.de/~mi.garcia/SoC2007/GymnastSlides.pdf`.

[50] Christopher J Daly and Miguel Garcia. Emfatic Language for EMF Development, 2005, 2007. `http://wiki.eclipse.org/Emfatic`.

[51] Werner Damm, Bernhard Josko, Amir Pnueli, and Angelika Votintseva. Understanding UML: A Formal Semantics of Concurrency and Communication in Real-Time UML. In Frank S. de Boer, Marcello M. Bonsangue, Susanne Graf, and Willem P. de Roever, editors, *FMCO*, volume 2852 of *LNCS*, pages 71–98. Springer, 2002.

[52] Merijn de Jonge. Pretty-Printing for Software Reengineering. In *Intnl. Conf. on Software Maintenance (ICSM 2002)*, pages 550–559. IEEE Computer Society Press, October 2002.

[53] Oege de Moor, Mathieu Verbaere, Elnar Hajiyev, Pavel Avgustinov, Torbjorn Ekman, Neil Ongkingco, Damien Sereni, and Julian Tibble. Keynote Address: .QL for Source Code Analysis. In *SCAM '07: Proc. of the Seventh IEEE International Working Conference on Source Code Analysis and Manipulation*, pages 3–16, Washington, DC, USA, 2007. IEEE Computer Society.

[54] Mike Barnett Rob DeLine, Manuel Fähndrich, K. Rustan, M. Leino, and Wolfram Schulte. Verification of Object-Oriented Programs with Invariants. *Journal of Object Technology*, 3(6):27–56, 2004. `http://www.jot.fm/issues/issue_2004_06/article2/index_html`.

[55] Birgit Demuth, Heinrich Hußmann, and Sten Loecher. OCL as a Specification Language for Business Rules in Database Applications. In Martin Gogolla and Cris Kobryn, editors, *UML*, volume 2185 of *LNCS*, pages 104–117. Springer, 2001.

[56] Prashant Deva. Folding in Eclipse Text Editors, March 2005. Eclipse Technical Article, `http://www.eclipse.org/articles/Article-Folding-in-Eclipse-Text-Editors/folding.html`.

[57] Jürgen Dingel, Zinovy Diskin, and Alanna Zito. Understanding and Improving UML Package Merge. *Software and Systems Modeling*, 2008. To Appear.

[58] Klaus R. Dittrich, Dimitris Tombros, and Andreas Geppert. Databases in Software Engineering: a Roadmap. In *ICSE - Future of SE Track*, pages 293–302, 2000.

[59] Kevin Donnelly and Matthew Fluet. Transactional Events. *SIGPLAN Not.*, 41(9):124–135, 2006.

[60] Jorge Horacio Doorn and Laura C. Rivero, editors. *Database Integrity: Challenges and Solutions*. Idea Group Publishing, 2002.

[61] Denis Dubé. Graph layout for domain-specific modeling. Master's thesis, School of Computer Science, McGill University, Montreal, Canada, 2006. http://moncs.cs.mcgill.ca/people/denis/files/thesis_HREF.pdf.

[62] Gilles Dubochet. On Embedding Domain-specific Languages with User-friendly Syntax. In *1st Workshop on Domain-Specific Program Development*, pages 19–22, 2006. LAMP-CONF-2006-003.

[63] Magali Duboisset, Francois Pinet, Myoung-Ah Kang, and Michel Schneider. Precise Modeling and Verification of Topological Integrity Constraints in Spatial Databases. In Lois M. L. Delcambre et al., editor, *ER*, volume 3716 of *LNCS*, pages 465–482. Springer, 2005.

[64] Alexander Egyed. Instant Consistency Checking for the UML. In *ICSE '06: Proceeding of the 28th Intnl. Conf. on Software Engineering*, pages 381–390, New York, NY, USA, 2006. ACM Press.

[65] Karsten Ehrig, Claudia Ermel, Stefan Hänsgen, and Gabriele Taentzer. Generation of Visual Editors as Eclipse Plug-ins. In *ASE '05: Proc. of the 20th IEEE/ACM Intnl Conf on Automated Software Engineering*, pages 134–143, New York, NY, USA, 2005. ACM Press.

[66] EJB 3.0 Expert Group. JSR 220: Enterprise JavaBeans, Version 3.0: EJB 3.0 Simplified API. Available at http://java.sun.com/products/ejb/docs.html, 2005.

[67] Tayfun Elmas, Shaz Qadeer, and Serdar Tasiran. Goldilocks: a Race and Transaction-aware Java Runtime. *SIGPLAN Not.*, 42(6):245–255, 2007.

[68] Elver Project. Teneo EMF Persistency, http://www.eclipse.org/emft/projects/teneo/, 2007.

[69] Matthias Erche, Michael Wagner, and Christian Hein. Mapping Visual Notations to MOF Compliant Models with QVT-Relations. In *SAC '07: Proc. of the 2007 ACM Symposium on Applied Computing*, pages 1037–1038, New York, NY, USA, 2007. ACM Press.

[70] Martin Erwig. Inductive graphs and functional graph algorithms. *J. Funct. Program.*, 11(5):467–492, 2001.

[71] Leonidas Fegaras and David Maier. Towards an Effective Calculus for Object Query Languages. In *SIGMOD '95: Proc. of the 1995 ACM SIGMOD Intl Conf. on Management of Data*, pages 47–58, New York, NY, USA, 1995. ACM Press. http://lambda.uta.edu/sigmod95.ps.gz.

[72] Leonidas Fegaras and David Maier. Optimizing Object Queries using an Effective Calculus. *ACM Trans. Database Syst.*, 25(4):457–516, 2000.

[73] Charles L. Forgy. Rete: a Fast Algorithm for the Many Pattern/Many Object Pattern Match Problem. *Expert systems: a software methodology for modern applications*, pages 324–341, 1990.

[74] J. Nathan Foster, Michael B. Greenwald, Jonathan T. Moore, Benjamin C. Pierce, and Alan Schmitt. Combinators for bidirectional tree transformations: A linguistic approach to the view-update problem. *ACM Trans. Program. Lang. Syst.*, 29(3):17, 2007.

[75] Martin Fowler. *Refactoring: Improving the Design of Existing Code*. Addison-Wesley Longman Publishing Co., Inc., Boston, MA, USA, 1999.

[76] Erich Gamma, John Vlissides, Ralph Johnson, and Richard Helm. *Design Patterns CD: Elements of Reusable Object-Oriented Software, (CD-ROM)*. Addison-Wesley Longman Publishing Co., Inc., Boston, MA, USA, 1998.

[77] Miguel Garcia. Formalizing the Well-formedness Rules of EJB3QL in UML + OCL. In T. Kühne, editor, *Reports and Revised Selected Papers, Workshops and Symposia at MoDELS 2006, Genoa, Italy*, LNCS 4364, pages 66–75. Springer-Verlag, 2006.

[78] Miguel Garcia. How to process OCL Abstract Syntax Trees, Eclipse Technical Article, 2007. http://www.eclipse.org/articles/article.php?file=Article-HowToProcessOCLAbstractSyntaxTrees/index.html.

[79] Miguel Garcia. Rules for Type-checking of Parametric Polymorphism in EMF Generics. In Wolf-Gideon Bleek, Henning Schwentner, and Heinz Züllighoven, editors, *Software Engineering 2007 – Beiträge zu den Workshops*, volume 106 of *GI-Edition Lecture Notes in Informatics*, pages 261–270, 2007.

[80] Miguel Garcia. Automating the Embedding of Domain Specific Languages in Eclipse JDT, Eclipse Technical Article, 2008. http://www.eclipse.org/articles/article.php?file=Article-AutomatingDSLEmbeddings/index.html.

[81] Miguel Garcia. Bidirectional Synchronization of Multiple Views of Software Models. In Dirk Fahland, Daniel A. Sadilek, Markus Scheidgen, and Stephan Weißleder, editors, *Proc. of the Workshop on Domain-Specific Modeling Languages (DSML-2008)*, volume 324 of *CEUR-WS*, pages 7–19, 2008.

[82] Miguel Garcia. Efficient Integrity Checking for Essential MOF + OCL in Software Repositories. *Journal of Object Technology*, Jul/Aug 2008. To appear.

[83] Miguel Garcia. Formalization of QVT-Relations: OCL-based Static Semantics and Alloy-based Validation. In Peter Friese, Simon Zambrovski, and Frank Zimmermann, editors, *Proceedings of the Second Workshop on MDSD Today*, pages 21–30. Shaker Verlag, October 2008. ISBN 978-3-8322-7627-0, http://www.sts.tu-harburg.de/~mi.garcia/pubs/2008/qvtr/QVTRelationsFormalization.pdf.

[84] Miguel Garcia and Ralf Möller. Certification of Transformation Algorithms in Model-Driven Software Development. In Wolf-Gideon Bleek, Jorg Räsch, and Heinz Züllighoven, editors, *Software Engineering 2007*, volume 105 of *GI-Edition Lecture Notes in Informatics*, pages 107–118, 2007.

[85] Miguel Garcia and Ralf Möller. Incremental Evaluation of OCL Invariants in the Essential MOF Object Model. In Thomas Kühne, Wolfgang Reisig, and Friedrich Steimann, editors, *Modellierung 2008*, volume 127 of *GI-Edition Lecture Notes in Informatics*, pages 11–26, 2008.

[86] Miguel Garcia and Paul Sentosa. Generation of Eclipse-based IDEs for Custom DSLs. Technical report, Software Systems Institute (STS), Technische Universität Hamburg-Harburg, Germany, Sep 2007. http://www.sts.tu-harburg.de/~mi.garcia/SoC2007/IDEalizeReport.pdf.

[87] Miguel Garcia and A. Jibran Shidqie. OCL Compiler for EMF. In *Eclipse Modeling Symposium at Eclipse Summit Europe 2007, Stuttgart,*

Germany, 2007. http://www.sts.tu-harburg.de/~mi.garcia/pubs/2007/ese/oclcompiler.pdf.

[88] Martin Giese and Daniel Larsson. Simplifying Transformations of OCL Constraints. In Briand and Williams [28], pages 309–323.

[89] Stephen Gilmore. Programming in Standard ML '97: A tutorial introduction. Technical Report ECS-LFCS-97-364, Laboratory for Foundations of Computer Science, Department of Computer Science, The University of Edinburgh, 1997.

[90] GMF Team. Eclipse Graphical Modeling Framework Tutorial, http://wiki.eclipse.org/index.php/GMF_Tutorial, 2007.

[91] Wolfgang Goerigk. Compiler verification revisited. *ACL2 Case Studies*, pages 247–264, 2000.

[92] Brian Goetz, Tim Peierls, Joshua Bloch, Joseph Bowbeer, Doug Lea, and David Holmes. *Java Concurrency in Practice*. Addison-Wesley Professional, 2005.

[93] Bob Goldberg. The DASL Language: Programmer's Guide and Reference Manual, TR-2005-128. Technical report, Sun Microsystems Research Labs, 1 2005. http://research.sun.com/techrep/2005/abstract-128.html.

[94] Michael J. C. Gordon. Mechanizing Programming Logics in Higher Order Logic. In *Current trends in hardware verification and automated theorem proving*, pages 387–439, New York, NY, USA, 1989. Springer-Verlag New York, Inc.

[95] James Gosling, Bill Joy, Guy Steele, and Gilad Bracha. *The Java(TM) Language Specification, (3rd Edition)*. Addison-Wesley Professional, July 2005.

[96] Dan Grossman. Type-safe Multithreading in Cyclone. *SIGPLAN Not.*, 38(3):13–25, 2003.

[97] Dan Grossman. Software Transactions are to Concurrency as Garbage Collection is to Memory Management. Technical Report 2006-04-01, University of Washington Department of Computer Science and Engineering, April 2006.

[98] Lars Grunske, Leif Geiger, and Michael Lawley. A Graphical Specification of Model Transformations with Triple Graph Grammars. In Alan Hartman and David Kreische, editors, *ECMDA-FA*, volume 3748 of *LNCS*, pages 284–298. Springer, 2005.

[99] Boris Gruschko, Friedrich H. Vogt, and Simon Zambrovski. The Use of TLA+ and Model Checking Tools in the Eclipse Environment. In *2nd International Workshop on Web Services and Formal Methods*, Versailles, France, 9 2005.

[100] Torsten Grust. *The Functional Approach to Data Management - Modeling, Analyzing and Integrating Heterogeneous Data*, chapter Monad Comprehensions. A Versatile Representation for Queries, pages 288–311. Springer Verlag, Sept 2003. ISBN: 978-3-540-00375-5.

[101] Torsten Grust and Marc H. Scholl. Translating OQL into Monoid Comprehensions—Stuck with Nested Loops? Technical Report 3a/1996, Dept. of Computer and Information Science, Database Research Group, U Konstanz, September 1996.

[102] Ashish Gupta and Iderpal Singh Mumick, editors. *Materialized views: Techniques, Implementations, and Applications*. MIT Press, Cambridge, MA, USA, 1999.

[103] Ali Hamie. Translating the Object Constraint Language into the Java Modelling Language. In *SAC '04: Proc. of the 2004 ACM Symposium on Applied Computing*, pages 1531–1535, New York, NY, USA, 2004. ACM Press.

[104] Chris Hankin. *Lambda Calculi: A Guide for Computer Scientists*. Graduate Texts in Computer Science, Vol 3. Oxford University Press, USA, 1995. ISBN 0198538405.

[105] E. N. Hanson, S. Bodagala, and U. Chadaga. Trigger Condition Testing and View Maintenance Using Optimized Discrimination Networks. *IEEE Transactions on Knowledge and Data Engineering*, 14(2):261–280, 2002.

[106] David Harel. From play-in scenarios to code: An achievable dream. *Computer*, 34(1):53–60, 2001.

[107] T. Harmon and R. Klefstad. Toward a Unified Standard for Worst-Case Execution Time Annotations in Real-Time Java. *Parallel and Distributed Processing Symposium, IPDPS 2007*, pages 1–8, March 2007. IEEE Computer Society.

[108] Tim Harris and Simon P. Jones. Transactional Memory with Data Invariants. In *First ACM SIGPLAN Workshop on Languages, Compilers, and Hardware Support for Transactional Computing*, 2006.

[109] John Harrison. Formalizing Dijkstra. In *Proc. of the 11th Intnl. Conf. on Theorem Proving in Higher Order Logics*, pages 171–188, London, UK, 1998. Springer-Verlag.

[110] David Hearnden, Kerry Raymond, and Jim Steel. MQL: a Powerful Extension to OCL for MOF Queries. In *EDOC '03: Proc. of the 7th Intl. Conf. on Enterprise Distributed Object Computing*, pages 264–276, Washington, DC, USA, 2003. IEEE Computer Society.

[111] Görel Hedin and Eva Magnusson. JastAdd: An Aspect-oriented Compiler Construction System. *Sci. Comput. Program.*, 47(1):37–58, 2003.

[112] Anders Hessellund. SmartEMF: Guidance in Modeling Tools. In *Companion to the 22nd ACM SIGPLAN Conf. OOPSLA '07*, pages 945–946, New York, NY, USA, 2007. ACM Press.

[113] Benjamin Hindman and Dan Grossman. Strong Atomicity for Java Without Virtual-Machine Support. Technical Report 2006-05-01, Dept. of Computer Science and Engineering, University of Washington, Seattle, WA, USA, May 2006.

[114] Ian Horrocks. *Constructing the User Interface with Statecharts*. Addison-Wesley Longman Publishing Co., Inc., Boston, MA, USA, 1999.

[115] Zhenjiang Hu, Dongxi Liu, Hong Mei, Masato Takeichi, Yingfei Xiong, and Haiyan Zhao. A Compositional Approach to Bidirectional Model Transformation. Technical Report METR 2006-54, Dept. of Mathematical Informatics, Graduate School of Information Science and Technology, The University of Tokyo, Bunkyo-Ku, Tokyo, Oct 2006. `http://www.keisu.t.u-tokyo.ac.jp/research/techrep/data/2006/METR06-54.pdf`.

[116] Shan Shan Huang, David Zook, and Yannis Smaragdakis. Statically safe program generation with SafeGen. In Robert Glück and Michael R. Lowry, editors, *GPCE*, volume 3676 of *LNCS*, pages 309–326. Springer, 2005.

[117] Thierry Hubert and Claude Marché. A Case Study of C Source Code Verification: the Schorr-Waite Algorithm. In *SEFM '05: Proc. of the Third IEEE Intnl. Conf. on Software Engineering and Formal Methods*, pages 190–199, Washington, DC, USA, 2005. IEEE Computer Society.

[118] Michael Huth. Some Current Issues in Model Checking. *Software Tools for Technology Transfer*, 8(4):1–10, 2006.

[119] Daniel Jackson. Automating First-Order Relational Logic. In *SIGSOFT '00/FSE-8: Proc. of the 8th ACM SIGSOFT Intnl Symposium on Foundations of Software Engineering*, pages 130–139, New York, NY, USA, 2000. ACM Press.

[120] Daniel Jackson. *Software Abstractions: Logic, Language, and Analysis*. The MIT Press, 2006.

[121] James E. Johnson, David E. Langworthy, Leslie Lamport, and Friedrich H. Vogt. Formal Specification of a Web Services Protocol. *Electr. Notes Theor. Comput. Sci.*, 105:147–158, 2004.

[122] Simon Peyton Jones. *Beautiful Code: Leading Programmers Explain How They Think*, chapter 24 (Beautiful Concurrency). O'Reilly Media, Inc., 2007.

[123] Simon Peyton Jones and Philip Wadler. Comprehensive Comprehensions. In *Proc. of the ACM SIGPLAN Workshop Haskell '07*, pages 61–72, New York, NY, USA, 2007. ACM Press.

[124] Frédéric Jouault, Jean Bézivin, and Ivan Kurtev. TCS: a DSL for the Specification of Textual Concrete Syntaxes in Model Engineering. In Stan Jarzabek, Douglas C. Schmidt, and Todd L. Veldhuizen, editors, *GPCE*, pages 249–254. ACM Press, 2006.

[125] Frédéric Jouault and Ivan Kurtev. On the Architectural Alignment of ATL and QVT. In *Proc. of the 2006 ACM Symposium on Applied Computing (SAC 06)*, pages 1188–1195, Dijon, France, 2006. ACM Press.

[126] JSR-45 Expert Group. JSR 45: Debugging Support for Other Languages, 2003.

[127] Kaarel Kaljurand and Norbert Fuchs. Verbalizing OWL in Attempto Controlled English. In *OWLED 2007*, 2007. http://attempto.ifi.unizh.ch/site/pubs/papers/owled2007_kaljurand.pdf.

[128] Richard B. Kieburtz. A Logic for Rewriting Strategies. *Electr. Notes Theor. Comput. Sci.*, 58(2), 2001.

[129] Adam Kieżun, Michael D. Ernst, Frank Tip, and Robert M. Fuhrer. Refactoring for Parameterizing Java Classes. In *ICSE'07, Proc. of the 29th Intnl. Conf. on Software Engineering*, Minneapolis, MN, USA, May 23–25, 2007.

[130] Oleg Kiselyov and Ralf Lämmel. Haskell's Overlooked Object System. Draft; Submitted for journal publication; online since 30 Sep. 2004; Full version released 10 September 2005, http://homepages.cwi.nl/~ralf/OOHaskell/paper.pdf, 2005.

[131] Gerwin Klein and Tobias Nipkow. A Machine-Checked Model for a Java-like Language, Virtual Machine and Compiler. *ACM Transactions on Programming Languages and Systems*, 28(4):619–695, 2006.

[132] Günter Kniesel. A Logic Foundation for Conditional Program Transformations. Technical Report IAI-TR-2006-1, ISSN 0944-8535, Computer Science Department III, University of Bonn, Germany, Jan 2006.

[133] Andrew J. Ko and Brad A. Myers. Barista: An Implementation Framework for Enabling New Tools, Interaction Techniques and Views in Code Editors. In *CHI '06: Proc. of the SIGCHI conference on Human Factors in computing systems*, pages 387–396, New York, NY, USA, 2006. ACM Press.

[134] A. Königs and A. Schürr. MDI - a Rule-Based Multi-Document and Tool Integration Approach. *Journal of Software & System Modeling*, 5(4):349–368, December 2006.

[135] Jernej Kovse. *Model-Driven Development of Versioning Systems*. PhD thesis, TU Kaiserslautern, Germany, August 2005.

[136] Viktor Kuncak and Daniel Jackson. Relational Analysis of Algebraic Datatypes. *SIGSOFT Softw. Eng. Notes*, 30(5):207–216, 2005.

[137] Andreas Kunert. Semi-automatic Generation of Metamodels and Models from Grammars and Programs. In *Fifth Intl Workshop on Graph Transformation and Visual Modeling Techniques*, Electronic Notes in Theoretical Computer Science, 2006.

[138] Marcel Kyas. An Extended Type-system for OCL Supporting Templates and Transformations. In M. Steffen and Gianluigi Zavattaro, editors, *Formal Methods for Open Object-Based Distributed Systems (FMOODS 2005)*, volume 3535 of *LNCS*, pages 83–98. Springer-Verlag, 2005.

[139] Ralf Lämmel, Simon Thompson, and Markus Kaiser. Programming Errors in Traversal Programs over Structured Data. *ENTCS*, 2008. To appear in Proc. of LDTA 2008.

[140] L. Lamport. Checking a Multithreaded Algorithm with +CAL. In *Proc. 20th International Symposium on Distributed Computing DISC 06*, 2006.

[141] Leslie Lamport. *Specifying Systems: The TLA+ Language and Tools for Hardware and Software Engineers*. Addison-Wesley Longman Publishing Co., Inc., Boston, MA, USA, 2002.

[142] Leslie Lamport. The +CAL Algorithm Language. In *NCA '06: Proc of the Fifth IEEE Intnl Symposium on Network Computing and Applications*, pages 5–10, Washington, DC, USA, 2006. IEEE Computer Society.

[143] Michael Lawley. Transaction Safety in Deductive Object-Oriented Databases. In Tok Wang Ling, Alberto Mendelzon, and Laurent Vieille, editors, *DOOD*, volume 1013 of *LNCS*, pages 395–410. Springer, 1995.

[144] Doug Lea. *Concurrent Programming in Java: Design Principles and Patterns, 2nd Ed.* Addison-Wesley Longman Publishing Co., Inc., Boston, MA, USA, 1999.

[145] Daan Leijen and Erik Meijer. Domain Specific Embedded Compilers. In *PLAN '99: Proc. of the 2nd conference on Domain-specific languages*, pages 109–122, New York, NY, USA, 1999. ACM Press.

[146] Johannes Leitner. Verifikation von Modelltransformationen basierend auf Triple Graph Grammatiken, March 2006. Diplomarbeit. `http://pes.cs.tu-berlin.de/pes/theses.php_id=25.html`.

[147] Matthew Lewis, Tobias Schubert, and Bernd Becker. Multithreaded SAT Solving. In *ASP-DAC '07: Proc. of the 2007 conference on Asia South Pacific design automation*, pages 926–931, Washington, DC, USA, 2007. IEEE Computer Society.

[148] K. J. Lienberherr. Formulations and Benefits of the Law of Demeter. *SIGPLAN Not.*, 24(3):67–78, 1989.

[149] Dongxi Liu, Zhenjiang Hu, and Masato Takeichi. Bidirectional Interpretation of XQuery. In *PEPM '07: Proc. of the 2007 ACM SIGPLAN symposium on Partial evaluation and semantics-based program manipulation*, pages 21–30, New York, NY, USA, 2007. ACM Press. `http://www.ipl.t.u-tokyo.ac.jp/~liu/PEPM2007.pdf`.

[150] Dongxi Liu, Zhenjiang Hu, Masato Takeichi, Kazuhiko Kakehi, and Hao Wang. A Java Library for Bidirectional XML Transformation. *JSSST Computer Software*, 24(2):164–177, May 2007. `http://www.ipl.t.u-tokyo.ac.jp/~hu/pub/jssst-cs06-liu.pdf`.

[151] Hanbing Liu and J. Strother Moore. Java Program Verification via a JVM Deep Embedding in ACL2. In Konrad Slind, Annette Bunker, and Ganesh Gopalakrishnan, editors, *TPHOLs*, volume 3223 of *LNCS*, pages 184–200. Springer, 2004.

[152] Na Liu, John G. Hosking, and John C. Grundy. MaramaTatau: Extending a Domain Specific Visual Language Meta Tool with a Declarative Constraint Mechanism. In *VL/HCC*, pages 95–103. IEEE Computer Society, 2007.

[153] David Mandelin, Lin Xu, Rastislav Bodík, and Doug Kimelman. Jungloid Mining: Helping to Navigate the API Jungle. *SIGPLAN Not.*, 40(6):48–61, 2005.

[154] Dragos Manolescu, Wojtek Kozaczynski, Ade Miller, and Jason Hogg. The Growing Divide in the Patterns World. In *IEEE Software*, volume 24, pages 61–67. July-Aug. 2007.

[155] Slavisa Marković and Thomas Baar. *Proc. of the 8th Intnl. Conf. on Model Driven Engineering Languages and Systems - MoDELS 2005 - LNCS*, volume 3713, chapter Refactoring OCL Annotated UML Class Diagrams, pages 280–294. Springer Verlag, October 2005.

[156] Kim Marriott and Sitt Sen Chok. QOCA: A Constraint Solving Toolkit for Interactive Graphical Applications. *Constraints*, 7(3-4):229–254, 2002.

[157] Kazutaka Matsuda, Zhenjiang Hu, Keisuke Nakano, Makoto Hamana, and Masato Takeichi. Bidirectionalization Transformation based on Automatic Derivation of View Complement Functions. In Ralf Hinze and Norman Ramsey, editors, *ICFP*, pages 47–58. ACM Press, 2007. http://www.ipl.t.u-tokyo.ac.jp/~hu/pub/icfp07.pdf.

[158] Jeff McAffer and Jean-Michel Lemieux. *Eclipse Rich Client Platform: Designing, Coding, and Packaging Java(TM) Applications*. Addison-Wesley Professional, 2005.

[159] Farhad Mehta and Tobias Nipkow. Proving Pointer Programs in Higher-Order Logic. *Inf. Comput.*, 199(1-2):200–227, 2005.

[160] Erik Meijer, Brian Beckman, and Gavin Bierman. LINQ: reconciling object, relations and XML in the .NET framework. In *SIGMOD '06: Proc. of the 2006 ACM SIGMOD Intnl. Conf. on Management of Data*, pages 706–706, New York, NY, USA, 2006. ACM Press.

[161] Stephan Merz. On the logic of TLA$^+$. *Computers and Informatics*, 22:351–379, 2003.

[162] Bertrand Meyer, Christine Mingins, and Heinz Schmidt. Providing trusted components to the industry. *Computer*, 31(5):104–105, 1998.

[163] Pascal Müllender. Übersetzung der deklarativen Modelltransformationssprache QVT-Relations in Operational Mappings. Diplomarbeit, Universität Augsburg, Germany, August 2007.

[164] Tobias Nipkow. More Church-Rosser Proofs (in Isabelle/HOL). In M. McRobbie and J.K. Slaney, editors, *Automated Deduction — CADE-13*, volume 1104 of *LNCS*, pages 733–747. Springer, 1996.

[165] Tobias Nipkow. Winskel is (Almost) Right: Towards a Mechanized Semantics Textbook. In *Proc. of the 16th Conference on Foundations of Software Technology and Theoretical Computer Science*, pages 180–192, London, UK, 1996. Springer-Verlag.

[166] Tobias Nipkow, Lawrence C. Paulson, and Markus Wenzel. *Isabelle/HOL — A Proof Assistant for Higher-Order Logic*, volume 2283 of *LNCS*. Springer, 2002.

[167] Joerg Nitzsche, Tammo van Lessen, Dimka Karastoyanova, and Frank Leymann. BPEL light. In *5th Intnl. Conf. on Business Process Management (BPM 2007)*. Springer, September 2007.

[168] Nathaniel Nystrom, Michael R. Clarkson, and Andrew C. Myers. Polyglot: An Extensible Compiler Framework for Java. *LNCS*, 2622:138–152, January 2003.

[169] Object Management Group. OMG UML 2.1.1 Superstructure Specification, formal/2007-02-05, Feb 2005.

[170] Object Management Group. Meta Object Facility (MOF) Core Specification, formal/06-01-01, Jan 2006.

[171] Object Management Group. OMG OCL Specification v2.0, formal/2006-05-01, May 2006.

[172] Object Management Group. OMG UML 2.1.1 Infrastructure Specification, formal/2007-02-06, Feb 2006.

[173] Object Management Group. MOF QVT Final Adopted Specification, formal/07-07-07, July 2007.

[174] David von Oheimb. *Analyzing Java in Isabelle/HOL: Formalization, Type Safety and Hoare Logic*. PhD thesis, Technische Universität München, 2001.

[175] David von Oheimb and Tobias Nipkow. Machine-checking the Java Specification: Proving Type-safety. In Jim Alves-Foss, editor, *Formal Syntax and Semantics of Java*, volume 1523 of *LNCS*, pages 119–156. Springer, 1999.

[176] Jorge-Luis Perez-Medina, Sophie Dupuy-Chessa, and Agnes Front. A Survey of Model-Driven Tools for User Interface Design. In *6th International Workshop on TAsk Models and DIAgrams (TAMODIA'2007, Toulouse, France, Novembre 2007)*, 2007.

[177] J. Steven Perry. *Java Management Extensions*. O'Reilly & Associates, Inc., Sebastopol, CA, USA, 2002.

[178] Benjamin C. Pierce. The Weird World of Bi-Directional Programming. Invited talk at ETAPS, 2006. `http://www.cis.upenn.edu/~bcpierce/papers/lenses-etapsslides.pdf`.

[179] Martin Plümicke and Jörg Bäuerle. Typeless Programming in Java 5.0. In *PPPJ '06: Proc. of the 4th international symposium on Principles and practice of programming in Java*, pages 175–181, New York, NY, USA, 2006. ACM Press.

[180] Detlef Plump. Essentials of Term Graph Rewriting. *Electronic Notes in Theoretical Computer Science*, 51:277–289, 2002.

[181] Steffen H. Prochnow. KIEL: Textual and Graphical Representations of Statecharts. `http://rtsys.informatik.uni-kiel.de/~rt-kiel/kiel/documents/talks/oberseminar-0511-spr/talk.pdf`, Nov 2005.

[182] Chris Raistrick, Paul Francis, John Wright, Colin Carter, and Ian Wilkie. *Model Driven Architecture with Executable UML*. Cambridge University Press, Cambridge, UK, 2004.

[183] Nicole Rauch and Burkhart Wolff. Formalizing Java's Two's-Complement Integral Type in Isabelle/HOL. In Thomas Arts and Wan Fokkink, editors, *Proc. 8th International Workshop on Formal Methods for Industrial Critical Systems*, volume 80 of *Electronic Notes in Theoretical Computer Science (ENTCS)*, pages 40–56. Elsevier, June 2003.

[184] Norbert Ritter and Hans-Peter Steiert. Enforcing Modeling Guidelines in an ORDBMS-based UML Repository. In *Intnl Resource Mgmt. Assoc. Conf. 2000 (Information Modeling Methods and Methodologies Track of IRMA 2000)*, pages 269–273. Anchorage, Alaska, May 2000.

[185] Anna Ruokonen, Imed Hammouda, and Tommi Mikkonen. Enforcing Consistency of Model-Driven Architecture Using Meta-Designs. In *European Conf. on MDA: Workshop on Consistency in Model Driven Engineering (C@MoDE 2005)*, pages 127–141, Nov. 2005.

[186] Max Schäfer, Torbjörn Ekman, and Oege de Moor. Sound and Extensible Renaming for Java. In Gregor Kiczales, editor, *23rd Annual ACM SIGPLAN Conference on Object-Oriented Programming, Systems, Languages, and Applications (OOPSLA 2008)*. ACM Press, Oct. 2008. To appear.

[187] Markus Scheidgen and Joachim Fischer. Human Comprehensible and Machine Processable Specifications of Operational Semantics. In David H. Akehurst, Régis Vogel, and Richard F. Paige, editors, *ECMDA-FA*, volume 4530 of *LNCS*, pages 157–171. Springer, 2007.

[188] Martijn M. Schrage. *Proxima – a presentation-oriented editor for structured documents*. PhD thesis, Utrecht University, The Netherlands, Oct 2004.

[189] Sagar Sen, Benoit Baudry, and Doina Precup. Partial Model Completion in Model Driven Engineering using Constraint Logic Programming. In *INAP'07 (Intnl. Conf. on Applications of Declarative Programming and Knowledge Management)*, Würzburg, Germany, 2007.

[190] Peter Sestoft. A Spreadsheet Core Implementation in C#. Technical Report TR-2006-91, IT University, Copenhagen, Denmark, Sept. 2006.

[191] Ajeet Shankar and Rastislav Bodík. DITTO: Automatic Incrementalization of Data Structure Invariant Checks (in Java). In *PLDI '07: Proc. of the 2007 ACM SIGPLAN Conf. on Programming Language Design and Implementation*, pages 310–319, New York, NY, USA, 2007. ACM Press.

[192] Jérôme Siméon and Philip Wadler. The Essence of XML. *SIGPLAN Not.*, 38(1):1–13, 2003.

[193] Dave Steinberg, Frank Budinsky, Marcelo Paternostro, and Ed Merks. *EMF: Eclipse Modeling Framework*. Addison-Wesley Professional, Boston, MA, USA, 2nd edition, 2008.

[194] Perdita Stevens. Bidirectional Model Transformations in QVT: Semantic Issues and Open Questions. In *Model Driven Engineering Languages and Systems*, pages 1–15. Springer, 2007.

[195] L. J. Stockmeyer. The Complexity of Decision Problems in Automata Theory and Logic. Technical Report MAC TR-133, MIT, Cambridge MA, Project MAC, 1974.

[196] E. Torlak and D. Jackson. The Design of a Relational Engine. Technical Report MIT-CSAIL-TR-2006-068, MIT CSAIL, 2006.

[197] Agathoniki Trigoni. *Semantic Optimization of OQL Queries*. PhD thesis, University of Cambridge, UK, October 2002.

[198] Jeffrey D. Ullman. A Comparison between Deductive and Object-Oriented Database Systems. In *DOOD*, pages 263–277, 1991.

[199] Antti Viljamaa and Jukka Viljamaa. Creating Framework Specialization Instructions for Tool Environments. *In: Proc. of the Nordic Workshop on Software Development Tools and Techniques (K. Osterbye, ed.), NWPER 2002, IT University of Copenhagen*, 2002.

[200] Joost Visser. Matching Objects without Language Extension. *Journal of Object Technology*, 5(8):81–100, 2006.

[201] Hai Wang, Jin Song Dong, Jing Sun, and Jun Sun. Reasoning Support for Semantic Web Ontology Family Languages using Alloy. *International Journal of Multiagent and Grid Systems, Special issue on Agent-Oriented Software Development Methodologies*, 2(4), December 2006.

[202] Junhua Wang, Soon-Kyeong Kim, and David Carrington. Verifying Metamodel Coverage of Model Transformations. In *ASWEC '06: Proc. of the Australian Software Engineering Conference (ASWEC'06)*, pages 270–282, Washington, DC, USA, 2006. IEEE Computer Society.

[203] Jos Warmer and Anneke Kleppe. *The Object Constraint Language: Getting Your Models Ready for MDA*. Addison-Wesley, Boston, MA, USA, 2003. ISBN 0321179366.

[204] Sam Weber, Hoi Chan, Lou Degenaro, Judah Diament, Achille Fokoue-Nkoutche, and Isabelle Rouvellou. Fusion: A System for Business Users to Manage Program Variability. *IEEE Transactions on Software Engineering*, 31(7):570–587, 2005.

[205] Wikipedia. Referential transparency — Wikipedia, the free encyclopedia, 2007. `http://en.wikipedia.org/wiki/Referentially_transparent`.

[206] Darren Willis, David J. Pearce, and James Noble. Efficient Object Querying for Java. In Dave Thomas, editor, *ECOOP*, volume 4067 of *LNCS*, pages 28–49. Springer, 2006.

[207] Manuel Wimmer and Gerhard Kramler. Bridging Grammarware and Model-ware. In Jean-Michel Bruel, editor, *MoDELS Satellite Events*, volume 3844 of *LNCS*, pages 159–168. Springer, 2005.

[208] Glynn Winskel. *The Formal Semantics of Programming Languages: An Introduction*. MIT Press, Cambridge, MA, USA, 1993.

[209] V.L. Winter, S. Roach, and F. Fraij. Dependable Software through Higher-Order Strategic Programming. Technical Report SAND2004-0868, Sandia National Laboratories, March 2004.

[210] Yingfei Xiong, Dongxi Liu, Zhenjiang Hu, Haiyan Zhao, Masato Takeichi, and Hong Mei. Towards Automatic Model Synchronization from Model Transformations. In *ASE '07: Proceedings of the twenty-second IEEE/ACM international conference on Automated software engineering*, pages 164–173, New York, NY, USA, 2007. ACM Press.

[211] Yoav Zibin, Alex Potanin, Mahmood Ali, Shay Artzi, Adam Kieżun, and Michael D. Ernst. Object and Reference Immutability using Java Generics. In *ESEC/FSE 2007: Proc. of the 11th European Software Engineering Conference and the 15th ACM SIGSOFT Symposium on the Foundations of Software Engineering*, Dubrovnik, Croatia, September 5–7, 2007.

Index

dynamic dependency graph, 234
    pruning, 248
Dynamic Programming, 231
dynamic semantics, 120, 180

EBNF to EMOF conversion, 122
    algorithms, 135
Eclipse
    JDT, 101
EMF Generics, 189
Enterprise JavaBeans, 225
equijoin, 250
Event Condition Action, 225
    design patterns, 226
Executable EMOF, 166
execution trace, 166
expressive power
    Ecore vs. UML2, 91

Focal, 147

Generalized Concept Inclusion (GCI),
    57
generic type
    declaration, 42
    invocation, 42
    subtyping, 43
generics, *see* parametric polymorphism
grammar
    conversion to EMOF, 30
graph marking, 167

Hoare logic, 163, 203
Hoare-style, 196
HOL-OCL, 203
Human-Computer Interaction (HCI), 154

IDE generator, 119

instrumentation code, 245
integrity checking, 205, 206
    main memory case, 230
integrity constraints, 205
integrity enforcement, 210
interceptor undeployment, 256
intermediate representation, 90

JPQL
    well-formedness, 20
JSR-220, 17
JVMTI, 256

key duplicates, 197
Kodkod, 65

lambda calculus, 202
LINQ, 250
lock, 252
logical consistency
    of behavioral specs, 5
    of structural specs, 5

M0-level, 184
memoization, 233
memory footprint, 242
memory model, 170
metamodel, 184
method interception, 245
misprediction handling, 249
model checking, 161
    definition, 8
model compiler, 159
model finding, 195
model inspection, 59
model transformation, 166
    validation, 172

model-driven
    language definition, 16
    software engineering, 15
monoid calculus, 211
    collection monoids, 215
monoid comprehension, 215
monoid homomorphism, 216
mutual forward references, 84

non-determinism, 189, 192

object store, 171
Object-Relational Mapping (ORM), 23
OCL functions
    aggregators, 246
    computational complexity, 219
    incrementalization, 233
    termination behavior, 243
OCL metamodel, 73
OCLASTView, 73
open compiler, 120

parametric polymorphism, 38
    EMOF, 38
parametric types
    automatic refactoring, 46
partial evaluation, 80
pattern matching, 183
pointer aliasing, 171, 233
profiling, 235
program inversion, 146
program verification
    HOL-OCL, 173
    KeY project, 173
programming language design, 2
proof tactic, 174
proof techniques, 201

query
    translation, 28
query language
    coverage, 207
    ease of manipulation, 207
    EJB3QL, 17
    evaluation fitness, 207
    execution plan generation, 220
    JPQL, 17
    optimization calculus, 207
Query-View-Transformation (QVT), 122
QVT-Relations, 182
    compilation, 190

refactoring, 92, 190
reference aliasing, 225
reference handshaking, 240
referential transparency, 232
Relational Logic, 55
Rete algorithm, 255
rewriting, 214
    confluence, 217
    termination, 217
ROI, 155
role hierarchy, 58
Role Membership Assertion (RMA), 58
round-tripping, 183, 254
rule engine, 226
rule engines, 256

schema mapping, 214
Schorr-Waite, 167
scope rules, 23
self-maintenance, 210
set comprehension, 199
shared-memory transactions, 251

GARCIA GUTIERREZ, Miguel Alfredo

http://www.sts.tu-harburg.de/people/mi.garcia

Angaben zu Person

Geburtsort	San Juan, Argentinien.
Staatsangehörigkeit	Argentinische, Spanische.

Schulausbildung

Grundschule in Argentinien.
Wirtschaftsgymnasium in Argentinien.

Studium

Studium der Informationssysteme an der Universidad Nacional de San Juan, Argentinien. Diplomabschlussprüfung, Thema der Diplomarbeit: "Application of Parallel Processing Techniques to the Long-Term Optimal Operation Planning of Large Hydro-Thermal Power Systems".

Master in Information and Media Technologies, TU Hamburg-Harburg, Germany. Thema der Master Thesis: "Software Systems Modeling: Requirements, Examples, Experience".

Professional Degree in Global Technology Management, Northern Institute of Technology, Germany.

Berufserfahrung

Software Engineer. Institute of Electrical Engineering, Universidad Nacional de San Juan, Argentinien.

Wissenschaftlicher Mitarbeiter, Institut für Softwaresysteme, Technische Universität Hamburg-Harburg, Germany.